MD ✓ 8/14/98

**HENRY COUNTY**
**LIBRARY SYSTEM**
DATE DUE

*Twayne's Studies in Short Fiction*

Gordon Weaver, General Editor
*Oklahoma State University*

**Shirley Jackson.** Werner Wolff—Black Star.

# SHIRLEY JACKSON

## _A Study of the Short Fiction_

_Joan Wylie Hall_

_University of Mississippi_

_TWAYNE PUBLISHERS_
An Imprint of Simon & Schuster Macmillan
New York

_Prentice Hall International_
London • Mexico City • New Delhi • Singapore • Sydney • Toronto

Twayne's Studies in Short Fiction Series, No. 42

Twayne Publishers
An Imprint of Simon & Schuster Macmillan
866 Third Avenue
New York, N.Y. 10022

Macmillan Publishing Company is a part of the Maxwell Communication Group of Companies.

**Library of Congress Cataloging-in-Publication Data**

Hall, Joan Wylie.
    Shirley Jackson: a study of the short fiction / Joan Wylie Hall.
        p.  cm. — (Twayne's studies in short fiction ; no. 42)
    Includes bibliographical references and index.
    ISBN 0-8057-0853-7 (alk. paper)
    1. Jackson, Shirley, 1919–1965—Criticism and interpretation.
2. Short story. I. Title. II. Series.
PS3519.A392Z69 1993
813'.54—dc20                        92-36432
                                                 CIP

10 9 8 7 6 5 4 3

Printed in the United States of America.

*For J. R. Hall,*
*Jennifer Hall,*
*and*
*Justin Hall*

# Contents

# Contents

# Preface

Shirley Jackson's fiction is as varied as her admirers, who include the poet Sylvia Plath, the horror novelist Stephen King, and the fabulist Isaac Bashevis Singer. Yet Jackson's reputation rests largely on a single shocking story written early in her career. "The Lottery" (1948) remains a popular selection in introductory literature classes, and critics still speculate on the meaning of Tessie Hutchinson's stoning in the town square. Jackson recorded the story for Folkways Records but was disappointed with productions made for radio and television. With some amusement, she reported on musical, pantomime, and ballet versions to her parents.[1] When she died in 1965, a large headline in the *New York Times* identified her as "Shirley Jackson, Author of Horror Classic."[2]

A few months later, however, Jackson's husband, Stanley Edgar Hyman, summarized her canon as "quite a few short stories and twelve books: six novels, a volume of short stories, two fictionalized memoirs, and three juveniles, one of them a play."[3] Hyman addressed his remarks to the large audience of the *Saturday Evening Post,* in conjunction with the posthumous printing of Jackson's story "The Possibility of Evil." He added that at her death Jackson had been working on a new novel, "savagely comic in tone," and a children's fantasy. As the author of several books of literary criticism, Hyman was unhappily aware that Jackson had been neglected by scholars and awards-granting institutions. Despite a "fair degree of popularity" and the "approbation of her fellow craftsmen," she still awaited the serious recognition won by many "inferior writers" of her time (Hyman, 63).

Critics have slowly begun to pay more attention to Jackson during the past 20 years, and feminist critics have begun to examine her humor and her female characters.[4] Aside from a few unpublished dissertations, however, only two full-length studies have appeared. Lenemaja Friedman's comprehensive *Shirley Jackson* (1975) surveys the body of her work, emphasizing Jackson's skill as "an entertainer, a born storyteller."[5] While Friedman discounts the mystique of magic and witchcraft often attached to Jackson by publicists, Judy Oppenheimer's *Private Demons: The Life of Shirley Jackson* (1988) argues that a dark side was an important element of her complex personality. Oppenheimer's biography posits a psychological basis for the neo-Gothic strain in Jackson's fiction. More prominent in her novels than in her short stories, Jackson's Gothicism places her in an important American tradition, ranging from Edgar Allan Poe and Nathaniel Hawthorne to William Faulkner, Flannery O'Connor, and John Hawkes. Because the scope of both Friedman's and Oppenheimer's studies is so broad, neither discusses Jackson's short stories at length, though both make special mention of "The Lottery."

"The Lottery" is just one of many excellent stories Jackson wrote over a 25-year period; especially good are "The Daemon Lover," "Flower Garden," "The Summer People," and "A Visit." Jackson published around 110 stories, more than 30 of which were semi-autobiographical, with most of these absorbed into her two family memoirs, *Life among the Savages* (1953) and *Raising Demons* (1957). She collected 25 of the earliest stories in *The Lottery; or, The Adventures of James Harris* (1949), a best-seller in the short-fiction genre. Hyman gathered 14 more stories, along with Jackson's incomplete last novel, in *Come Along with Me* (1968). Several of the uncollected stories appeared in now-forgotten magazines of the 1940s and 1950s, such as *Peacock Alley* and *Charm*, but many were sold to such popular periodicals as the *New Yorker*, *Playboy*, *Harper's*, and *Good Housekeeping*. Whether her mood was comic or serious, Jackson often wrote of ordinary characters—typically women in their twenties and thirties—who become enmeshed in extraordinary situations that either free them or, more often, trap them. Merging the real and the surreal, the best of these stories recall the fiction of Franz Kafka (whose influence Jackson disclaimed), Singer, Jorge Luis Borges, and Joyce Carol Oates.

The Shirley Jackson Papers at the Library of Congress contain manuscripts of most of the published stories and about 50 unpublished stories. Most of the latter were written early in Jackson's career—some probably dating back to 1936–37, the year she spent at home writing a thousand words a day before transferring from the University of Rochester to Syracuse University—and are generally not very good. On a personal information form she filled out for Syracuse in 1937, Jackson wrote that she was attending college "to further my writing career."[6] "For her entire adult life," Hyman observed in 1965, "she regarded herself as a professional writer, one who made a living by the craft of writing" (Hyman, 63).

In letters to her parents and literary agents, Jackson several times distinguished her serious fiction (short and long) from the stories she wrote to produce a steady income. She told her parents in November 1949 that she was writing one "popular story" about her children each month because "it's keeping a name for me, building up a following, opening new markets with plenty of money, and helping to support us while I take my time with the novel [*Hangsaman* (1951)]" (SJP, Box 3).

Like Jackson, several of her contemporaries with a literary reputation published not only in the *New Yorker* but also in women's magazines. Kay Boyle wrote for *Woman's Home Companion*; John Cheever and J. D. Salinger, for *Mademoiselle*. Ray Bradbury and other science fiction writers of the 1940s and early 1950s found a market in *Charm*. Jackson was unique, however, for publishing so regularly in so many of these journals directed exclusively at a female readership, while also submitting stories—as Boyle and Jean Stafford did—to magazines like *Harper's*. Her name is the only one that is now at all familiar in issue after issue of *Ladies Home Journal* and *Good Housekeeping*. Sylvia Plath, who had hoped to meet Jackson in June 1953 after her selection to *Mademoiselle's* College Board, was unusual in aspiring to publish, like Jackson, in both *Ladies Home Journal*–which Plath mocked but read avidly—and the *New Yorker*. Unfortunately, Jackson's discovery of an appealing formula and a lucrative market distracted critical attention from the balance of her short fiction, which was much more important to her. "Housewife humor," Lynette Carpenter argues, has led "traditional male critics" to exclude Shirley Jackson from literary history (1988, 144, 143).

✦

Part 1 of this study opens with a discussion of *The Lottery*, a carefully ordered short-story cycle that reveals the range of Jackson's talent. "After You, My Dear Alphonse" displays the sensitivity to social problems common to much American fiction of the 1930s and 1940s. "The Daemon Lover" and "The Renegade" introduce figures who will recur in Jackson's work—the unmarried urban woman and the country housewife, both subject to anxiety and crisis. A third female type, the malicious older woman, appears in "Trial by Combat" and "Men with Their Big Shoes." "The Tooth" and "The Lottery" place contemporary horrors in a context of myth and ritual. The second chapter of Part 1 treats the *Come Along with Me* stories, which focus on women under stress in a variety of situations, including the failed suicide of "Janice" and a bizarre encounter with a demonic stranger in "The Rock." A final chapter on several uncollected stories emphasizes Jackson's concern with obstacles to attaining a secure sense of identity. From the nameless housewife-writer of the family sketches to the village newcomer in "Home," her often divided characters struggle to declare their selfhood.

Part 2, "The Writer," reprints excerpts from Jackson's lectures on fiction writing, along with previously unpublished material from the Library of Congress that relates to her short stories. An early interview with the *New York Times* and a short biography by Hyman suggest the breadth of Jackson's reading and the enjoyment she derived from writing. Part 3, "The Critics," collects scholars' comments on several short stories, including, of course, "The Lottery."

✦

I hope this study will encourage readers to discover for themselves the many attractions of Shirley Jackson's short stories. A skilled practitioner of several popular genres, she saw herself as an innovator in the area of domestic comedy. (Desi Arnaz asked if she would write a screenplay for Lucille Ball.)[7] A civil rights advocate from her college days, she can still be appreciated for effective portrayals of discrimination in stories like "Flower Garden" and "A Fine Old Firm." Her truly shocking stories—"The Lottery" and the Gothic "A Visit," for example—are few in number, but their impact is undiminished. Perhaps of greatest interest to today's readers, however, are the many stories in which unsuspecting women suffer more credible shocks. Thrown off balance, deprived of control, these imperilled females embody a postwar sensibility of dislocation and loss. Their sex, Jackson strongly implies, is no badge of protection; rather, it almost ensures their defeat.

## Notes

1. Letter to Geraldine and Leslie Jackson, November 1951, Shirley Jackson Papers, Box 3, Library of Congress, Washington, D.C.; hereafter cited in text as SJP.

2. "Shirley Jackson, Author of Horror Classic, Dies," *New York Times*, 10 August 1965, 29.

3. Stanley Edgar Hyman, "Shirley Jackson 1919–1965," *Saturday Evening Post*, 18 December 1965, 63; hereafter cited in text. With minor revisions, Hyman's tribute to Jackson was reprinted as the preface to his collection of several of her works, *The Magic of Shirley Jackson* (New York: Farrar, Straus & Giroux, 1966). Jackson also wrote book reviews, which Hyman does not mention. Jackson's pieces for the *New York Times Book Review* are listed in the Bibliography, but letters in the SJP suggest she probably published additional reviews elsewhere.

4. See, for example, Lynette Carpenter, "The Establishment and Preservation of Female Power in Shirley Jackson's *We Have Always Lived in the Castle*," *Frontiers* 8, no. 1 (1984): 32–38; Carpenter, "Domestic Comedy, Black Comedy, and Real Life: Shirley Jackson, a Woman Writer," in *Faith of a (Woman) Writer*, ed. Alice Kessler-Harris and

William McBrien (Westport, Conn.: Greenwood, 1988), 143–48 (hereafter cited in text); Tricia Lootens, "'Whose Hand Was I Holding?': Familial and Sexual Politics in Shirley Jackson's *The Haunting of Hill House*," in *Haunting the House of Fiction: Feminist Perspectives on Ghost Stories by American Women*, ed. Lynette Carpenter and Wendy K. Kolmar (Knoxville: University of Tennessee Press, 1991), 166–92; Thelma J. Shinn, *Radiant Daughters: Fictional American Women* (Westport, Conn.: Greenwood, 1986), 48–57, 75–78; Nancy Walker, "*Agelaste* or *Eiron*: American Women Writers and the Sense of Humor," *Studies in American Humor*, n.s. 4, nos. 1, 2 (1985): 116, 121; Walker, *A Very Serious Thing: Women's Humor and American Culture* (Minneapolis: University of Minnesota Press, 1988), 31, 33–35, 48–49, 65–66, 125, 145.

5. Lenemaja Friedman, *Shirley Jackson* (Boston: Twayne Publishers, 1975), x.

6. Shirley Jackson's "Information for Personnel Division" form (1937) in "Alumni: Shirley Jackson" file, George Arents Research Library, Syracuse University, Syracuse, N.Y.

7. See the letter from literary agent Carol Brandt to Shirley Jackson, 20 October 1961, SJP, Box 6.

# Acknowledgments

I am grateful for permission to use the following material:

Frontispiece reproduced with the permission of the photographer, Werner Wolff, and Black Star.

Excerpts from *The Lottery*, by Shirley Jackson. Copyright 1948, 1949 by Shirley Jackson. Copyright renewed © 1976, 1977 by Laurence Hyman, Barry Hyman, Mrs. Sarah Webster, and Mrs. Joanne Schnurer. Reprinted by permission of Farrar, Straus & Giroux, Inc.

Excerpts from the Introduction to *The Magic of Shirley Jackson*, edited by Stanley Edgar Hyman. © 1965, 1966 by Stanley Edgar Hyman. Reprinted by permission of Farrar, Straus & Giroux, Inc.

Excerpts from stories in *Come Along with Me*, by Shirley Jackson, and from the Preface by Stanley Edgar Hyman. Copyright 1948, 1952, © 1960 by Shirley Jackson. Copyright 1944, 1950, © 1962, 1965, 1968 by Stanley Edgar Hyman. Reprinted by permission of Viking Penguin, a division of Penguin Books USA Inc.

"Notes on Shirley Jackson," by Stanley Edgar Hyman, from the Shirley Jackson Papers, Library of Congress. Used by permission of Phoebe Pettingell Hyman.

"Biographical Material," by Shirley Jackson, from the Shirley Jackson Papers, Library of Congress. Used by permission of Sarah H. Stewart.

"Talk with Miss Jackson," by Harvey Breit, from the *New York Times Book Review*. Copyright 1949 by The New York Times Company. Reprinted by permission.

"Notes on an Unfashionable Novelist," by Shirley Jackson, from the Shirley Jackson Papers, Library of Congress. Used by permission of Sarah H. Stewart.

"The Unloved Reader," by Shirley Jackson, from the Shirley Jackson Papers, Library of Congress. Used by permission of Sarah H. Stewart.

Excerpts from "Experience and Fiction," "Biography of a Story," and "Notes for a Young Writer" from *Come Along with Me*, by Shirley Jackson. Copyright 1952, 1948, © 1960 by Shirley Jackson. Reprinted by permission of Viking Penguin, a division of Penguin Books USA Inc.

Excerpts from four of Shirley Jackson's letters to Geraldine and Leslie Jackson, Shirley Jackson Papers, Library of Congress. Used by permission of Sarah H. Stewart.

Outlines of "Elizabeth" and "I Know Who I Love," by Shirley Jackson, Shirley Jackson Papers, Library of Congress. Used by permission of Sarah H. Stewart.

Excerpts from *Private Demons: The Life of Shirley Jackson*, by Judy Oppenheimer. © 1988 by Judy Oppenheimer. Reprinted by permission of The Putnam Publishing Group.

Excerpts from "Sanctuary: Shirley Jackson's Domestic and Fantastic Parables," by James Egan, from *Studies in Weird Fiction*. Reprinted by permission of James Egan, Professor of English, University of Akron, Akron, Ohio.

"'Farther than Samarkand': The Escape Theme in Shirley Jackson's 'The Tooth,'" by Richard Pascal, from *Studies in Short Fiction*. © 1982 by Newberry College. Reprinted by permission.

Excerpts from "'The Lottery': Symbolic Tour de Force," by Helen E. Nebeker, from *American Literature*. © 1974 by Duke University Press. Reprinted by permission.

Excerpts from "The Stoning of Mistress Hutchinson: Meaning and Context in 'The Lottery,'" by Fritz Oehlschlaeger, from *Essays in Literature*. Reprinted by permission of Western Illinois University.

Excerpts from "A Marxist/Feminist Reading of Shirley Jackson's 'The Lottery,'" by Peter Kosenko, from the *New Orleans Review*. Reprinted by permission.

✛

Three libraries provided essential resources for my study of Shirley Jackson. I greatly appreciate the help of Diane Cooter and Amy Doherty of the George Arents Research Library, Syracuse University; James H. Hutson, Alice Birney, Charles Kelly, and Frederick Bauman of the Manuscript Division, Library of Congress; Bill Clark and Martha Swan of the interlibrary loan department, the John Davis Williams Library, University of Mississippi.

The week I spent reading the Shirley Jackson Papers at the Library of Congress was supported by a travel grant from the National Endowment for the Humanities and a faculty development grant from the College of Liberal Arts, University of Mississippi. The College of Liberal Arts and the university's Office of the Vice Chancellor for Academic Affairs provided grants in aid of publication. I thank these institutions for their belief in the value of the project.

S. T. Joshi generously shared his own bibliographical research on Shirley Jackson, adding significantly to my list of uncollected stories. His forthcoming book, *The Modern Weird Tale*, will include a long chapter titled "Shirley Jackson: Domestic Horror." I am also grateful to Judy Oppenheimer, Jackson's biographer, for corresponding with me. Werner Wolff, who photographed Jackson soon after the publication of *The Lottery* in 1949, was instrumental in providing the frontispiece for this study; I thank him for his kind help. Sarah H. Stewart, Shirley Jackson's daughter and literary executrix, made a major contribution by allowing me to quote from the Shirley Jackson Papers and to reprint, in Part 2, several lengthy passages and complete texts not previously published.

Gordon Weaver, general editor of Twayne's Studies in Short Fiction, has been generous and prompt with his guidance from the start. I also very much appreciate the advice and expertise of Liz Traynor Fowler, Vida Petronis, Melissa Solomon, and Barbara Sutton of Twayne Publishers. Ms. Fowler, in particular, was instrumental in initiating this study.

The patience and the word-processing skills of Sara Selby, Kristen Sulser, and Kathy Williams of the University of Mississippi English Department were indispensable.

Among the many friends who loaned books, helped locate bibliographical material, and offered other important help and encouragement are Huafu Paul Bao, Jack Barbera, Polly Stevens Fields, Benjamin Franklin Fisher IV, Doreen Fowler, David Galef, Anne Gowdy, Colby H. Kullman, T. J. Ray, and Cynthia Shearer. For crucial assistance at every stage of this book's development, I am especially thankful to J. R. Hall.

*Part 1*

# THE SHORT FICTION

# The Lottery as a Short-Story Cycle

## The Man in a Blue Suit and Other Unifying Devices

In *The Lottery; or, The Adventures of James Harris* Shirley Jackson organized 25 of her short stories into a five-part book. Although 17 of the stories had already been published in such magazines as *Mademoiselle* and the *New Yorker*, Jackson had probably been writing with a collection in mind for several years. A note on contributors to the 1944 volume *Cross-Section: A Collection of New American Writing* announced she was working on a book of stories to be published early in 1945.[1] The Shirley Jackson Papers in the Library of Congress include undated manuscripts, probably from 1946 or 1947, of title and contents pages for a collection named "The Intoxicated." Among the 40 stories listed are several never published by Jackson; not listed are "The Lottery" and nine other stories from *The Lottery*.[2] When the book finally appeared in 1949, Jackson's title capitalized on the dramatic response to the publication of "The Lottery" in the 26 June 1948 *New Yorker*. So closely has her fame been identified with the one story that subsequent paperback editions have modified or eliminated her subtitle, thus obscuring the volume's loose coherence.

The Farrar, Straus & Giroux paperback, which has gone through several printings since 1982, notes the original title on the back of the title page and retains Jackson's division of the contents but is itself entitled *The Lottery and Other Stories*, deflecting the reader's attention from the book's many allusions to James Harris. Even more revisionary is a Fawcett Popular Library printing of 1975, whose title page and garish cover refer only to *The Lottery* and whose contents page eliminates Jackson's text divisions. Consequently, the stories seem to be chapters of a bizarre novel; this edition's preliminary blurb outlines an action more melodramatic than any created by Jackson: "From the moment you enter a village where age-old rites of evil lead to modern horror, and encounter a lover who enslaves the soul of every woman he touches, you will be gripped by a fascination that will not let you go until the final shocking revelation."[3] From front cover ("The most eerie and haunting work of our time") to back ("A GEM OF SATANIC

3

SHOCK"), the Fawcett edition suggests a singleness of tone and plot that does not accurately represent the short-story format.

Jackson's book is, in fact, neither as disjointed as the first paperback implies nor as tightly composed as the second insists. Although Susan Garland Mann does not mention Jackson in her guide to more than 120 short-story cycles, the format of *The Lottery; or, The Adventures of James Harris* is similar to that of James Joyce's *Dubliners*, Sherwood Anderson's *Winesburg, Ohio*, and Ernest Hemingway's *In Our Time*.[4] References to James Harris are the most obvious link between Jackson's stories. Harris is explicitly identified in six stories, and his presence extends to several more.[5] For example, the "tall, graceful man in a blue suit" who makes a one-sentence appearance at the end of "The Intoxicated," the book's first story, demands a second look when we hear James Harris described by his fiancée in the second story, "The Daemon Lover": "He's rather tall, and fair. He wears a blue suit very often."[6]

James Harris's failure to arrive for his own wedding and his lover's conviction that he is hiding from her inevitably influence the reader's response to all further mention of the names "James" and "Harris." When we learn in "The Renegade" that the Walpoles' dog has been killing chickens at the Harris place, we are inclined to sympathize with the distraught Mrs. Walpole. The narrator calls attention to the family name by obscuring it when Mrs. Harris phones with the bad news: "The voice—it was a woman—said, 'I'm sorry to bother you, but this is—'and gave an unrecognizable name" (71). Through the three-page conversation, Mrs. Harris is described only as "the voice" and "the other woman," but the voice speaks "with relish" (71), insinuating that "if Mrs. Walpole wanted to fight . . . she had picked just the right people" (73). In the original *Harper's* version of "The Renegade" the angry couple is identified later in the story (by Mrs. Walpole's neighbor, Mrs. Nash) as the Kittredges.[7] By changing the name to Harris in *The Lottery*, Jackson efficiently adds this rural conflict to Harris's more typically urban "adventures."

Similar revisions in other stories strengthen the interrelatedness of the collection. When "A Fine Old Firm" appeared in the *New Yorker*, Mrs. Concord told Mrs. Friedman that her son Charles would join the law firm of Satterthwaite and Ferguson after his military service and thus needed no introduction to Mrs. Friedman's husband's partnership, Grunewald, Friedman, and White.[8] The transformation to "Satterthwaite & Harris" in *The Lottery* (196) combines with Mrs. Concord's anti-Semitism to produce a tense conclusion to the women's superficially pleasant conversation. A name substitution in "The Tooth" is even more ominous. The *Hudson*

*Review* story describes a housewife whose trip to the dentist leads to her running off with Ray, a poetic man in a blue suit whom she meets on the bus.[9] "The Tooth" is placed near the end of *The Lottery*, and here Ray becomes Jim, evoking the elusive "daemon lover" James Harris of the second story.

The collection's many references to a Mr. Harris and to Jim, Jimmy, Jamie, and James—often paired with the Harris surname—culminate in the epilogue, a seven-quatrain ballad excerpt that constitutes the last of the book's five parts (305–6). The poem depicts a woman who has been lured from her family by a mysterious lover, whose "cloven foot" she discovers only after she has joined him on shipboard. Although he promises to show her "how the lilies grow / On the banks of Italy," he sinks the ship, admitting "the mountain of hell" is their true destination. At the end of the ballad Jackson identifies the work as "James Harris, the Daemon Lover (Child Ballad No. 243)"; her source is the philologist Francis Child's monumental collection, *English and Scottish Ballads* (1883–98). The plot of the ballad relates to several of Jackson's stories, from "The Daemon Lover" and "The Tooth" to the humorous "Dorothy and My Grandmother and the Sailors," whose narrator describes a visit to a battleship with her nervous mother and grandmother.

Jackson restores to James Harris some of the demonic character that Stanley Edgar Hyman, in an essay on Child's ballads, finds so disappointingly diluted in American renderings of the "Daemon Lover" ballad. "In the American texts," says Hyman, "the wife of a house carpenter elopes with her sailor beau, the ship springs an accidental leak (in one Virginia text nothing happens to it at all), and the wife regrets her impetuosity."[10] In citing Child, Jackson injects the magic and the supernatural elements that "slough off readily" in domesticated versions, "even where they seem to be the ballad's point" (Hyman 1963, 263–64). Moreover, her portrayals of James Harris offset "the toning down of the frank sexuality of the ballads in America" (Hyman 1963, 265).

In a *New York Times* review Donald Barr complained that the recurrences of James Harris's name in widely differing circumstances "give a false unity to the book and confuse the meaning of individual stories."[11] As Barr implies, the several James Harrises do not seem to be a single, consistent character. The diversity of the descriptions, however, may be credited to the devil's own shape-shifting nature, as well as to Jackson's fascination with role playing and complex personalities. One feature many of her Harrises have in common—whether single or married, passive or aggressive, renamed or new to *The Lottery*—is the profession of writing. Jackson links the James Harris stories to several others in the collection that reflect a diversified literary tradition. These range from "After You, My Dear Alphonse," with its echoes of the comic strip "Alphonse and Gaston," to "Come Dance with Me in Ireland," whose title is clarified by a shabby character who knew Yeats and who quotes the poet's "Come out of charity, come dance with me in Ireland" (225), a poem derived in turn from a medieval ballad. "Pillar of Salt" evokes the biblical story of Lot's wife, and "Seven Types of Ambiguity" alludes to William Empson's 1930 book, a classic of literary criticism.

Jackson's literary allusions also unite *The Lottery* into a short-story cycle. Much as Joyce Carol Oates parodies, counterpoints, and otherwise refers to familiar works of fiction in the short-story collection *Marriages and Infidelities* (1972), Jackson seems intent on emphasizing the literariness of her text. That books and readers appear throughout *The Lottery* is not surprising considering Jackson's and Hyman's reading habits. Judy Oppenheimer estimates that their personal library consisted of 30,000 to 40,000 books.[12] Furthermore, books are an important means of characterization in Jackson's novels. In *The Road through the Wall* (1948), for example, she contrasts two young women by describing the stories they read. Marilyn Perlman methodically works her way through Thackeray for the sake of her vocabulary, while the more childish Harriet Merriam prefers Louisa May Alcott. Harriet wonders whether a girl will move into the neighborhood house-for-rent: "they would be like in *Little Women*, and Harriet's friend would be Jo (or just possibly Beth, and they could die together, patiently)."[13] This romantic vision of death is brutally opposed by the murder and suicide of two local children at the end of the story. A book similarly echoes Jackson's plot in *The Sundial* (1958), where old Mr. Halloran reads about Robinson Crusoe's struggles, while his family and their hangers-on stock up the mansion in the expectation the world will soon end. A reference to long-overdue library books at the beginning of *We Have Always Lived in the Castle* (1962) foreshadows the confrontations between the Blackwood sisters and their hostile town, and the narrator's preference for fairy tales prepares the reader for Mary Katherine's creation of a private world "on the moon."

The emphasis on reading in *The Lottery* is nevertheless unusual, even among Jackson's works, if only for the number of characters involved in the act, from a teenager who reads Caesar in Latin class in "The Intoxicated" to a private secretary who carries *The Charterhouse of Parma* "for effect" in "The Villager" (49). This emphasis is especially noticeable when we compare *The Lottery* with 14 stories Hyman collected in *Come Along with Me* after Jackson's death. Whereas Hyman's selections span a 27-year period, all the *Lottery* stories date from the 1940s, and so we can trace Jackson's preoccupation with the written word in the earlier work to her self-consciousness as a novice writer. In her study of Willa Cather's early fiction Sharon O'Brien describes a corresponding abundance of literary allusions, which O'Brien attributes to "the woman writer's need to declare herself a descendent of the male literary tradition to which she fears she does not belong."[14] While Jackson too may have felt the need to provide herself with a legitimate ancestry, she early on revealed as many ties to women authors and to an oral tradition of myth and ballad-making as to the male literary canon. In interviews, she admired Samuel Richardson, André Gide, and E. M. Forster but also Fanny Burney, Jane Austen, Susan Ferrier, the Brontës, Ivy Compton-Burnett, and—in Jackson's opinion, the best contemporary writers in the short-story form—Katherine Anne Porter and Elizabeth Bowen.[15]

To the varied literary allusions and recurring ballad figure James Harris in *The Lottery* may be added yet another connective device—the excerpts from a witchcraft treatise that introduce the book's first four parts. Although Donald Barr objects that these epigraphs, like the reappearances of James Harris, produce a "false unity" (Barr, 4), they explicitly order Jackson's diverse material into book form.[16] The four passages from Joseph Glanvill's *Saducismus Triumphatus; or, Full and Plain Evidence Concerning Witches and Apparitions* (1689) divide the volume into groups of six or seven stories. The epigraph to the book's first part anticipates the demonic journey described in the Child ballad of the epilogue: "She saith, That after their Meetings, they all make very low Obeysances to the Devil, who appears in black Cloaths, and a little Band. He bids them Welcome at their coming, and brings Wine or Beer, Cakes, Meat, or the like. He sits at the higher end. . . . They eat, Drink, Dance and have Musick. At their parting they use to say, *Merry meet, merry part*."[17] The passage colors the reader's perception of the cocktail party in "The Intoxicated," the keynote story. The drink, the music, and especially the preview of global disaster at the kitchen table are unpleasantly reminiscent of the gathering described by an alleged witch in Glanvill's record of confessions.

The Glanvill passages preceding the next three parts hint at the hidden mysteries that motivate human behavior; one passage presents the devil as a sexual partner and even more directly than the "Daemon Lover" ballad does. *Saducismus Triumphatus* also provides names for three characters in the volume's longest story, "Elizabeth." The protagonist, not identified in full until the eighth page, has a namesake in Elizabeth Style, whose dealings with the devil are reported at great length in the witchcraft treatise

(Glanvill, 345–62). In her loneliness and frustration, Jackson's Miss Style similarly seeks help from Jim Harris, forgetting "his heavy face, his thin voice" (191). The physical torments to which Elizabeth Style subjects the teenage Elizabeth Hill in Glanvill's account parallel Miss Style's sarcastic jibes at Daphne Hill, an awkward young secretary. Finally, Robert Hunt, frequently cited by Glanvill as a reliable witness, provides a name for the old family friend whose invitations Elizabeth insensitively rejects.

Glanvill's editor, Coleman O. Parsons, remarks that Glanvill influenced many later storytellers and incorporated into his own books such narrative techniques as the heightening of suspense (Glanvill, vii–xvii). In drawing on Glanvill, Jackson achieves the same effect Poe does when he cites Glanvill on "the mysteries of the will" three times in the story "Ligeia." Though the passage may be spurious—Poe's editors have not been able to locate it—the epigraph suggests what Parsons describes as Glanvill's "verbal, atmospheric, and technical appeal to Poe" (Glanvill, xvi). A final attraction Glanvill may have held for Poe, the linking of "the rational to the irrational" (Glanvill, xvi), is a major focus of *The Lottery*.

This conjunction supplies a recurring plot pattern in which Jackson's characters are distanced from the familiar and the reasonable as they become involved in situations that, at worst, recall the demonic encounters of the Child ballad and of *Saducismus Triumphatus*. Although references to James Harris and to Glanvill's witches frame and punctuate the book with the supernatural, most of the collection's unsettling moments are more mundane. Even the most incredible experiences, those of the jilted fiancée in "The Daemon Lover" and the runaway housewife in "The Tooth," could be explained in psychological rather than supernatural terms. Jackson herself demythologizes the Salem witchcraft trials in her children's book on the subject by frequently referring to the villagers' gossip and personal motivations. In an afterword to the paperback edition of *The Witchcraft of Salem Village*, she actually questions the existence of the devil and witches and finds more convincing sources for the "epidemic" in group hysteria or a bread fungus.[18] Yet the epilogue to *The Lottery* offers no such assurance, and the reader of the ballad is left in a state of shock that replicates the final condition of Jackson's typical protagonist.

In my discussion of the individual stories, I follow Jackson's four-part division of the 25 works. Her arrangement is not chronological by date of composition, nor does she separate previously published stories from new pieces. What unity there is within each group inheres chiefly in the family status of the characters. The first six stories—"The Intoxicated," "The Daemon Lover," "Like Mother Used to Make," "Trial by Combat," "The

Villager," and "My Life with R. H. Macy"—focus on singles, one of them a woman who lives alone while her husband is serving in the army. The next seven stories—"The Witch," "The Renegade," "After You, My Dear Alphonse," "Charles," "Afternoon in Linen," "Flower Garden," and "Dorothy and My Grandmother and the Sailors"—are concerned with children, and in three instances children are portrayed with their domineering grandmothers. The six pieces in the third group— "Colloquy," "Elizabeth," "A Fine Old Firm," "The Dummy," "Seven Types of Ambiguity," and "Come Dance with Me in Ireland"—are the least susceptible to generalization, but most of them portray married women (Elizabeth Style of "Elizabeth" wishes she were married) who speak about their husbands or children to friends or others outside the family. Aside from "Elizabeth," whose protagonist is in fact involved in a long-term relationship as passionless as most of the marriages in *The Lottery*, "Seven Types of Ambiguity" is the only story in the group that does not center on married women. Appropriately titled, this story is curious for several reasons, including its portrayal of James Harris as a polite bookseller with no apparent love interest. A married couple does visit the book shop, but their relationship is secondary to the husband's interaction with a fellow customer. The final group of six stories—"Of Course," "Pillar of Salt," "Men with Their Big Shoes," "The Tooth," "Got a Letter from Jimmy," and "The Lottery"—depicts a series of couples whose marriages undergo unusual pressures. References to James Harris are most frequent in the first group of stories, but some form of his name appears in at least two stories in each of the sections that follow. This common thread epitomizes the underlying theme of the intrusion of the irrational into the rational, or the unfamiliar into the familiar, a motif of menace that radiates from the James Harris tales to infect most of the relationships in the book.

## Group One: Balancing Acts

"The Intoxicated" introduces the tone of menace by describing an uneasy encounter between an unnamed party guest and the teenage daughter of his host and hostess. Although the title applies most obviously to the male visitor, who is uncomfortably aware of his inebriation, it is also relevant to the excited intensity of Eileen, who disturbs his retreat from the noisy living room. Their conversation across the kitchen table is the first of several verbal duels in *The Lottery*, a disconcerting dialogue that leaves the visitor irritated and even shocked. Eileen's imagination, articulateness, and reflection relate her to many of the embattled teenagers in Jackson's longer fiction, from Marilyn Perlman in *The Road through the Wall* and Natalie Waite in *Hangsaman* (1951) through Mary Katherine Blackwood in *We Have Always Lived in the Castle*, her last completed novel. Preliminary small talk about the changing times makes the guest nervous; he feels Eileen's "tone had been faintly surprised, as though next he were to declare for an arena with gladiators fighting wild beasts, or the solitary circular waltzing of a madman in a garden" (4–5).

Their conflict, aggravated by differences of age and sex, comes to a climax when Eileen describes a paper she is writing about the future. She foresees the man's death in the rubbish of fallen churches, apartment houses, schools, and office buildings, but she imagines herself among the survivors of an earth-shaking cataclysm: "'Things will be different afterward,' she said. 'Everything that makes the world like it is now will be gone. We'll have new rules and new ways of living'" (7).[19] Since the kitchen provides no real refuge from the pressures of the cocktail party, the guest returns to the living room, where his hostess is talking earnestly with a James Harris look-alike, "a tall, graceful man in a blue suit" (8). When the now sober visitor describes Eileen to his host as an "extraordinary girl," the father "ruefully" shakes his head and concludes, "Kids nowadays" (8).

Earlier versions of "The Intoxicated" end on a more clearly threatening note. In what seems to be the earliest of three drafts, Jackson stops not with the host's rueful words, but with the guest's realization that the two men share an unvoiced terror:

> Suddenly in his host's eyes and tightened mouth he found the fear, the insistent nagging, ("When they come, when they come with their songs and their bright new words, with their gaiety and their cruelty, where will we hide? What will preserve us, who will protect us, what can save us then?").
> And he said brightly, looking down into his glass, "She's going to be a fine woman, someday." (SJP, Box 16)

In reworking the conclusion for the published version, Jackson progressively removed all direct allusion to either man's distress. Another important revision is the transformation of a "heavy red-faced man in a grey suit," who speaks with the hostess in all three drafts, to a graceful man in blue, a substitution whose significance becomes apparent only in the next story. This technique of concealing the ugly and the fearful offsets the full horror of Eileen's vision, but the disturbing quality of that vision anticipates the experiences of many characters in *The Lottery*.

"The Daemon Lover," one of Jackson's most powerful stories, introduces James Harris by name and is in many ways a more representative work than "The Intoxicated." Because it had already appeared in print in *Woman's Home Companion* as "The Phantom Lover," she may have decided to grant the lead position in *The Lottery* to a previously unpublished story, especially one whose apocalyptic perspective would set the tone for the more personal disasters of successive stories.[20] Because Jackson publicly commented on very little of her writing, her remarks to a *New York Times* interviewer on the genesis of "The Daemon Lover," as illustrative of her compositional method, are noteworthy: "Someone told me an anecdote, just a few sentences. (Sort of like Henry James, you know.) I like thinking about it, turning it around, thinking of ways to use a situation like that in order to get a haunting note. It gets quite real. I think of what other thing it will go with, while I'm washing the dishes. But I do it because it's fun, because I like it" (Breit, 15). The book's epilogue reveals that one thing Jackson found to go with the anecdote was Child Ballad No. 243, a poem that supplied the "haunting note" in the person of James Harris.

Another element of her design may have been Elizabeth Bowen's "The Demon Lover," written in London during World War II and included in the short-story volume *Ivy Gripped the Steps* (1946). In her preface Bowen states that the stories, though written separately and published first in magazines—as most of Jackson's were—have a "cumulative and collective meaning that no one of them, taken singly, has by itself." The volume, she adds, is "an organic whole: not merely a collection but somehow—for better or worse—a book."[21] The same could be said of the coherence of *The Lottery; or, The Adventures of James Harris*. Although the wartime climate that unites Bowen's stories is virtually absent from Jackson's book (except for a few references to soldiers and sailors), both writers were repeatedly drawn toward portrayals of extreme mental states. Thus in her preface Bowen comments on the hallucinations and the claustrophobia experienced by many of her characters. She numbers the "ruthless young soldier lover" who returns to London in 1941 after a 25-year absence in "The Demon Lover" among the "questionable" ghosts in the book, "for are they subjective purely?" (Bowen, xii). It is tempting to explain away the demon lover in Jackson's story as an illusion of the age-conscious, lovesick protagonist (especially in light of the original title, "The Phantom Lover"), but Jackson too creates an objective reality for James Harris. The two stories end quite differently: Bowen's demon lover reclaims his one-time fiancée, while Jackson's Jamie Harris deserts his fiancée of one week on the day set for their wedding. Both conclusions are nightmarish. Each woman forfeits

11

her familiar domestic world, and each receives terrifying confirmation of her early sense of a strangeness in the love relationship.

The ending of Jackson's story is foreshadowed in her opening description of the unnamed protagonist: "She had not slept well; from one-thirty, when Jamie left and she went lingeringly to bed, until seven, when she at last allowed herself to get up and make coffee, she had slept fitfully, stirring awake to open her eyes and look into the half-darkness, remembering over and over, slipping again into a feverish dream" (9). The subject of her remembering is unclear. Is she nervous about the coming marriage, or is she perhaps uneasy that she has begun a sexual relationship with Jamie before the wedding? The "sudden horror" she feels when she realizes that she has not changed the bedsheets, and her tactics "to avoid thinking consciously of why she was changing the sheets" (10), could indicate either anxious anticipation or guilt. Still, changing the bathroom towels three times in the course of the morning seems compulsive, and her accidental ripping and prompt mending of her girlish print dress may be sexually suggestive.

The fiancée's uneasiness begins long before Jamie fails to arrive at the scheduled hour of 10. The note she attempts to write to her sister Anne to announce the marriage only increases the woman's anxiety by reminding her of something odd in the courtship. Hesitant in mid-sentence—"I can hardly believe it myself, but when I tell you how it happened, you'll see it's even stranger than that . . . " (9)—she tears up the page, then turns to consider her depressingly limited wardrobe. She hesitates over the clothes as she had hesitated over the letter. Eager to appear soft and feminine, she nevertheless is repelled at the sight of herself in the mirror wearing a dress whose wide skirt "looked irresistibly made for a girl, for someone who would run freely, dance, swing it with her hips when she walked" (11). Angrily, she accuses herself of trying to look prettier than she is. Applying the proper makeup is "another delicate balance between looking as well as possible, and deceiving as little" (12). The woman "cruelly" reminds herself that, though the marriage license says she is 30, her real age is 34.

The reader infers that the fiancée's life is a series of such delicate balancing acts. Like most of Jackson's protagonists, she loses her customary equilibrium when a totally unexpected counterforce destroys the hard-won balance. Jackson, like Poe, is interested in the mental states that influence characters' responses to such forces—the drunkenness of the man in "The Intoxicated" and the chronic alcoholism of the narrator in Poe's "The Black Cat," for example. James Harris is a more formidable adversary than the teenage Eileen, but the fiancée's anxiety at his failure to meet her as planned is intensified by a sleepless night, a lack of food, a headache, a surplus of caffeine from her many cups of coffee, and, finally, the trail of snide remarks that follows her urgent search through the city. Like the boy Robin, who desperately seeks the financial and emotional support of an urban cousin in Hawthorne's "My Kinsman Major Molineux," she too seems trapped in a maze of streets that echo with the hostile laughter of tradesmen and local residents. People repeatedly shut their doors on both suppliants.

Each encounter with a stranger thus prepares the fiancée for the end of her journey. Arriving at an apartment to which she has been directed by a sarcastic boy, she thinks "suddenly, with terror, What shall I say if Jamie is there, if he comes to the door?" (27). She now seems as frightened at the possibility of his presence as she is at his absence. The voices she had heard fall silent, and the only sound is "something that might have been laughter far away." Coincidentally, her final recollection of her parting from James Harris the night before is his "laughing down the hallway" (12). When the woman knocks at the other door in the dirty hallway, it swings open on a messy attic. A bright-eyed rat watches her, "its evil face alert" (27). Stumbling, she closes the door on her skirt, tearing for a second time the dress she had mended in preparation for her wedding. In the days that follow, she returns to the apartment frequently and again hears low voices and laughter: "She came on her way to work, in the mornings; in the evenings, on her way to dinner alone, but no matter how often or how firmly she knocked, no one ever came to the door" (28). Earlier, she had dreamed of quitting her job for a "golden house-in-the-country future" when Jamie became an established writer (12). Her dream is destroyed: still a working woman, she moves between her neat apartment and the shabby building where James Harris has shut her out of his life.

The fiancée realizes she should report Jamie to the police as a missing person, but she knows how foolish she would look explaining he had not arrived for the wedding: "She couldn't tell them any more than that, could not say, 'Yes, it looks silly, doesn't it, me all dressed up and trying to find the young man who promised to marry me, but what about all of it you don't know? I have more than this, more than you can see: talent, perhaps, and humor of a sort, and I'm a lady and I have pride and affection and delicacy and a certain clear view of life that might make a man satisfied and productive and happy; there's more than you think when you look at me'" (23). By striking so cruelly at her fragile dignity, James Harris sends his fiancée on a tortured journey as painful as the ship voyage to hell described in the Child ballad. While few characters in *The Lottery* suffer equivalent losses, many of Jackson's women—and a couple of her men—find their pride and their very sense of self as delicate a fabric as the fiancée's print dress.

The other four stories in Jackson's first group repeat in a minor scale the notes of shock and dislocation sounded in "The Intoxicated" and "The Daemon Lover." Less nightmarish than "The Daemon Lover," these works nevertheless resemble in several ways the existentialist novels and absurdist plays of the postwar years. Like the unnamed protagonists of the first two stories, these characters too are thrown off balance and scramble to secure an identity. At times, they can resolve the crisis only by assuming another identity, which introduces an odd sense of doubleness, a sort of doppelgänger effect. The fact that all the central characters in the first group of stories act without the support, or even the presence, of other family members, emphasizes their essential loneliness. Sometimes Jackson, like the absurdist playwrights, turns this situation to comic effect, but her comedy—like that of Samuel Beckett, Eugène Ionesco, and Harold Pinter—invariably contains an element of threat.

James Harris again embodies the threat in the next story, "Like Mother Used to Make." In her biography of Jackson, Judy Oppenheimer describes a true-life source for the incident, involving Stanley Edgar Hyman (Oppenheimer, 102). This peculiar sequel to "The Daemon Lover" ends with a man, not a woman, shut out of an apartment that harbors the laughing Mr. Harris. Ironically, David Turner is driven from his own neat home, which James Harris, now described as "a very large man" (35), unwittingly invades. Mr. Harris is admitted by his co-worker, David's neighbor and dinner guest, Marcia. From David's apartment, she presses the buzzer that opens the lobby door after Harris, visiting for the first time, rings her doorbell. Invited in for dessert, Harris assumes that the apartment is Marcia's and that she has baked the delicious pie to which the title alludes. Smiling conspiratorily at David, Marcia easily plays the role of hostess, and David withdraws to wash dishes in the kitchen. When he finally returns to the living room, David speaks awkwardly, and Mr. Harris watches him impatiently. Marcia's "Sit down, Davie, won't you?" is delivered in a tone he recognizes as "the one hostesses used when they didn't know what else to say to you, or when you had come too early or stayed too late. It was the tone he had expected to use on Mr. Harris" (38). Accepting the identity of unwelcome guest, David says his farewells "much more genially than he intended" (39). Marcia closes the door on him as he thanks her for the dinner, and he retreats down the hall to her sloppy apartment.

The situation is humorous but almost as incredible as the plight of the jilted fiancée in "The Daemon Lover," and finally almost as disturbing. Sitting on Marcia's unmade bed, David looks around at her scattered laundry and wind-strewn papers: "It was cold, and it was dirty, and as he thought miserably of his own warm home he heard faintly down the hall the sound of laughter and the scrape of a chair being moved" (40). In both stories, James Harris precipitates the protagonist's exclusion, not only from a physical place but also from emotional sustenance. Both the fiancée and David Turner respond mechanically to their losses. While the woman fruitlessly returns to the closed door, David attempts to restore order by attacking the chaos of Marcia's apartment: "Wearily, David leaned over and picked up a paper from the floor, and then he began to gather them up one by one" (40). Jackson's revision of an early draft radically changes the tone of her original conclusion, where David (there named Jamie Turner) giggles down the hall to Marcia's apartment, elated they have together made "a fool out of a big guy like that." The "big guy" is innocently named Harold Lang in this early form, and James Turner whistles as he picks up Marcia's papers, confident "if Lang stays over there even an hour . . . I can get this place looking pretty good" (SJP, Box 16).

Analogous to the cluttered attic in "The Daemon Lover," Marcia's rooms in the revised version of "Like Mother Used to Make" represent the dark side of life that most of Jackson's characters seem fated to confront. David realizes that Marcia's apartment is an upsetting double of his own: "This apartment was not agreeable for him to come into; it was exactly the same as his: foyer, kitchenette, living-room, and it reminded him constantly of his first day in his own apartment, when the thought of the careful home-making to be done had left him very close to despair" (31). After his long hours of exertion, only one reminder of the original bleakness remains to worry David; the falling plaster in one corner of his living-room ceiling is a "perpetual trouble to him," and "no power on earth could make it less noticeable" (30). With paint, plants, and carefully selected furnishings, he has otherwise created "the most comfortable home he had ever had" (31). He keeps his single door key "safely" in his pocket, where it gives him a false sense of protection, "the only way into his warm fine home."

Marcia and David are as different as the decor of their apartments. Not only does she lack his neatness, but her loud speech contrasts with his quietness. At the same time, the two are similar in exhibiting a blend of gender characteristics. Reversing the usual male-female stereotypes, Jackson shows David's pleasure in domestic matters—he is "tenderly" accumulating a complete set of silverware (32)—and she describes his blush of pleasure at Marcia's praise. Marcia, on the other hand, is portrayed as a working woman (named "Billie" in the draft) who is "always hungry"; she fills her dinner plate "without admiring the serving silver" (34). Although she calls David "honey" in front of James Harris, their relationship does not appear to be a romantic one. In contrast to David, the large Mr. Harris exudes an oppressive masculinity. To Marcia's amusement and David's distress, he "thickly" announces smoke is good for plants as he lights a cigar. Then he "heartily" holds out a hand, which David "limply" shakes as he leaves his apartment to the outsiders (39). In this final twist, David's "urgency to be rid of them both" (37) is relieved, but only at the cost of surrendering his home. Since Marcia clearly tells him goodnight, he may be providing the setting of the latest of "the adventures of James Harris."

Apartments are also strangely invaded in the next two stories, "Trial by Combat" and "The Villager," and in both the motif of doubleness recurs. The "combat" of the first work is restricted to the small-scale skirmishes of two women in a New York roominghouse, but the husbands of both have served in the army, and the title expresses the tension that runs through most of the book. Emily Johnson indirectly accuses her downstairs neighbor, Mrs. Allen, of stealing several items from her furnished room and hopes the thefts will stop. The next day, however, a cheap pair of earrings and two packs of cigarettes are missing, and she subsequently enters Mrs. Allen's apartment, where she finds all her stolen possessions in the dresser. When Mrs. Allen suddenly returns, the startled Emily explains that a terrible headache forced her to come looking for aspirin. "Let's not say any more about it," responds Mrs. Allen, either kindly or threateningly. Triumphant in combat, she promises to come up later, "just to see how you feel" (47).

As in "Like Mother Used to Make," the apartments, as well as the persons who live there, are disconcertingly alike and different. Mrs. Allen's room is "directly below her own" (41), and when Emily first pays a call she sees immediately that the apartment is "almost like her own—the same narrow bed with the tan cover, the same maple dresser and armchair; the closet was on the opposite side of the room, but the window was in the same relative position (42). Emily describes the 60-year-old Mrs. Allen as a mathematical doubling of herself: "More than twice as old as I am, Emily thought, while she stood in the doorway, and a lady still" (42). Neither woman has children; their husbands are gone (Mr. Allen dead and Mr. Johnson apparently overseas); both like flowers; and both mask their frustrations with politeness, a common feature of Jackson's women. When Mrs. Allen catches her in the act of spying, Emily wonders what the older woman could be waiting for "with such a ladylike manner," and when Emily speaks, she recognizes the similarity: "My voice is almost ladylike, too, she thought" (47).

The women are also alike in their efforts to make homes of their small apartments, but the task is not easy, and these homes remain as susceptible to assault as those in the preceding stories. Mrs. Allen tells Emily she has repeatedly complained to the landlady that "you can't make people feel at home if you put all the same furniture in the rooms" (42). Emily has bought asters to brighten her room, but she knows they fade quickly. She "pleadingly" expresses her fear that someone has a key to her door, and when Mrs. Allen explains that all the keys in the building open all the old-fashioned locks, Emily insists, "It *has* to stop" (45). Her key provides no more security than David Turner's in "Like Mother Used to Make." Emily's final reluctance to confront Mrs. Allen with the evidence of theft may stem from her identification with the older woman. When she enters the widow's room on her spying mission, Emily experiences "a sudden sense of unbearable intimacy with Mrs. Allen" (46). Staring for the third time at a picture of a dignified-looking Mr. Allen in uniform, she reflects, "They must have had such a pleasant life together, and now she has a room like mine, with only two handkerchiefs of her own in the drawer" (46).

Mrs. Allen is pitiful, but she also has a sinister side that relates her more closely to James Harris than to Emily Johnson. An early instance of the several menacing old ladies in Jackson's fiction, she symbolically erodes Emily's sense of self by stealing her initial pin. In taking "one of a set of china dogs" (41), she further attacks the younger woman's wholeness, while also suggesting that she and Emily constitute a set. Emily wrongly assumes that "her losses were trivial" (41); her original certainty that she can deal with the situation logically is thwarted by the illogical attacks of Mrs. Allen.

The trespassers who explore a modest apartment in "The Villager" are not thieves, but one of them is a smiling Mr. Harris, come to answer a classified ad for furniture for sale. By chance, he enters shortly after the arrival of the protagonist, Hilda Clarence, who is there on the same mission. (A note on the door from the absent resident invited Miss Clarence, who had made an appointment, to wait in the unlocked flat.) Hilda lets Mr. Harris think she is Nancy Roberts, a dancer who lives in the apartment with her husband, Arthur. Nancy's scattered books remind Hilda that 15 years ago she herself had come to the city with the dream of becoming a dancer, and she is striking a pose when Mr. Harris walks in. Hilda identifies not only with Nancy but with Mr. Harris, an urban newcomer who plans to get a job and practice his writing craft at night, much as she had become a stenographer to support her now-abandoned goal of dancing professionally.

But after she lies to Mr. Harris that she *is* a dancer, he intrusively wanders around the apartment. The discomfort he inflicts is mild compared to his impact in earlier stories, but when he looks into the dirty bathroom Hilda winces, and when he opens the kitchen door she explains she does not cook much. Neither does Mr. Harris, who pleasantly remarks he needs a wife, evoking a shudder in the reader and perhaps regret on Hilda's part that she has so convincingly adopted the persona of Nancy. Miss Clarence heads for home alone, not waiting to confront her double, but the slight exertion of the dance pose leaves its mark, and the story ends, as most of Jackson's do, on a note of pain: "Her shoulders ached" (56).

Hilda Clarence in several ways resembles the unlucky fiancée of "The Daemon Lover." Another unmarried working woman, Miss Clarence too is about 35 and conscious of her appearance (49). Her pride in her competence as a well-paid private secretary is reminiscent of the fiancée's confidence in her personal worth. Both women smoke nervously and become increasingly impatient, frequently checking the time as they are kept waiting past a scheduled hour. Jackson strengthened the similarities between the two stories by renaming Mr. Atkins from the *American Mercury* version of "The Villager" as Mr. Harris.[22] The Robertses' old wooden building, the dingy hallway, and the shiny maple furniture in their messy living room compare unfavorably with Miss Clarence's beige and off-white furnishings and her modern apartment house, much as the fiancée's neat rooms contrast with the garret of "The Daemon Lover." Though Hilda Clarence's quest from her Greenwich Village home is much less anguished than the fiancée's disillusioning journey, they both make trips into darkness.

"My Life with R. H. Macy," on the other hand, is the one really humorous work in this first division of stories. Shirley Jackson's earliest piece in a national publication, it appeared in the *New Republic* during Christmas week of 1941.[23] In contrast to the minor annoyances that characters experience at the start of the typical Jackson story, "My Life with R. H. Macy" opens with a shock. The calm third-person narrator of the first five stories is replaced with the distraught voice of a victim who begins in medias res: "And the first thing they did was segregate me. They segregated me from the only person in the place I had even a speaking acquaintance with; that was a girl I had met going down the hall who said to me: 'Are you as scared as I am?'" (57). Close to the ending mood of the preceding stories, the sense of isolation and displacement is undercut immediately after the speaker answers "yes." The rest of the story sounds like a parody of the tone of menace and the themes of doubleness and identity common to the previous pieces and to many of the succeeding ones. Though disconcerting in this context, the shift in tone provides comic relief that Jackson may have considered necessary. One of the few autobiographical sketches incorporated into *The Lottery*, "My Life with R. H. Macy" reveals her tendency to recognize the absurd in the mundane and also anticipates her outpouring of fictionalized autobiography in the 1950s.

As the title indicates, the narrator's agony results from her employment at the huge New York department store. Early in "The Villager" Hilda Clarence is compared to the many other young adults who moved from small towns to Greenwich Village with "plans to work in Macy's or in a bookshop until they had enough money to pursue their art" (49). The speaker in "My Life with R. H. Macy" exaggerates that Macy's alone has 11,700 employees, all of them so much depersonalized that each supervisor is named Miss Cooper and the clerks are called by their numbers, 13-3138 in her case. Workers have additional numbers for their locker, time clock, cash box, cash register, cash-register drawer, and cash-register-drawer key. A misfit from the first day, the protagonist reports for training in a red velvet afternoon dress, while the other young women wear tailored suits. She is further alienated by the special language of Macy's: "Comp. keep for ref. cust. d.a. no. or c.t. no. salebook no. salescheck no. clerk no. dept. date M" (58). The store's secular rituals—incongruously performed against a backdrop of the Christmas season—subsume individuals into groups, units, and departments. Told she cannot wear her hat while punching the clock, the nonconforming speaker leaves for another part of the store, "bowing timidly at the time clock and its prophet" (58). She is sent to lunch three times in one day because the counter head in the book department confuses her with 13-6454 and 13-3141. When she finally sells a copy of her assigned book, *The Stage-Struck Seal*, she destroys the "duplicate triplicate" because she does not know how to file it. Confused by a customer's request for a different title, she is stared at by a fellow employee who illogically explains that "philosophy, social sciences and Bertrand Russell were all kept in dictionaries" (60).

Like most of Jackson's frustrated women, this one comes to a moment of crisis, but her response frees her from a routine that threatens to destroy her individuality. Falling downstairs after her second day of work, she tears her stockings, an accident that—unlike the unfortunate ripping of the fiancée's dress in "The Daemon Lover"—is comically resolved. The narra-

tor rejects the doorman's detailed instructions for getting a free replace-
ment and reclaims her identity by buying herself a new pair and exiting
through the customers' entrance. Her subsequent long letter to her former
employer is sarcastically signed with the total of all her Macy's numbers,
divided by 11,700. At the story's end she is characteristically bruised but,
unique among the protagonists of the first part of *The Lottery*, uncharacteristically jubilant. Although Jackson invokes the comic spirit in several
stories that follow, no other central character maintains or recovers a
comparable state of command. The menace embodied by James Harris and
other strangers in the first group of stories spreads through the rest of the
book as friends and family members compound such outside threats to the
delicately balanced protagonists. Thus opposed, Jackson's characters have
no more chance of maintaining their equilibrium than the "stage-struck
seals" that the sympathetic Macy's clerk says she "possessively" tends (59).

## Group Two: Rebellious Sons and Daughters

In contrast to the loners of *The Lottery*'s first six stories, the seven stories in
the second part focus on women and girls in family settings; husbands are
frequently absent or subordinated to background roles. As their titles
insinuate, "The Witch" and "The Renegade," the first two stories, have
affinities with the first part. The frightening experiences of the two mothers
in these stories are all the more terrible in light of their children's casual
responses. The mothers in the second part's remaining five stories are also
confounded by their sons and daughters, but in less startling ways. Much
as "My Life with R. H. Macy" renders Jackson's usual themes in a comic
mode, most of the works in the second part translate her concerns with
anxiety and a sense of self into more realistic situations than those depicted
in the first set of stories. Accordingly, the element of the bizarre and the
incredible diminishes, though a feeling of strangeness and uneasiness
remains throughout.

In a break from the claustrophobic rooms and urban settings of the first
several stories, "The Witch" takes place on a train passing through an
attractive landscape. While the introductory lines of each story in the first
group portray a lone adult, "The Witch" begins with a family tableau: a
talkative four-year-old, Johnny; his mother, who is quietly reading; and a
baby girl, who occupies herself with toast and a rattle. At the start, the only
disquieting detail is the baby's tendency to "slip slowly sideways," but she
is "strapped securely," and her mother straightens her whenever she slides
halfway down the seat (63). The one time she bangs her head, her brother

Johnny pets her feet until she laughs; he is rewarded with a lollipop. The mother herself is initially so secure that she responds with an automatic "fine" to the boy's constant chatter, even to his unusual claim to have sighted a witch outside. But, as often happens in *The Lottery*, the initial sense of control is jeopardized by an outsider, in this case a fellow passenger who fascinates the son but so upsets the mother that her original calm is eventually shattered.

The intruder remains unnamed, but as he enters the coach he looks like an aging James Harris. With his "pleasant face" (as in "The Villager"), his blue suit (reminiscent of "The Daemon Lover"), and his cigar (as in "Like Mother Used to Make"), the friendly traveler charms the child as effectively as Mr. Harris intrigued the women in the earlier stories. The man's blue suit is an addition to Jackson's original manuscript (SJP, Box 19). The boy responds to him with ready laughter, as Marcia responded to James Harris in "Like Mother Used to Make." Like the exclusive laughter associated with Jamie Harris in "The Daemon Lover," the good humor shuts out the mother. Though anxious when the white-haired stranger sits down by her son, she soon relaxes and returns "peacefully" to her book, not joining in the conversation.

The crisis thus arrives unexpectedly. A memory of his childhood, which the old man introduces in fairy-tale fashion—"Once upon a time"—suddenly becomes an unbelievable account of savagery, worthy of the Brothers Grimm. The man tells Johnny that he had a sister ("just like yours") on whom he lavished gifts before pinching her to death and dismembering her. The mother's smile fades as she helplessly opens and closes her mouth. Before she manages to ask the storyteller to leave, her son "eagerly" draws out the fact that a bear ate the dead girl's head. Boy and man laugh repeatedly at the distressed mother, threatening to chop off her head and the baby's too. After the stranger excuses himself to leave the car, the woman "urgently" tells Johnny he was just teasing, but the boy, settling down with a fresh lollipop, concludes, "Prob'ly he was a witch" (67).

Robert L. Kelly, who calls the story a "Satanic gem," finds a "subtle link of evil" in the correspondence between Johnny's sucker and the outsider's cigar.[24] When Johnny comments that his father smokes cigars too, the man's retort that *all* men do "raises the possibility that this man also has a paternal claim." Kelly's suggestion is especially intriguing in light of the father's absence from the coach and the gradual alignment of the man and the boy against the woman and the baby girl. The several doubles in Jackson's book incline the reader to view Johnny and the visitor as another such pair. Certainly they seem to speak the same language. When the boy asserts he is 26, the man ignores the woman's corrective "Four" and "politely" repeats "Twenty-six" (65). Instead of ignoring Johnny's references to witches, as his mother has previously done, the stranger takes him seriously and asks whether he has found many. Johnny's innocent delight in the man's sadistic tale inspires the boy to project a similar denouement for his mother. When the woman threatens to call the conductor, he anticipates, "The conductor will *eat* my mommy" (67). The child's ignorant cruelty is mirrored in the deliberate brutality of the man, who unfeelingly asks the mother whether he has frightened her. The stranger's story line is an exaggerated version of the many *Lottery* plots in which unsuspecting victims, like Johnny's mother, are abruptly confronted and deprived of control, even the control of their own voices. Most of these victims lack any defense equivalent to the strap that saves Johnny's baby sister from serious slips.

"The Renegade" is an especially effective rendering of this basic plot. Again a horrified mother is dumbstruck to see the cruelty of strangers echoed in her children. In "The Witch" the nameless mother's maternal role is emphasized by consistent references to "the mother"; she is never "the woman." Similarly identified by her family relationship, the protagonist of "The Renegade," the mother of twins Judy and Jack, is always called "Mrs. Walpole." Mrs. Walpole too is initially portrayed alone with her children, though a self-absorbed Mr. Walpole joins her in the kitchen after the twins leave for school. Like the sliding baby in "The Witch," the "loitering" twins are an initial, though mild, source of concern for their mother, who is irritated that they might miss the bus. She experiences the "wading-through-molasses feeling of trying to hurry children" (69). Also like the preoccupied mother in the preceding story, who at first repeats "fine" to Johnny's most outrageous assertions, Mrs. Walpole "mechanically" calls her children's names.

In contrast to the other woman, however, Mrs. Walpole clearly struggles from the start to maintain her composure. Not only has the alarm clock failed to go off, but the coffee is too slow and the eggs too soft. With no time even to drink her juice, she has to make an effort to greet Mr. Walpole pleasantly and to prepare his breakfast "patiently." Her mind is "full of unfinished sentences that began, 'Don't you think other people ever have any feelings or—'" (70), sentences she never pronounces. But Mrs. Walpole has just brought matters under control when the ring of her telephone, an "unbearable intrusion," announces her downfall just as abruptly as the stranger's entrance in the railroad coach in "The Witch."

The phone call clarifies at least one meaning of the story's title. According to an angry neighbor, the ominously named Mrs. Harris, the Walpoles' dog, Lady, has overnight become a violent killer of chickens. The news affects Mrs. Walpole much as the man's ugly story affected Johnny's mother. She is silent so long the caller asks, "Hello?" before Mrs. Walpole can voice her denial: "That's perfectly ridiculous" (71). Mrs. Walpole seems unusually attached to the dog; in her opinion Lady is "quiet, competent, exceedingly tolerant," qualities that seem more descriptive of the woman herself. It pains her to picture Mr. Harris, who luckily forgot to take his shotgun to the chicken yard, chasing the dog with a stick. Mrs. Walpole speaks weakly; bewildered, she is seized with a "sudden unalterable terror" as she faces "an evil situation she had never known before" (72–73). Reminiscent of the fiancée in "The Daemon Lover," Mrs. Walpole then begins a journey through the village that confirms her apprehension. Spread by the Harrises, news of Lady's attack precedes her, and she—like the fiancée—is the object of knowing looks. In both stories, the evil inheres not simply in the original act of betrayal but in the cruelty of townspeople who further distress the woman victim, for Mrs. Walpole is the story's main victim.

Mrs. Walpole's encounters become increasingly grueling as one person after another offers advice. While her neighbor Mrs. Nash merely suggests a sturdy chain, old Mr. White thinks Lady should be killed, the grocer favors tying a "ripe" dead chicken around her neck, and a male customer at the grocery recommends putting the dog in a pen with a protective mother hen who would scratch out her eyes. The worst suggestion is relayed at the end by the Walpole children, who have been talking with Mr. Shepherd, a "genial man" who gives nickels to the twins and takes boys fishing. The children laughingly describe a spiked collar that would strangle Lady as she pulls at a rope when made to chase chickens. Judy and Jack compete to add gruesome details and sound effects. Recalling Johnny in "The Witch," Jack dramatically concludes, "The spikes cut her head off" (83). Mrs. Walpole is sickened as she watches the twins, "with their hard hands and their sunburned faces laughing together, their dog with blood still on her legs laughing with them" (83). She seeks comfort in the doorway view of "cool green hills" and a "peaceful sky," but when she closes her eyes she suddenly feels "the harsh hands [an echo of the children's "hard hands"] pulling her down, the sharp points closing in on her throat" (83).

Mrs. Walpole's final identification with the female dog is shockingly explicit, but it helps to explain why she is "indescribably depressed" after receiving Mrs. Harris's call (74). For Mrs. Walpole, with her outward restraint and inward turmoil is herself a "renegade" of sorts. She strains to sound "pleasant" when Mr. White asks whether Mr. Walpole has a gun to shoot Lady, trying "not to let her hatred show in her face" (77). Her alarm at the "deliberate, malicious pain" Lady has "inflicted" (81) suggests her fearfulness of releasing her own suppressed violence; again the terms in which she thinks of the dog seem more applicable to a person. Disturbed by "the murderous brutality a pretty dog like Lady could keep so well hidden in their home" (81), Mrs. Walpole perhaps recognizes a similar doubleness in herself. As a mother of fraternal twins, she could be especially conscious of the splits in her own life. The identity Mrs. Walpole feels with Lady may be the reason she does not correct the men in the grocery store when they several times refer to the dog as "he" and "him." Mrs. Walpole neither repeats the pronoun nor calls Lady by name, though the avoidance forces her to speak impersonally of "the dog" (79).

Mrs. Walpole can relate to Lady not only as a female whose usual good manners mask her inner tension, but also as an outsider in the community. The family's recent move from the city has entailed many adjustments, especially for Mrs. Walpole. Although she looks to the landscape for relief at the end of the story, she is generally ill at ease in the country setting. Mrs. Walpole realizes they are "still city folk and would probably always be city folk, people who owned a chicken-killing dog, people who washed on Tuesday, people who were not able to fend for themselves against the limited world of earth and food and weather that the country folk took so much for granted" (74). She is reminded daily of her helplessness, driven always to ask others' advice on everything from trash disposal to weather-stripping and baking. Mrs. Walpole contrasts her inadequacy with the efficiency of Mrs. Nash, who dispenses freshly baked doughnuts early in the morning, wearing a "shockingly clean house dress" in her "freshly washed" kitchen (75). To Mrs. Walpole, her neighbor's bright house, sturdy table, and good kitchen smells are "all symbols somehow of Mrs. Nash's safety, her confidence in a way of life and a security that had no traffic with chicken-killing, no city fears" (76). Mrs. Walpole's own insecurity is further emphasized when the sunlight that crosses Mrs. Nash's kitchen doorway is later juxtaposed with the "dark shadow" that crosses the sunlight in the Walpoles' kitchen entrance as Lady returns (81). It is a moment of dark illumination that relates Mrs. Walpole to several of Jackson's earlier protagonists. The dog is spotted with the blood that makes the woman turn "helplessly" to the pantry, where she blindly removes the first cans she touches for the children's lunch.

Mrs. Wilson, the central character in "After You, My Dear Alphonse," at first seems to have more in common with the capable Mrs. Nash than with the hesitant Mrs. Walpole. She bakes gingerbread, serves a nutritious lunch, and hospitably invites her son Johnny's playmate—sight unseen—to join him for the meal. Mrs. Wilson is not burdened with Mrs. Walpole's crippling anxiety, nor does she experience a sudden moment of horror comparable to that of the mother in "The Witch." Nevertheless, she is another of Jackson's divided women. Though scrupulously polite and even charitable, Mrs. Wilson conceals deep insecurities that prevent her from treating Johnny's friend as an individual. From the moment Boyd passes through the kitchen doorway and she sees he is black, she is on guard. Most of the story is told in dialogue, and there are no passages similar to the many in "The Renegade" where the narrator expresses Mrs. Walpole's suppressed emotions. But Mrs. Wilson's words and her concluding action suggest that she too feels fundamentally threatened.

The story's title, a familiar line from the comic strip "Alphonse and Gaston," is relevant to the exaggerated civility with which Mrs. Wilson addresses Boyd. M. Thomas Inge, who cites Faulkner's reference to the cartoon in *Light in August,* says Alphonse and Gaston "reside more in the popular consciousness and language as representatives of excessive politeness rather than as comic strip characters."[25] Inge explains that the two Frenchmen adhere so strictly to their mannerly phrases and gestures they are "immobilized" when disasters occur. Mrs. Wilson's speech too is automatically polite but paralyzingly unsuitable to the minor crisis of Boyd's appearance at the lunch table. The title has a more obvious connection with Johnny and Boyd. By playfully repeating "After you, my dear Alphonse" to each other at the beginning, middle, and end of the story, the two friends display their fellowship and, at the same time, their impotence against a world where even kind people like Mrs. Wilson can be insensitively cruel. As Carol Cleveland remarks, the story "speaks lightly but tellingly of racial prejudice."[26]

Mrs. Wilson's prejudice is evident chiefly in the stereotypes that underlie her conversation with Johnny and Boyd. Ironically, she seems determined to have Johnny treat Boyd fairly. She assumes her son is casting the black child in a slave's role since Boyd enters the house with an armload of kindling wood. Johnny "mildly" explains the wood is "dead Japanese" and Boyd is carrying the pile because it came from his place (86). The boys continue to disabuse Mrs. Wilson of her misconceptions about Boyd's appetite, his father's job, the number of his siblings, and his plans for the future. On this last subject, Johnny, caught up in his war games, remarks that they will both become tank drivers. While Mrs. Wilson seems intent on finding nonexistent differences between the two children, the boys' innocent responses show how much they have in common. She feels "defeated" when Johnny mentions that Boyd's father is a foreman, and she quickly changes the subject when Johnny wonders why she thinks Boyd's mother has a job; "You don't work," he reasonably points out (87). Unable to abandon her prejudices, Mrs. Wilson takes a "deep breath" as she works up to her final question, but her sentence is left incomplete as Boyd's "puzzled expression" greets her offer of a bundle of second-hand clothes (88).

Thwarted in her repeated efforts to sympathize, she withdraws the one thing that Boyd really needs. Reaching for another piece of gingerbread, he finds the plate lifted from the table by Mrs. Wilson, whose sudden irritation is noticed by the boys. Cuttingly, she observes, "There are many little boys like you, Boyd, who would be very grateful for the clothes someone was kind enough to give them" (89). Mrs. Wilson never sees that Boyd is a virtual double of her own son. In fact, Johnny's table manners and grammar, as revealed in the course of the meal, are somewhat inferior to those of the always polite but finally confused visitor, who stares at Mrs. Wilson's turned back as Johnny pulls him to the door. The boys' final exchange prevents the story from ending on too heavy a note but also puts the mother in her place. Mrs. Wilson overhears the departing Boyd quietly ask Johnny whether she is still mad. Johnny is not sure, but he does know, "She's screwy sometimes." Linking Johnny's white mother with *his* black one, Boyd identifies with his friend one more time: "So's mine" (89).

Despite the humorous tone and the socially sensitive theme, "After You, My Dear Alphonse" leaves the reader with a familiar protagonist: a dumbfounded character whose sense of home and security are menaced by the unexpected intrusion of an outsider. Like the other married women thus far in *The Lottery*, Mrs. Wilson faces her challenge without the aid of her husband; Johnny describes his father to Boyd as a "little guy" who would not hurt a flea (87). As in "Trial by Combat" brief military references place a small-scale conflict in the context of a world at war. But the disturbing laughter of several earlier characters, including the alarming children in "The Witch" and "The Renegade," has an innocent, though still exclusionary, parallel in the giggles of Boyd and Johnny. In a more significant variation on her usual pattern, Jackson depicts Boyd as a harmless outsider, and Mrs. Wilson as a protagonist whom it is difficult to pity. Her oven and her tempting gingerbread are uncomfortably reminiscent of the witch in the fairy tale "Hansel and Gretel."[27]

The centerpiece in the largest group of stories, "Charles" presents the book's most humorous treatment of the beleaguered mother. First published as fiction in *Mademoiselle*, the semi-autobiographical story was later incorporated into Jackson's family chronicle, *Life among the Savages*.[28] Next to "The Lottery" "Charles" is the most frequently anthologized piece from Jackson's collection, and probably for a similar reason: both end with an unforgettable scene that suddenly forces the reader to reconsider the whole preceding sequence of events. The mild tension of the opening, as the narrator's son Laurie sets off for kindergarten, ending "an era of my life" (91), hardly prepares us for the startling denouement. But, as frequently happens in Jackson's stories, the tension so steadily increases that the central character, Laurie's mother, is finally forced to take action.

"Charles" is the third story in a row to stage the family drama around the kitchen table. This is the center to which the newly independent Laurie returns each noon to report on the latest exploits of his classmate, the Charles of Jackson's title. Like the children in "The Witch" and "The Renegade," Laurie relishes reporting acts of violence and cruelty. He is entertained rather than upset when Charles hits the teacher, kicks the teacher's friend, or punches a boy in the stomach. Laurie grins "enormously," jokes with his father, and laughs "insanely" between accounts of the morning's events (92). Unusual for a father in *The Lottery*, Laurie's is not only present, but also supportive of his wife, whose questions and reactions are typically more urgent than his own. When she asks her husband whether kindergarten might be too "unsettling" for Laurie, he assures her everything will be all right (92).

Like most of Jackson's women, the unnamed mother tries to contain her fears. She responds "heartily," for example, when Laurie describes Charles's refusal to do exercises. But she also becomes "passionately" intent on meeting Charles's mother, and she goes to the neutral ground of a PTA assembly alone, no husband by her side. Once there, she is restless, "scanning each comfortable matronly face, trying to determine which one hid the secret of Charles. None of them looked to me haggard enough" (96). She resembles the questing women in "The Daemon Lover" and "The Renegade" as she cautiously approaches Laurie's teacher for help, and her quest too ends in humiliation. Unexpectedly learning that Laurie has had some adjustment problems, the surprised narrator quickly assigns the blame to Charles. The first protagonist in *The Lottery* to laugh, she sympathizes with the teacher for having her hands full with Charles in her class, but she laughs alone. With the teacher's closing words, another of Jackson's women is abruptly enlightened, and speechless as a result: "'Charles?' she

27

said. 'We don't have any Charles in the kindergarten'" (96). The narrator had studied every face but her own for signs of the worry she bears as the anxious mother who unknowingly harbors "the secret of Charles."

In the last three stories in the second group, Jackson broadens her focus on families to include a third generation. Grandmothers are powerful forces in each case, and the challenges issued them by their children or grandchildren form a central conflict in all three. In several ways resembling "Charles," "Afternoon in Linen" portrays Harriet, a 10-year-old who deceives her grandmother, embarrassing the woman in front of others. The opening sentence depicts a peaceful scene, a cool room with a view of flowering bushes, that in no way prepares for the final moment of humiliation. An allusion later in the paragraph, however, anticipates the reversal. The two women and two children who gather in the formal room all wear linen, a coincidence that quickly leads the precocious Harriet to identify with an episode from *Through the Looking-Glass*, a fantasy based on reversals. Her grandmother, dressed in white, reminds her of Lewis Carroll's gentleman in white paper, and "I'm a gentleman all dressed in pink paper, she thought" (97).

Harriet is also an Alice, ill-at-ease at the tea party held by her grandmother, Mrs. Lennon. To protect herself from Howard Kator's mocking laughter, she tells the boy's mother that Mrs. Lennon has lied about Harriet's ability to write poems. As Mrs. Lennon pressures her granddaughter to recite, the amused Howard, "his mouth open and a great delight growing in his eyes," becomes a Cheshire cat to Harriet's Alice (99). Mrs. Lennon herself finally reads one of Harriet's poems—recalling the many inset poems in the Alice books—only to have the girl announce she copied the piece from a library book. The incredulous grandmother allows Harriet to remove from her "unresisting" hand the sheaf of papers, which the girl protectively holds behind her back, "away from everyone" (102). The most obvious connection between "Afternoon in Linen" and the preceding stories in the second group is the confounding of Mrs. Lennon, the gracious hostess who thought she was in control of the situation. But Harriet is of interest too as a youthful version of the several characters in the book whose sense of dignity and security is threatened. Jackson's original ending made the threat more explicit by stating that the girl held her papers "in back of her, safe" (SJP, Box 15). Harriet shares her first name with a similarly distressed child in Jackson's *The Road through the Wall*, the miserable Harriet Merriam, whose mother invades her privacy by looking through the letters, poems, and other private writings in her desk.

"Flower Garden," another treatment of betrayal of self and others, is among Jackson's best stories. Like "After You, My Dear Alphonse" it criticizes racism but probes much further into the pressures that cause an otherwise sympathetic character to turn on persons of a different race and social class. One of Jackson's longest stories (at 30 pages), it also develops symbolic settings in more detail than is usual in *The Lottery*. Although elements of the absurd and the bizarre are absent, "Flower Garden" exhibits most features of a typical Shirley Jackson story: the besieged female protagonist, the initial uneasiness that grows to desperation, the presence of doubles, the impact of the outsider, and the calm, third-person narrative voice. A striking exploration of the family relationships central to the book's second section, the story is also a superior example of the several stories on social issues that Jackson wrote throughout the 1940s.

The flower garden of the title is the major symbol of the story. Planted by Mrs. MacLane, a young widow who moves to a small Vermont town to begin a new life, the garden flourishes under the care of Mr. Jones, a black man. By the end of the summer, however, the grass turns brown and the roses are dying. A violent thunderstorm blows a neighbor's branch onto the garden, and a discouraged Mrs. MacLane tells Mr. Jones to leave it for the next owner; she and her son will return to the city, where, she says, she will never have to see another garden. The fate of her flowers parallels Mrs. MacLane's rejection by the town; after an early period of warm welcome, she is shunned for her friendliness to Mr. Jones and his children.

While the reader's sympathy is directed to the Joneses and the MacLanes, Jackson complicates that response by relating events from the perspective of one of the townspeople, Helen Winning. This perspective marks a major change from an early, much shorter version of "Flower Garden" that told the story from the viewpoint of Mrs. Hanson, as Mrs. MacLane was originally named (SJP, Box 15). Mrs. Winning, not Mrs. MacLane, is Jackson's typically divided protagonist, and though she finally sides with the village against the outsiders, it is not without a struggle. In fact, Mrs. Winning's struggle, rather than Mrs. MacLane's fall from favor, is the main interest of the story. Although the action is not related in the townswoman's voice, her initial envy and admiration of Mrs. MacLane are unmistakable, as is her identification with the town and with the Winnings, "the oldest family in town" (103). As the newest family in town, Mrs. MacLane and Davey introduce a color and vitality that Mrs. Winning finds irresistible. She had once hoped to buy their cottage herself, but has grown used to living in the old family house on the hill, where her mother-in-law holds "the position of authority" (104).

The contrast between the cozy, newly refurbished cottage and the large cold house represents Helen Winning's conflict. When Mrs. MacLane shows Mrs. Winning her small green and rose bedrooms, Helen sighs, thinking of the "oddly-matched, austere bedrooms in the big Winning house" (111). Mrs. Winning feels a "quick wonderful relief" when she sees Mrs. MacLane has furnished the small home exactly as she might have "if she were eleven years younger" (109). Mrs. MacLane is about 30, and the slightly graying Mrs. Winning is probably about 40, but 11 years is also the period she has lived in the hereditary house, where she and her mother-in-law have come to look alike, "as women will who live intimately together, and work in the same kitchen and get things done around the house in the same manner" (103). In one brief seasonal span, from late winter to late summer, Helen grows even more like the older Mrs. Winning. But Mrs. MacLane has a temporary liberating impact on Helen, who surprises herself by telling the newcomer about her desire for the little house: "Why did I say that, she wondered; it had been a very long time since young Mrs. Winning had said the first thing that came into her mind" (108). Mrs. Winning also thinks "wistfully" of the garden Mrs. MacLane will create; maple trees are so thick around the Winning house that only a row of nasturtiums will grow there, carefully tended by Helen.

The smiling, hopeful Mrs. MacLane so affects her caller that Helen makes several suggestions for reciprocal visits to the Winning house, "and all without the permission of her mother-in-law" (111). The older Mrs. Winning is irritated when Helen comes home late, driven there by guilt over the meat she bought an hour earlier at the grocery and "dinner for the Winning men" (111). The younger Howard Winning kisses his mother but only nods to his wife on his way to the table with the oldest and the youngest Howard Winning. Surveying three generations of silent, efficient eaters, Helen is struck, "today more poignantly than ever before, that she had at least given them another Howard, with the Winning eyes and mouth, in exchange for her food and her bed" (112).

Helen's inner bitterness and sense of estrangement from the family are in conflict with her exterior politeness and spirit of cooperation, reminiscent of Mrs. Walpole in "The Renegade." In "Flower Garden" too an unforeseen crisis makes the strain intolerable. At first, Helen's friendship with Mrs. MacLane provides an escape from the tension at home. It blossoms along with the cottage garden, through days that are "miraculously long and warm" (115). But the idyl does not outlast the summer. Mrs. MacLane's angry response when Davey and Howard call young Billy Jones "nigger" suddenly puts Helen on the defensive. From this point on family ties and communal pressure render the bonds of friendship as fragile as the beautiful blue bowl in the center of Mrs. MacLane's living room. After Mr. Jones, Billy's father, comes to work in the MacLanes' garden, Helen is so "incredulous," "indignant," and "embarrassed" that she discontinues her daily visits (123).

On her first shopping trip without Mrs. MacLane, she has a disturbing conversation with Mrs. Harris, an unpleasant woman who laughingly asks about Mr. Jones and ridicules Mrs. MacLane's green and yellow sandals. Helen realizes the bright shoes are "inevitably right" for Mrs. MacLane, but she begins to worry what the town is saying about the MacLanes since Mrs. Harris invariably repeats the local gossip. When she mentions her annoyance with Mrs. Harris to her mother-in-law, the older Mrs. Winning unexpectedly blames Lucy Harris's bad temper on "that man of hers" (125).

The apparent cruelty of this latest Mr. Harris anticipates Helen's very visible cruelty toward the MacLanes. Weeks after the encounter with Mrs. Harris, another villager, Mrs. Burton, asks Helen whether she minds if Davey MacLane is not invited to a children's party. The younger Mrs. Winning feels troubled, but for her own sake, not on the MacLanes' behalf. Injecting the "weight of the old Winning house into her voice," she not only denies she cares but with malice "carefully" adds that Mrs. MacLane is, after all, "like a second mother to Billy" (129). Then, catching sight of Mrs. MacLane, who may have overheard, the two women laugh, recalling the brutal laughter of earlier stories. During a subsequent exchange with Mrs. MacLane, a courteous but evasive Helen enjoys sounding "exactly like Mother Winning" (131).

When an end-of-summer storm hurls Mrs. Burton's tree branch onto Mrs. MacLane's fading flowers, the town's triumph over the small family is almost complete. Mrs. Burton glances at the damage before symbolically shutting her door against Mrs. MacLane. Helen Winning, starting down the hill on her daily trip to the store, turns without responding to the greetings of both MacLanes. She moves "with great dignity, back up the hill toward the old Winning house" (134). In thus identifying with the ironically named Winnings, Helen seems to resolve her sense of separation from the family, but she loses even more than Mrs. MacLane does. With this final retreat to the dark homestead, Shirley Jackson wisely rewrote her original conclusion, in which the Mrs. Winning character (first called Mrs. Worthing) gave a big going-away party for the departing woman, who cheerfully announced that she would have a garden wherever she went.

"Dorothy and My Grandmother and the Sailors" follows anticlimactically on the disheartening last scene of "Flower Garden." Like "My Life with R. H. Macy," the story seems deliberately positioned at the end of a section to offset the preceding gloom with a comic reprise of many familiar elements. As in "Afternoon in Linen" and "Flower Garden," an authoritarian grandmother expects women of the younger generation to meet her standards. The moments of anxiety and panic common to previous stories recur. So, less menacingly, do the mealtime gatherings frequent in the second group of stories. Every meal in "Dorothy and My Grandmother and the Sailors" is at a restaurant and includes ice cream, however—a holiday spirit unusual for *The Lottery*. Equally unusual is the shift from the typical domestic setting in the eastern United States to the male world of a battleship anchored in San Francisco Bay. The first-person narrative relates the story to "My Life with R. H. Macy" and "Charles," but this "I" is unique for creating an atmosphere of nostalgia. The opening sentence depicts a scene as attractive as Mrs. MacLane's short-lived flower garden or the glimpse through Mrs. Lennon's living-room window: "There used to be a time of year in San Francisco—in late March, I believe—when there was fine long windy weather, and the air all over the city had a touch of salt and the freshness of the sea" (135). Shirley Jackson generally reserved the first-person point of view for her most obviously autobiographical short stories, and the account of the shipboard excursion relates a childhood adventure with her friend Dorothy Ayling.

Despite its origins in fact and its almost vaudevillian humor, "Dorothy and My Grandmother and the Sailors" has a special connection with the James Harris ballad that comprises Jackson's epilogue to the book. The grandmother of the title seems to view each sailor as a potential demon lover and her two young charges as likely victims. Thus she rejoices when the narrator, who strays from the rest of the group, is found "in time" (139). In a more typical Jackson story, the protagonist's sudden perception that she has wandered alone into alien territory would be much more terrifying. Even in the context of a sightseeing expedition, it is an uneasy moment when "the lady [whose dress she was following] turned around and I realized that it was not my mother and I was lost" (138–39). Rescue comes in the person of "a tall man in a uniform with lots of braid" (139), a maritime version of the tall blue-suited James Harris of earlier stories. The grandmother grabs the girl from his side and retreats backward with her to join the mother, who nervously shakes her daughter while asking, "Aren't you ashamed?" (139). The episode so alarms both older women that they put an end to the annual springtime tradition of visiting the fleet, but the story does not end with the daughter's shaming. A second adventure on the journey to town involves Dorothy as well as the narrator. Both girls are panic-stricken when two sailors sit beside them at the movie theater. A wailing Dorothy clutches the grandmother, who assures her she will be safe at home with the older women. The story concludes prosaically with a reference to Dot's new gray coat, bought along with a matching one for the narrator, on the long day in the city: "She wore it all that year" (141).

Though the mood is very different, the plot recalls Helen Winning's eventual withdrawal from the possibilities for a freer life represented by Mrs. MacLane and her colorful house in "Flower Garden." The 12-year-old girls too are pulled from their predictable lives in suburban Burlingame to the excitement of the city and the ship. All the older women in the story, though, are intent on shielding them. Even Dot's mother "earnestly" tells the two to stay away from sailors; she herself is "never well enough" to go shopping in the city (136). The battleship becomes a metaphor for the broader male realm. It is hostile ground, where the girls and women tread "cautiously" and look about "apprehensively." In contrast, the narrator's Uncle Oliver (Jackson's own "Uncle Clifford" in her original manuscript [SJP, Box 15]), an ex–navy man who escorts them aboard, touches the paint "affectionately" (137). Gathering a small group of men and boys about him to discuss the ship's radio system, he is oblivious to his niece's misadventure. As in most of Jackson's stories, men are either ineffectual or disconcerting. Initiated into this awareness at the age of 12, the two girls do not complain as they retire to their Burlingame homes and to the sheltering warmth of their identical coats.

## Group Three: Language Arts

A more heterogeneous group than the first two parts of *The Lottery*, the next six stories continue to explore male-female relationships, but children are much less in evidence than they were in the second group. As in the preceding section, the women are married, or at least in a long-term relationship with a man; men are more prominent than they were in most of the earlier stories, and they are often in conflict with women. Although the action is as realistic as it was in the last five stories, the element of the strange or the absurd so characteristic of the first group (and of the first two stories of the second) occasionally recurs, especially in verbal exchanges. Characters frequently manipulate each other in these stories, and words are often their weapons. Communication, a problem for many of Jackson's protagonists, becomes almost impossible at several points, leading to feelings of estrangement and displacement. Moreover, literary allusions and other references to writing are especially prominent in this section, emphasizing the power of the word—sometimes in contrast to the powerlessness of Jackson's characters.

The title of the first story, "Colloquy," alerts the reader to a focus on language and relationships. Jackson's short stories contain a high percentage of conversation, but "Colloquy" is an extreme example. The narrator has little to add to Mrs. Arnold's nervous discussion with a physician; moreover, much of the woman's worry seems to derive from the sudden failure of language to express meaning. Two of her comments to the doctor begin, "When I was a little girl," as she contrasts the simple ways and speech of the past with the chaos of the present. She "hysterically" explains that her husband's anger over his inability to buy a copy of the *Times* led to his jumbled outburst on "social planning on the local level and surtax net income and geopolitical concepts and deflationary inflation" (147). When she asks whether everyone is insane, the doctor "severely" advises her to pull herself together: "In a disoriented world like ours today, alienation from reality frequently—" (147). An incredulous Mrs. Arnold echoes his key words—"Disoriented," "Alienation," "Reality"—as she stands and exits.

The physician's jargon relates him to the pompous Mr. Arnold and thus reduces the "competent-looking and respectable" man (145) to an object of satire. Linda Trichter Metcalf remarks that both men utter words "removed from the operational frame of human activity, and drawn from vocabularies that have no roots in the content of the wife's world."[29] But the doctor's interrupted assessment of Mrs. Arnold's problem also summarizes and illustrates the themes of several stories in *The Lottery*. Appropriately, "Colloquy" is the first story in Jackson's contents page for the projected collection "The Intoxicated" (SJP, Box 16). The physician's comments sound surprisingly like Stanley Edgar Hyman's remarks in the preface to *The Magic of Shirley Jackson* (1966), where he describes Jackson's "fierce visions of dissociation and madness, of alienation and withdrawal, of cruelty and terror" as "a sensitive and faithful anatomy of our times, fitting symbols for our distressing world of the concentration camp and the Bomb" (*MSJ*, viii).

The title character in "Elizabeth" has a milder communication problem than Mrs. Arnold, but her underlying discontent is just as serious. Far from being intimidated by words, she deals with them daily as a fiction editor (the position Shirley Jackson held on the Syracuse University literary magazine), and she often uses them dishonestly or cruelly. Perfunctorily reading a new client's manuscript, she copies a paragraph into her own notebook to use in a story she is writing. Her letter to the author follows a formula, and she randomly consults the manuscript to praise a character before delivering a sales pitch for professional editing services. More of an aggressor than Jackson's typical women characters, Elizabeth does not even bother to be polite when she fires the new office secretary, Daphne Hill. Envying the young woman's attractiveness, she criticizes her dress and her untidy hair, then lies that Robert Shax, the head of the literary agency, wants Daphne to quit the job. Elizabeth is similarly ruthless when an old family friend calls with a message from her father and an invitation for the evening; she says she has an important dinner appointment and hangs up before the elderly Mr. Hunt finishes talking. Earlier in the day, she had thrown a plaintive letter from her father into the trash. She resents being reminded of the home she willingly left behind: "They hang on to me, she thought; they're holding me back, with their letters and their 'Yrs. afftly.,' and their sending love back and forth" (177).

The home Elizabeth has established for herself in New York is not a real home either; it can assume a "sham appearance of warmth and welcome" when she needs "a place to hide in" (150), but the single armchair in the one-room apartment is hard and the gray paint on the end table is chipped. Her dusty kitchen is as ill-furnished as the kitchen in "The Villager," and her former competence at cooking has dwindled, "with the rest of her daily life," to "a miniature useful only as a novelty on rare occasions" (189). Even her body has shrunken to an unappealing thinness. The narrator sums up Elizabeth as "a rather unhappy and desperate young woman with little or no ability to make things gracious" (188).

In her desperation, Elizabeth especially resembles the fiancée of "The Daemon Lover," and she too is unfortunate in her men. Her employer-boyfriend's most extravagant display of affection is a pat on her head, and when he says, "We get along pretty well, don't we, Liz?," she simply answers, "Fine" (159). The response is as automatic and perhaps as untruthful as the "fine" with which she earlier reacted to the drugstore clerk's announcement that he had sent his newly completed play to a rival agency. Cynical about her relationship with Robbie, Elizabeth studies him coolly during their argument over Daphne: "He thinks I'm awed, she thought, he's a man and he's cowed me" (169). But she still looks to men for an escape from her boring life.

Finally, Elizabeth phones Jim Harris, the firm's one successful client and now an ex-client because of a fight with Robert Shax. Although he sounds as ordinary as the cigar-smoking Mr. Harris in "Like Mother Used to

Make," his signed photograph on the office wall is a troubling icon, a constant reminder of the agency's major loss. For Elizabeth, he is the final hope for a better life, and she refuses to be put off by his evasive references to a visiting kid sister when she pressures him to meet her for dinner. She transforms him in her imagination from a heavy-faced man with a "thin voice" to "a stranger, a gallant dark man with knowing eyes who watched her across a room"; she fantasizes that he is "a quiet troubled man" who loves her and who, like Elizabeth, needs "sunlight, a warm garden, green lawns" (191). In identifying Jim Harris with her dream world, Elizabeth makes of him the mysterious lover that he proves to be in "The Daemon Lover" and, even more dramatically, in "The Tooth," a story in the final section of *The Lottery*.

Unfortunately for Elizabeth, Jim is probably no more willing to play the role of romantic rescuer than Jamie was in "The Daemon Lover." "Elizabeth" ends the way the other story began, with careful preparations on the woman's part, but no guarantee the eagerly awaited caller will ever arrive. At one time, Jackson had planned to write a novel about Elizabeth. The action was to parallel "the discovery and condemnation of a witch" as Elizabeth, metaphorically in league with the devil (her employer, Robert Shax), progressed to a "figurative destruction": her decision to return to her childhood home to keep house for her father.[30] Interestingly, the production of words provides the livelihood of the devil and his cohorts in "Elizabeth."

In "A Fine Old Firm," as in "Elizabeth," cold women symbolically long for the warmth of the sun, but their manipulative ways leave them in the shadows. This next story, with its restrained portrayal of anti-Semitism, has even more in common with "Flower Garden," where Helen Winning yearned for springtime and then rejected the fruitfulness represented by Mrs. MacLane. Like the two generations of Winning women in "Flower Garden," Helen Concord and her mother in the end present a politely cool front to a generous outsider, Mrs. Friedman; the family names of the Winnings and the Concords are equally ironic. "A Fine Old Firm" originally appeared in the *New Yorker*, whose typical stories were, and often still are, less concerned with plot development than with the subtleties of situation and character.[31] Jean Stafford's biographer, Charlotte Margolis Goodman, speculates that many of Stafford's stories might have followed this model because of the early encouragement of Katharine White, the *New Yorker's* fiction editor.[32] White may similarly have influenced Shirley Jackson, whose "Trial by Combat," "After You, My Dear Alphonse," "Afternoon in Linen," "Colloquy," and "Come Dance with Me in Ireland"—all first published in the *New Yorker*—de-emphasize action and stress a civilized confrontation of opposing characters. Dialogue conceals and reveals much in these clashes. It is a story type that can be found in Jackson's earliest fiction for journals at Syracuse University in 1938 and as late as "A Great Voice Stilled," published in *Playboy* in 1960.

Reminiscent of "Trial by Combat" and "After You, My Dear Alphonse," the quiet battle in the foreground takes place against the backdrop of world war. Bob Friedman and Charles Concord are army friends, stationed "far away" (195). Their friendship leads Mrs. Friedman, dressed in a warm fur coat, to call unexpectedly on Mrs. Concord, whose house is within a few blocks of hers. A more formal woman than Mrs. Friedman, Mrs. Concord does not echo the caller's easy laughter, and she continues to call her son "Charles" while Helen and Mrs. Friedman refer to him as "Charlie." Both Concord women seem to resent the long-distance friendship that has developed between Mrs. Friedman and Charlie. They do not offer refreshments, nor do they suggest a return visit to their cold living room, but their greatest rebuff is Mrs. Concord's politely automatic rejection of Mrs. Friedman's suggestion that her husband might find a place for Charlie in his law firm. Apparently with no thought of consulting her son, she explains that Charles will join Satterthwaite & Harris, a "fine old firm" in which Mr. Concord's grandfather was a partner (197). Like the Winning homestead in "Flower Garden," the old firm carries the weight of a long tradition. In contrast, the friendship of the two young soldiers seems tenuous, as susceptible to family pressure as the boyish brotherhood of Johnny and Boyd in "After You, My Dear Alphonse" or the short-lived companionship of Helen Winning and Mrs. MacLane. Destined to bind himself to Mr. Harris, Charles will probably find it expedient to dissociate himself from the Friedmans and the opportunity for personal freedom that their name implies.

Respectability matters so much to Mrs. Concord that it makes her cruel in her refusal of Mrs. Friedman's offer. Decorum in word and action is equally important to Mrs. Wilkins in "The Dummy," though here too decorum masks fear and disgust. Mrs. Wilkins selects a restaurant that is twice described as "respectable" in the opening sentence, and she nostalgically contrasts an ugly ventriloquist in the floor show with a "nice" young singer in the "nice" programs of the past. After dismissing the dummy act as "coarse," she "primly" turns her attention to her ice cream. The aloof Mrs. Wilkins, however, injects herself into a subsequent three-way dispute among the ventriloquist, his dummy, and his girlfriend or wife; slapping the obnoxious mannequin, she spontaneously produces a rather tasteless show of her own. The distorted figure, with its disembodied speech, is an exaggerated version of wooden humans like Mrs. Wilkins.

Although Mrs. Wilkins and her friend Mrs. Straw leave with dignity, like the affronted Helen Winning at the end of "Flower Garden," they seem more lifeless than the dummy Marmaduke in the instant before Mrs. Wilkins attacks. Wordlessly, Mrs. Wilkins's mouth "opened, and shut again," and Mrs. Straw "watched blankly" (207). Distanced by poor seats and their lack of interest, the two women had been able to ignore the comedy routine between the ventriloquist Joey and the "grotesque wooden copy of the man" (203). But they are close enough to the entertainers' table to hear the nasty conversation that follows between Joey and a woman Mrs. Straw belittles as "our friend in the green dress" (204). Schizophrenically, the ventriloquist addresses the woman with increasing crudeness in Marmaduke's voice; his own tones conceal the anger he projects through the dummy. Thus the grinning mannequin loudly insults her after she pleads with Joey to be quiet and to stop drinking: "Just because a man wants to have a good time she has to freeze up like an icebag" (206-7). The ventriloquist responds to this insinuation of frigidity by warning Marmaduke to "talk nicer to your old mother," but the dummy vulgarly recommends that the "old bag" can "get back on the streets" if she is unhappy with Joey's attempt to enjoy himself (207).

Mrs. Wilkins's disdain for the spectacle does not adequately explain the violence of her response. In directing her slap at the dummy, she transfers her anger much as Joey does. The source of this anger may lie in her unexpected identification with the girl in green, Marmaduke's "old mother." Mrs. Wilkins appears to link the dummy with her son Walter, whose name comes up throughout her conversation with Mrs. Straw. "Seems like there's a lot he doesn't tell us," she complains to her friend (201). Perhaps she hears Walter, not Joey, in Marmaduke's derision and momentarily forgets whom she is striking. The illusion that the dummy is real continues even after the two women stiffly leave. The ventriloquist and the girl look together at the "slumped" and finally silent figure, and she reaches over to straighten his head as if he has drunk himself into the stupor she had dreaded to see in Joey.

In his burlesque duplication of Joey, the dummy is a dramatic image of the many other doubles and role players in *The Lottery*, from Hilda Clarence's pose as Nancy Roberts in "The Villager" to Laurie's creation of a fractious alter ego in "Charles." Marmaduke is an especially uncanny counterpart: "where the man was small and ugly, the dummy was smaller and uglier, with the same wide mouth, the same staring eyes, the horrible parody of evening clothes, complete to tiny black shoes" (203). As Cullen Murphy observes in an *Atlantic* essay, there is "something surreal and ghastly" about a dummy; Murphy cites the several cases in which "dark forces" control the figures in television shows like "The Twilight Zone" and "Night Gallery," as well as in a film which preceded Jackson's story by a few years, the 1945 *Dead of Night*.[33] Also disconcerting is the ventriloquist's separation of language from a human source. When a wooden replica of life is endowed with speech, the effect is akin to that in "Colloquy," where men sound like machines.

The split setting of a two-level bookstore introduces another group of disjunctions in "Seven Types of Ambiguity." Dennis Welch posits a "possible ruse in the story and a subtle ambiguity based on the ruse and suggested by the story's title."[34] The ruse involves a contradiction between speech and intent, reminiscent of the contrast between Joey's conciliatory words and the anger he projects through Marmaduke. Welch believes the interest a young character expresses in William Empson's *Seven Types of Ambiguity* masks his collusion with the store owner, Mr. Harris, to unload the book on a naive customer. Welch does not mention the other James Harris stories, but his reading would relate the seemingly benign proprietor to the several earlier Harrises, with their devious behavior. An alternative reading, however, could preserve Mr. Harris's culpability and add to it that of the middle-aged shopper, while rendering the young college student, Mr. Clark, innocent of mercenary designs. Instead of questioning the boy's motives in several times mentioning Empson, we might ask why the customer, who benefits from the boy's advice in selecting the books he has come to buy, does not reward him by giving him a work he so obviously wants but cannot afford. Perhaps envying the 18-year-old's superior education, the man asks Mr. Harris to add the single odd volume to all the neatly matched sets of nineteenth-century British novels he has chosen. Instead of discouraging the purchase, Mr. Harris simply glances up and then adds one more figure to his price list.

Welch credits Shirley Jackson with intentional ambiguity and thus does not insist on his interpretation to the exclusion of others. Moreover, his essay, one of the few written on a Jackson story other than "The Lottery," has the virtue of imaginative attention to the text that Stanley Edgar Hyman praises in a chapter on Empson in *The Armed Vision: A Study in the Methods of Modern Literary Criticism*. Published in 1948, the year before *The Lottery* collection, *The Armed Vision* says that Empson's book contains "the most elaborate and probably the finest close reading of poetry ever put down, the fantastic, wonderful, and almost endless spinning out of implications and linguistic possibilities."[35] The spiral stairs to the bookstore's basement room become a metaphor for Empson's intricate readings and for Jackson's surprising twists of plot. "Watch the bottom step," warns Mr. Harris. "There's one more than people think" (210).

There is not only one more step, but also one more story to the shop than is obvious from the main level, again suggestive of Jackson's layers of meaning. The "little upstairs bookshop," a "neat small store" attended by a girl, provides entry to Mr. Harris's very different preserve (209). The underground room seems enormous, its rows of tall bookcases, lines of book tables, and piles of books on the floor lit by dirty ceiling lights that customers are to turn off as they "grope" their way back to Mr. Harris's cluttered desk with their purchases. In contrast to the best-sellers and art books on display upstairs, the basement stock is for more serious readers. Mr. Harris acts as if the large cold room is a man's domain. Although the wife of the middle-aged customer enters the basement first and seems more at ease there than her husband, Mr. Harris leads her to his chair near the coal stove, where she remains seated until her husband signals "Ready, Mother?" at the end of the story (216). The man twice says that "we" would like to buy some books, but the woman makes only one request, for *Jane Eyre*, and the husband and Mr. Clark search through the stacks without any further suggestions from her. A male–female opposition is evident too in Mr. Clark's remark that the woman would be pleased with a set of Jane Austen as well as the set of Brontës, while choosing Dickens, Meredith, and Thackeray for the man. Characterized mainly through her soft voice, the wife remains disappointingly silent when her husband and Mr. Harris complete the sale with the last-minute addition of Empson, a book that the buyer, who used to enjoy Dickens and Twain, will probably never read.

Another text, Yeats's "I Am of Ireland," provides the title for "Come Dance with Me in Ireland," which was selected for *The Best American Short Stories, 1944*. John O'Flaherty, the old man who quotes Yeats in the story, gains dignity from his association with the poet and his poetry, despite a humiliating encounter with three women whose concerns are more prosaic. The impoverished Mr. O'Flaherty is ringing Mrs. Archer's doorbell to sell shoelaces when he almost faints. Much as Mrs. Wilson attempts to impose her charity on Boyd in "After You, My Dear Alphonse," Mrs. Archer and her friends force inappropriate help on the elderly beggar. Mrs. Archer and the middle-aged Mrs. Corn, together with the unmarried Kathy Valentine, speak about him in the third person as if he is not present, and many of their comments are insulting. Mrs. Corn is sure he is drunk. Kathy claims that "these people eat things like heaps of fried potatoes and eggs and—" (222), yet Mr. O'Flaherty barely touches the large meal Jean Archer dutifully prepares. The women introduce themselves as Miss or Mrs., reserving their first names, but Kathy Valentine calls Mr. O'Flaherty John. Mrs. Archer worries that her husband, Jim (the worst name a man can have in *The Lottery*), might not approve of her generosity to the old man. Mrs. Corn protectively removes the Archer baby from his sight.

When Mr. O'Flaherty suddenly announces, "I knew Yeats," Kathy Valentine dimly responds, "Let me see—he was the writer, wasn't he?" (225). He then recites, "'Come out of charity, come dance with me in Ireland,'" a jibe at the awkward charity of the three women.[36] When the departing man tells Mrs. Archer, "We are of two different worlds, Madam" (226), he does not simply mean he is from what Kathy patronizingly calls "the old country" (225). He may be alluding to Yeats's "Sailing to Byzantium," with its contrast between the timeless world of art and the decaying sensual world represented by the useless meal and also by the Archer baby: "Whatever is begotten, born, and dies" (Yeats, l. 6). The materialistic world, says Yeats, is "no country for old men" (l. 1), for there "an aged man is but a paltry thing, / A tattered coat upon a stick" (ll. 9–10). Recalling the poem's scarecrow metaphor, the story twice mentions John O'Flaherty's "long, shabby black overcoat" (219), which no one invites him to remove.

The narrator's several references to the Archer baby boy contrast to the repeated identification of Mr. O'Flaherty as "the old man," evoking not only the image of the life cycle in "Sailing to Byzantium" but also the description of the young mother in Yeats's "Among School Children." The poem's aging narrator wonders whether the woman

> Would think her son, did she but see that shape
> With sixty or more winters on its head,
> A compensation for the pang of his birth,
> Or the uncertainty of his setting forth?
> (Yeats, ll. 37–40)

The maternal trio in Jackson's story is powerless to shield the Archer baby from a sad old age. Mr. O'Flaherty symbolically emphasizes his ties with them all by sarcastically leaving his handful of shoelaces on the floor for Mrs. Archer: "For your kindness. Divide them with the other ladies" (225). Before turning to go, he repeats the title passage—"Come dance with me in

Ireland" (226)—to imply there can be a more joyful sort of giving than the women's shallow charity.

Insensitive at heart, the three women resemble the Concord women of "A Fine Old Firm" and the Winning women of "Flower Garden," along with Mrs. Wilson of "After You, My Dear Alphonse." In contrast to Flannery O'Connor's exploration of salvific "moments of grace," Jackson often exposes such moments of gracelessness. Yeats's metaphor of the dance in all three of his poems mentioned above portrays a harmony unattainable by most of Jackson's protagonists, victims and victimizers alike. Their last names and their small sacrifice of eggs and figs for his lunch promise a fertile love that Kathy Valentine, Mrs. Archer (perhaps an allusion to Cupid), and Mrs. Corn cannot fully share with the man who knew Yeats.

## Group Four: The Triumph of James Harris

The climactic last group of six stories is the grimmest in *The Lottery*. Pressures on the married female protagonists are so relentless and ubiquitous it seems almost inevitable the victim of the lottery in the final story should be one of their number. In contrast to the comic and satiric stories that conclude the first three sections of the book, "The Lottery" starkly proclaims the defeat of Jackson's most familiar character: the woman caught off guard. Despite touches of humor in the first and next to last stories in this section, the central characters in the other four stories are as desperate as the fiancée in "The Daemon Lover" and Mrs. Walpole in "The Renegade." In none of the preceding sections is the experience of losing control as fatal to the welfare of the women as a group.

The opening story, "Of Course," handles the theme lightly by depicting a housewife's unnerving encounter with her new neighbors, Mrs. Harris and James Junior. "*Nice* people, obviously," Mrs. Tylor thinks as she watches the two get out of a taxi (229), but when she learns of James Senior's many odd prohibitions, she eagerly agrees to accompany her young daughter to the movies, even though she has just volunteered to entertain the Harris boy for the afternoon. Mrs. Tylor's staccato repetition of the title phrase echoes several earlier women—Mrs. Walpole and Elizabeth Style, for instance—whose automatic politeness is hardly expressive of their true feelings. In relaying her husband's disapproval of movies, radios, newspapers, and bridge games, Mrs. Harris likewise masks the anxiety that betrays her only once, when she "uncomfortably" laughs: "You'll be thinking my husband is crazy" (232).

In her manuscript, Jackson called the scholarly writer of Elizabethan monographs Mr. Stuart rather than Mr. Harris, and his son was Charles James Stuart, a humorous composite of the names of the post-Elizabethan Stuart kings (SJP, Box 17). The revisions drop the wordplay to suggest that the menacing spirit of James Harris will live on in a new generation. Though this Mr. Harris—eschewing the *New Republic* and the *New York Times*—seems more eccentric than hazardous, his wife's account of him makes Mrs. Tylor feel "the way she felt when she was irrevocably connected with something dangerously out of control" (232), a sensation that recurs many times in the remaining stories.

Among the best portrayals of lost control is "Pillar of Salt," where a New Hampshire housewife becomes so overwhelmed by her perception of a disintegrating New York City that she is immobilized on a crowded street. Jackson emphasized the woman's growing uneasiness by excising from the manuscript a half-page account of a domestic ritual of dusting and cleaning that temporarily allayed Margaret's restlessness and made her "happy and ready for dinner" (SJP, Box 19). Briefer revisions also contribute to the seriousness of the story; for example, Margaret's husband, Brad, accompanies her to New York not simply for a vacation, as he did in the early version, but to view new products for his hardware store. Originally described as leaving the borrowed city apartment to look at farm machinery, he contemplates blowtorches in the final version, an action more in line with Margaret's vision of destruction. The title "Pillar of Salt" is another product of revision, a change from a phrase that was crossed out in the manuscript, almost obscuring the Hitchcockian word *vertigo*. Lot's wife, who was transformed to a salt pillar for her rebellion in looking back upon the burning of Sodom, epitomizes the many women in *The Lottery* who numbly sense their once solid worlds falling to ashes.[37]

Ironically, the train ride that brings Brad and Margaret to New York begins with "extreme pleasure" (235). At first they smile at occasional signs of breakdown: the repaired Empire State building (recently hit by a plane), the loose door of one taxi and flat tire of another. Margaret's good mood changes at a friend's party in a neighborhood where, according to a man who stands next to her in the noisy room, "someone's always getting killed" (240). A handwritten revision in Jackson's manuscript identifies the fellow guest as "a tall man in a blue suit," as if he has wandered out of the cocktail hour in "The Intoxicated," but the final version inexplicably omits the guarded reference to James Harris. To Margaret's embarrassment, she flees the crowded apartment when people on the street shout "fire"; and though the fire proves to be two buildings away, a "faint feeling of insecurity tagged her the next day" (241). Brad seems unaffected, but Margaret becomes more and more distressed. The toy cash registers, shopping carts, and telephones she notices while shopping for gifts for her children appear to be "hideous little parodies of adult life" (242). She nervously perceives decay everywhere; the very granite of buildings is "eroding unnoticed" (243), and time itself becomes distorted, with "every hour forty-five minutes long, every day nine hours, every year fourteen days" (243). Like the fiancée in "The Daemon Lover," Margaret is reluctant to voice her fears, "afraid to face the knowledge that it was a voluntary neck-breaking speed, a deliberate whirling faster and faster to end in destruction" (244).

A respite on Long Island, at a strangely familiar beach, recalls a vista Margaret has often entered in her imagination. A tune she remembered on the train from home recurs, "the symbol of the golden world she escaped into to avoid the everyday dreariness that drove her into writing depressing stories about the beach" (246). She laughs in recognition but answers "falsely" when Brad asks her to explain the humor in the "Godforsaken landscape." That Margaret is a writer and a woman of imagination comes as a surprise to the reader, but Margaret has no more success than Elizabeth Style or the demon lover's fiancée in bringing her fantasies to life. Instead, the gray and godforsaken landscape prevails. When a human leg washes up on the dunes, her Long Island host nonchalantly connects it with "one of these killings" (247), but the hysterical Margaret is convinced people are starting to come apart. Back in the city, she tries to calm herself, though the symbolic tune is now "nasty," with a "burden of suavity and expensive perfume" (248). Finally, she turns into the "pillar of salt" of the title while attempting to cross a street to her temporary apartment. She knows that, in wondering how people manage to beat the traffic light and reach the building, "she was lost" (252).

A similar doom befalls a younger housewife in "Men with Their Big Shoes." The title is Mrs. Anderson's derisive explanation for the dirt brought into the house where she serves as a cleaning woman for the "young Mrs. Hart," as she is twice called in the opening paragraph. Jackson's emphasis on her naïveté and inexperience is reminiscent of Hawthorne's depiction of the innocent protagonist of "Young Goodman Brown," and Mrs. Hart too is led close to despair by an older guide. In contrast to the cynical Mrs. Anderson, who has been unhappily married for 37 years, Mrs. Hart at the outset is very fortunate: it is her "first summer living in the country, and her first year being married and the mistress of a house; she was going to have her first baby soon, and it was the first time she had ever had anyone, or thought of having anyone, who could remotely be described as a maid" (255). She seems to have realized the country-house dream of the demon lover's fiancée. But when Mrs. Anderson insinuates Mr. Hart might be unfaithful, Mrs. Hart's "faint small uneasiness" about the older woman becomes a "sickening conviction" (256). Mrs. Anderson slyly arranges to move into the Harts' spare room (intended for the baby), arguing that a woman "who's older and knows a little more . . . might see a little more, too, maybe" (264). Wordlessly staring at the housekeeper, Mrs. Hart recognizes "with a sudden unalterable conviction that she was lost." This repetition of the "lost" Margaret's feelings in "Pillar of Salt" emphasizes the shared anguish of the women in the final section of *The Lottery*.

While homes were threatened in "Trial by Combat," "Like Mother Used to Make," and other stories, Mrs. Anderson's attack on the Harts' marital relationship is especially devastating. The housekeeper speaks often and bluntly of gender differences and conflicts that were hinted at in "The Witch," "The Dummy," and "Seven Types of Ambiguity." First, she contrasts men, who dirty the floors with their big shoes, to women: "A woman, you watch them, she always puts her feet down quiet" (255). But the offensive footprints are emblems of more serious, moral missteps. Mrs. Anderson believes all men treat their wives shabbily, whether by drinking, gambling, or chasing other women: "There's nothing any woman can do but make sure when she does have to get out she sure has some place to go," she warns Mrs. Hart (261). When she grimly concludes that fewer women would marry if they knew how their husbands would turn out, Mrs. Hart inadequately responds that "a successful marriage is the woman's responsibility" (261). Mrs. Anderson's innuendos capitalize on the younger woman's reticence in discussing sexual matters. For instance, Mrs. Hart quickly heads for the back door when Mrs. Anderson complains Mr. Anderson was at her all night again—"Not a minute's sleep for me" (259)—but she returns to her seat when it becomes clear he was shouting at his wife to get out. Mrs. Hart also seems ambivalent about her pregnancy, "irritably" smoothing her dress and wishing she could get into "decent" clothes again (263). Finally, her desperately cheerful smile yields to Mrs. Anderson's cruelly "knowing smile" (264).

All the anxieties and yearnings of Jackson's women culminate in the experience of Clara Spencer of "The Tooth." The original title, "Persephone," echoes in her surname and suggests that Clara's dreamlike journey to New York in the company of a mysterious stranger comprises an underworld descent (SJP, Box 18). If Clara is Persephone, Jim—who intercepts her on her long bus ride to the dentist's office—must be Pluto, god of the dead. Clara seems most full of life, however, when she rejects her past and runs, hand in hand with Jim, simultaneously on a city street and "barefoot through hot sand" (286). She is a Persephone who lacks any desire to return to her distant home and family.

Much as the Greek myth emphasizes the mother-daughter bond, "The Tooth" initially stresses the relationship between Clara and the unnamed man who is repeatedly identified as "her husband." Approaching the late-night bus that will take her from their small town to the city, Clara anxiously clings to his arm. Although she has been too rushed to dress herself properly, she has carefully arranged for the husband's meals and the children's care. Mr. Spencer also sounds solicitous, melodramatically stating he could not forgive himself if the painful tooth "turned out to be something serious" and he let Clara go to "this butcher up here" (266). His alarm is less appropriate to the anticipated dental extraction than it is to major surgery, perhaps of a gynecological nature. The sexual symbolism is made more explicit when the husband "accusingly" reminds Clara the tooth has troubled her repeatedly since he has known her and that she even had a toothache on their honeymoon (267). Clara's surprised "Did I?" suggests a powerful repression of the whole episode. The codeine, whiskey, and sleeping pill she has taken to blunt the present pain so far remove her usual inhibitions that her meeting with Jim in the "strange prison" of a bus is the start of a shocking liberation.

Richard Pascal sympathetically describes Clara's journey as a "quest for self-gratification and pure personal freedom," but he believes that, despite the upbeat tone of the ending, "Jim is a fantasy and she may be insane."[38] Pascal's footnoted comment on other appearances of Jim Harris in *The Lottery* obscures the significance of this final sighting of the tall man in a blue suit. In the context of the book's epilogue—Child Ballad No. 243—Jim is no fantasy but a charming stranger who lures the drab housewife with his attentiveness and his poetic speech: "'Even farther than Samarkand,' he was saying, 'and the waves ringing on the shore like bells'" (270). Before her tooth is removed, Clara remains on guard against Jim, who is several times identified as "the strange man" (270–71). She goes alone from the bus stop to the dentist's office, where her tooth now seems "the only part of her to have any identity" (276). Under the gas mask, she hallucinates that she is running down a corridor toward a laughing Jim, who awaits her with open arms. The dental surgeon presides over a sacrificial ceremony that metaphorically uproots Clara's past. "God has given me blood to drink," she cries to the nurse after the extraction (281). Still half asleep, she makes her way to the ladies' room, only to discover that in losing the tooth she has indeed lost her old identity. Not only does she fail to recognize her pale and worried face in the mirror, but she throws away her "C" lapel pin that she pulls off "with a feeling of relief" (285). With her hair freed from its clasp and her face clumsily brightened with lipstick and rouge, the refashioned woman walks "purposefully" to the elevator and is joined outside the building by Jim, who transports her to his exotic world as surely as Pluto transported Persephone.

Coming near the end of the book, "The Tooth" brings *The Lottery* full circle, back to the dowdy thirtyish woman and the laughing seducer who promised her a pastoral life in "The Daemon Lover." Given James Harris's history, Clara's departure with Jim is as hopeless a close as the fiancée's cruel rejection by Jamie in the early story. Though she escapes from the dull routine of domesticity, Clara blindly advances into another kind of bondage. Toni Reed describes the victims of the archetypal demon lover as "women who have stepped outside the accepted perimeters of society in some way," as Clara does by abandoning her conventional life. Typically these women are destroyed, physically or psychologically, because of "their own sense of powerlessness."[39]

Although James Harris figures only peripherally in the next to last story and not at all in "The Lottery," these two final pieces violently reinforce the theme of female impotence and male control. "Got a Letter from Jimmy" recalls the equally brief "Colloquy" by dramatizing gender differences in a dialogue format with minimal narrative commentary. Judy Oppenheimer identifies the origins of the story in an argument between Jackson and Stanley Edgar Hyman over his refusal to open a letter from an estranged friend, Walter Bernstein (Oppenheimer, 104–5). The Library of Congress manuscript is entitled "Letter from David" (SJP, Box 16), but Jackson insists on a connection between the frustrated housewives of this story and "The Tooth" by changing the name of the writer to Jimmy. In both cases Jim somehow alienates the women from their husbands. The unnamed protagonist also recalls Mrs. Anderson of "Men with Their Big Shoes" by harshly contrasting the sexes: "Sometimes, she thought, stacking the dishes in the kitchen, sometimes I wonder if men are quite sane, any of them. Maybe they're all crazy and every other woman knows it but me, and my mother never told me and my roommate just didn't mention it and all the other wives think I know" (287). The three-page play of nerves breaks off with the wife's deadpan decision to murder her husband and to bury him in the basement: "Under the cellar steps, she thought, with his head bashed in and his goddam letter under his folded hands, and it's worth it, she thought, oh it's worth it" (289).

47

The woman's repressed anger jars with the dinnertime activities in which she is engaged. In her ability to mask passionate thoughts with a polite running conversation, she resembles Mrs. Walpole of "The Renegade," but her rage is even greater, though her cause seems much more trivial than Mrs. Walpole's distress over her dog. She several times thinks "My God" and "Oh, God"—expletives she censors from her mild remarks to her husband. She dramatically anticipates he would break her arm if she accepted his challenge to open the letter herself. Although her determination to kill him should be taken no more seriously than her plan to steal the letter and scramble it with his eggs the next morning, the disparity between her silent monologue and her spoken words is characteristic of Jackson's more seriously threatened protagonists, from the demon lover's fiancée and Emily Johnson in the first group of stories to Mrs. Tylor and Margaret in this last section. Moreover, the mental violence of "Got a Letter from Jimmy" serves as a prelude to the physical violence of "The Lottery," whose closing scene releases the pent-up tensions of the preceding 24 stories.

This most famous of Jackson's works, originally printed in the *New Yorker*, achieves new significance from its position at the end of the volume. Like so many other stories in the book, "The Lottery" concludes with the defeat of a woman, in this case a horrible and final defeat, since Tessie Hutchinson is stoned to death by her townspeople when she draws the winning slip in the annual ritual of the lottery. Many critics emphasize the story's mythic elements, especially the rite of the scapegoat, a victim who must suffer for the well-being of the community. Among Jackson's papers at the Library of Congress is a library book check-out card from her college days for James Frazer's *Golden Bough*, a compendium of myth and folklore that Stanley Edgar Hyman discusses at length in *The Tangled Bank: Darwin, Marx, Frazer and Freud as Imaginative Writers*.[40] Jackson credited a Syracuse University instructor with providing the material for "The Lottery" in his Introduction to Folklore course (Friedman, 21). In the most detailed treatment of myth in the story, Helen E. Nebeker comments on the date, the characters' names, and the lottery equipment, particularly the three-legged stool that supports the box holding the slips of paper: "as old as the tripod of the Delphic oracle, as new as the Christian trinity."[41]

Shirley Jackson's account of writing "The Lottery" in her lecture "Biography of a Story" is more entertaining than illuminating. Most of the speech consists of excerpts from the hundreds of letters the *New Yorker* received in an unprecedented show of reader response. Jackson identifies three "themes" in these letters: "bewilderment, speculation, and plain old-fashioned abuse."[42] But she avoids any discussion of her own theme. When the *New Yorker* asked that she comment on the work, she said it was "just a story I wrote" ("Biography," 212). Hyman, on the other hand, remarks in his preface to *The Magic of Shirley Jackson*, "She was always proud that the Union of South Africa banned 'The Lottery,' and she felt that *they* at least understood the story" (*MSJ*, viii). His emphasis on the contemporary relevance of her fiction suggests "The Lottery" has at least as much in common with "After You, My Dear Alphonse," "Flower Garden," and "A Fine Old Firm" as it does with such mythically based stories as "The Daemon Lover" and "The Tooth."

Recent critical responses have pursued the direction indicated by Hyman. Peter Kosenko's Marxist-feminist reading concludes that the "democratic illusion" produced by the lottery is "an ideological effect that prevents the villagers from criticizing the class structure of their society."[43] Similarly, Joseph Church accuses Mr. Summers, the director of the lottery, of manipulating the "ostensibly democratic event."[44] According to Church, Tessie Hutchinson's cry of complaint is "a critical voice that states the truth about an unjust social arrangement." Fritz Oehlschlaeger adds that women are particular victims of the lottery, whose "real and continuing function" is "the encouraging of fertility within marriage, along with the patriarchal domination that accompanies it."[45] To lessen their own odds of winning the lottery, women produce large families, but their resistance to male authority is "subtly evident," says Oehlschlaeger. He notes, for example, Mrs. Adams's rebellious observation that "some places have already quit lotteries" (297).

Several assumptions of these critics weaken their arguments that the lottery and the social structure are biased against workers and/or women. Kosenko, for example, remarks that the townspeople address Bill Hutchinson rather than his wife when she arrives late, "since she 'belongs' to Bill" (Kosenko, 29). Yet Tessie has a friendly exchange with Mrs. Delacroix before two or three other neighbors assure Bill, who must be nervous at her absence, that she is making her way through the crowd. Kosenko also accuses Mr. Summers of wearing blue jeans "to convince the village that he is just another one of the common people," a pose that is undercut by the white shirt "more appropriate to *his* class" (Kosenko, 30). Perhaps Mr. Summers's clothing, like his greetings to the lottery participants, simply reflects his attempt to combine dignity and informality. Oehlschlaeger too makes statements that are impossible to substantiate. Because Tessie's fourth child, Davy, is noticeably younger than his siblings, he deduces she has had "recent difficulty in conceiving children" and, having passed her prime for childbearing, is "an extremely appropriate victim of a ceremony designed to promote fertility" (Oehlschlaeger, 264).

Such inferences are debatable, but, in focusing on the gender of the lottery's victim, Kosenko and Oehlschlaeger reach a conclusion toward which the whole book has been tending: women are especially prone to losing. Surely men have drawn the marked slip in the past. The deceased Mr. Watson, whose son Jack nervously selects a paper for himself and his mother, may have been a previous lottery winner. But, given the pattern established in most of the preceding stories in *The Lottery* collection, a woman is the more likely protagonist in any painful ritual of Jackson's invention, whether it be a broken engagement, a dental operation, or a community stoning.

Coincidentally, Jackson's "Biography of a Story" links the composition of "The Lottery" to a familiar woman's rite. According to Jackson, the story occurred to her three weeks before its publication while she was engaged in the maternal routine of pushing her daughter and the day's groceries uphill toward home in a stroller on "a bright June morning when summer seemed to have come at last" ("Biography," 211). She humorously speculates the strain of the final 50 yards could have "put an edge" to "The Lottery," but the act of writing was unusually effortless. Aside from "one or two minor corrections," the version she sent her agent was virtually identical to her original draft, she says. And the *New Yorker* fiction editor asked only that she change the date she had mentioned in the story to coincide with the day the magazine was issued: 27 June (actually 26 June). Since the first four pages of Jackson's preliminary manuscript are missing from the Jackson Papers, we cannot determine her intended date. Nebeker and others have remarked that the date 27 June "alerts us to the season of the summer solstice with all its overtones of ancient ritual" (Nebeker, 102), and perhaps the allusion was originally even more pointed.

"The Lottery" file at the Library of Congress does clarify a few other features of the story's history, however. A marginal comment on the *New Yorker* galley proof contradicts Jackson's account of composition in "Biography of a Story" by noting "Eleanor March 16, 1948" and "*New Yorker* April 12, 1948" (SJP, Box 17). Apparently Jackson completed the story several weeks earlier than her lecture suggested, calling into doubt her reference to an inspirational early summer stroll. More important, her revisions were more extensive than she indicated in the speech. Several of the changes are indeed minor. For example, there is no blank space in the manuscript after Mr. Summers completes the roll call with "Zanini" (298). Immediately after adding the space, Jackson changed her transitional

"Then" to "After that." But other revisions are more substantive. Occasionally, the changes responded to remarks in the margin of the manuscript, some of them in the form of questions and imperatives. The careless handwriting resembles Jackson's own, but it could be that of Stanley Edgar Hyman, who often discussed her writing with her. (Jackson rarely, if ever, addressed herself as "you" in the margins of her work.) Reacting to a marginal "Better say what they did!," she added the following sentences to Steve Adams's exchange of greetings with Joe Summers: "They grinned at one another humorously and nervously. Then Mr. Adams reached into the black box and took out a folded paper. He held it firmly by one corner as he turned and went hastily back to his place in the crowd, where he stood a little apart from his family, not looking down at his hand" (296).

Three revisions clarify statements in the original manuscript. After Mr. Summers asked Janey Dunbar whether she had a grown boy to draw for her in the absence of her injured husband, a comment in the margin inquired, "Wouldn't he know? Small place." Jackson subsequently explained, "Although Mr. Summers and everyone else in the village knew the answer perfectly well, it was the business of the official of the lottery to ask such questions formally. Mr. Summers waited with an expression of polite interest while Mrs. Dunbar answered" (295). Similarly, Jackson changed "Mr. Summers said" to "Mr. Summers asked formally" (299) when a marginal note remarked, "Here again, he'd know"—in this case, how many children the Hutchinsons have. Both of these emendations emphasize the ceremonial aspect of the lottery. The most important clarification, however, concerns Tessie's distraught shout when her husband draws the marked lottery slip. Originally, Tessie had accused Mr. Summers, "You made him take it." Addressing the margin's query, "Could you make this a little clearer?," Jackson rephrased the charge to remove the possible implication of force on Mr. Summers's part: "You didn't give him time enough to take any paper he wanted" (298). Joseph Church quotes this passage to support his claim that "Summers and company have rigged the lottery so that they'll never be chosen" (Church, 11), but the original wording would have given much stronger support to his argument.

Another major change appears on a separate scrap of paper that does not correspond to any marginal remark in the draft. In a much reworked typed passage, with several cross-outs and handwritten insertions, Jackson added some of the most familiar lines in the story, Old Man Warner's complaint that "'next thing you know, they'll be wanting to go back to living in caves, nobody work any more, live *that* way for a while. Used to be a saying about lottery in June, corn be heavy soon. First thing you know, we'd all be eating stewed chickweed and acorns. There's *always* been a lottery,' he added petulantly. 'Bad enough to see Mr. Summers up there joking with everybody.'"[46] The addition underwent minor changes in punctuation and a modified reference to Mr. Summers as "young Joe Summers" in the published version of "The Lottery" (297). Barbara Allen's folkloristic reading suggests the fertility proverb "makes it clear that the ceremony is associated with the success of the year's crop and, by implication, with the community's continued existence."[47] Yet, as Nebeker explains, for several of the villagers, the "present rite" differs from the "meaningful ritualistic slaughter of the past" (Nebeker, 104). With its post office, bank, coal business, and grocery store, the village economy may have grown enough beyond its agricultural foundation to weaken an earlier faith in the necessity of fertility ceremonies. The storyteller observes that "in some towns there were so many people that the lottery took two days and had to be started on June 26th" (291).

The large cast of characters and the communal action distinguish "The Lottery" from the rest of Jackson's book, and most critics view the story as either an indictment of unthinking adherence to outmoded ways or a critique of an unjust class system. But we should not overlook Tessie Hutchinson's relationship to the many other women who fight losing battles in *The Lottery* collection. Like most of Jackson's housewives, she grows increasingly insecure, even in the company of her family. Her late arrival for the drawing in the town square signals her initial uneasiness. Given the nature of the lottery, Tessie's casual "Clean forgot what day it was" (294) is hard to accept, unless she has repressed the memory as Clara Spencer in "The Tooth" repressed the painful aspect of her honeymoon. After Tessie charges Mr. Summers with rushing her husband into drawing the marked slip for the Hutchinsons, Bill himself orders her to be quiet. Unlike such housewives as Mrs. Hart ("Men with Their Big Shoes") and Mrs. Walpole ("The Renegade"), Tessie is not reduced to polite rejoinders. Frantically, she demands that her married daughter Eva take a chance along with the rest of the family in the second phase of the lottery, even though Mr. Summers gently reminds her that daughters draw with their husbands' families. Before Tessie finally reaches into the battered lottery box, she looks around "defiantly" (300), and Bill has to force the paper from her hand to reveal the black spot to the crowd.

Two of her children, Nancy and Bill Jr., are too busy smiling and laughing in relief at their own safety to express any sorrow for their mother, and Tessie reaches out "desperately" as the townspeople, including her youngest child, advance with stones in their hands (301). Her final scream,

"It isn't fair, it isn't right" (302), is cut short as the crowd surrounds her. In death, Tessie becomes the last and the most permanently silenced of the large, confounded sisterhood in *The Lottery; or, The Adventures of James Harris*. Though she is stirred to a brief resistance that contrasts with the more usual passivity of Jackson's protagonists, she shares with most of them—girl, woman, and the occasional man—the bleak epiphany that she is lost.

# Come Along with Me:
# Three Decades of Stories

During the 1950s and 1960s, Shirley Jackson was so busy working on book-length fiction that Bernice Baumgarten, her agent, quickly cleared out a backlog of early stories. In a letter to her parents in October 1954, Jackson noted she would have to get busy because *McCall's* had bought her last remaining unsold piece (SJP, Box 3). Early in 1955 she commented that the market—rebounding from a slump early in the decade—was tremendous; Baumgarten had just sold a new story for $1,500, and Jackson was preparing to type two more (letter to her parents from January or February 1955 [SJP, Box 3]). Her reputation remained strong, and several stories were bought for television production. Jackson told her parents that the televised version of "The Lottery" in the summer of 1950 was so "lousy" she felt "horribly embarrassed" (letter from June or July 1950 [SJP, Box 3]), but she continued to sell stories to such programs as "Danger" and "Cameo Theater." Letters to and from her agents are full of details on reprint rights, especially for "The Lottery." Two years before Jackson's death, Baumgarten's successor, Carol Brandt, said every editor in New York was eager to get a story from her (letter to Jackson from Brandt, 19 March 1963 [SJP, Box 6]).

Despite the success of *The Lottery*, however, Jackson did not compile another book of short fiction. In *Life among the Savages* (1953) and *Raising Demons* (1957) she worked several previously published stories about her four children into episodic family memoirs. A defensive letter explained to her parents that she wrote such stories for *Good Housekeeping* and *Woman's Home Companion* "simply for money" (ca. 9 November 1949 [SJP, Box 3]). At $1,000 apiece, she could not afford to "try to change the state of popular fiction today, and since they will buy as much of it as I write, I do one story a month, and spend the rest of the time working on my new novel [*Hangsaman*, published in 1951] or on other stories." Jackson added, "I won't write love stories or junk about gay young married couples, and they won't take ordinary children stories, and this sort of a thing [stories like "My Son and the Bully," in the October 1949 *Good Housekeeping*] is a compromise between their notions and mine, and is unusual enough so that I am the only person I know of who is doing it." She again distinguished her "one popular story a month" from her more serious fiction before complaining about the paperback marketing strategy for her first novel, *The Road through the Wall* (1948): "changing the name, putting a lurid cover on the book, and playing it up as some fantastic, love-among-the-haystacks routine."

In 1966, the year after Jackson died, Stanley Edgar Hyman edited *The Magic of Shirley Jackson*—a gathering of the two family memoirs; *The Bird's Nest* (1954), a carefully researched novel about a woman with a split personality; and 11 short stories, all previously published in *The Lottery*. The book, along with Hyman's preface, pays tribute to Jackson's versatility and craftsmanship: "Shirley Jackson, like many writers, worked in a number of forms and styles, and she exploited each of them as fully as she could" (*MSJ*, vii). Hyman notes that her commitment to "producing art in salable forms" was "curiously old-fashioned" (*MSJ*, viii) and objects that "obituary references to her in such terms as the 'Virginia Werewolf of seance-fiction writers' show a considerable obliviousness to her meanings and purposes" (ix). *The Magic of Shirley Jackson* was the first of two major efforts Hyman made toward modifying narrow assessments of Jackson's career. While the contents of this first book had appeared in earlier volumes closely supervised by Jackson herself, Hyman's second editorial project was a more original undertaking: *Come Along with Me: Part of a Novel, Sixteen Stories, and Three Lectures* (1968). The title refers to a six-chapter segment of the novel Jackson was working on at her death, amounting to only 26 printed pages. Hyman identifies the lectures as speeches Jackson presented at colleges and writers' conferences. "Experience and Fiction" is accompanied by "The Night We All Had Grippe," a family story published by *Harper's* in 1952, and "Biography of a Story" is accompanied by "The Lottery," which had also been reprinted in *The Magic of Shirley Jackson*. "Notes for a Young Writer" was inspired by Jackson's daughter Sarah, who helped her brother Barry, her father, and Hyman's second wife, Phoebe Pettingell, to assemble the book.

The bulk of the volume consists of 14 stories. Hyman explains that these were chosen from about 75 uncollected stories as "the best, or those best showing the range and variety of her work over three decades."[48] He dates each selection and arranges them chronologically, from 1938 to 1965. Either sharing or respecting Jackson's low opinion of the fictionalized family narratives, Hyman includes only one representative of that genre, the popular "Pajama Party" (1957), published as "Birthday Party" by *Vogue* in 1963 and reprinted in *The Best American Short Stories, 1964*. Hyman claims that the "economy and power" of "Janice"—the earliest story in *Come Along with Me*—is "surely prophetic of her later mastery" (vii), but Jackson achieved this mastery quite early. The stories from the late 1940s in both *The Lottery* and in the posthumous gathering already bear the Jackson hallmarks: a polished style and a chilling effect. Library of Congress drafts of several stories in *Come Along with Me* demonstrate, however, that such mastery often involved extensive revision, even in stories of the 1950s and 1960s. Some of the new stories rival the achievement of the best in *The Lottery*. Hyman thought that "The Summer People," for example, was probably superior to "The Lottery" (Oppenheimer, 132).

The stories in this second collection, like those in *The Lottery*, range from the realistic to the fantastic. The most common character is again an anxious woman, though in three stories she is older than the usual protagonist of *The Lottery*. Although James Harris does not reappear, four stories contain similar characters who exert their power over sexually vulnerable women. All four of these stories date from about 1946 to 1951, and Jackson had planned to include one of them, "I Know Who I Love," in *The Lottery*.[49] Even at his most threatening, however, the figure of the seductive, possibly demonic, male is again just one of several forces that overwhelm this new group of women. Lacking the Glanvill epigraphs, the Child ballad epilogue, and the many Harris references that framed the female experience in *The Lottery*, *Come Along with Me* does help to undercut Jackson's "Virginia Werewolf" label, as Hyman intended. Moreover, all 14 stories evince Jackson's continuing resolve to construct plots very different from the "love stories" and "junk about gay young married couples" that dominated the magazine market of her time. If there is a sameness to her story lines, she at least offered an alternative to the domestic romances that were the typical fare of *Mademoiselle*, *Charm*, *Ladies Home Journal*, and *Saturday Evening Post*, whose Norman Rockwell covers express the dominant mood that Jackson repeatedly challenged.

The three earliest, and least substantial, stories in Hyman's gathering suggest the direction Jackson's short fiction might have taken had it not been for the success of *The Lottery*. Like contemporaneous stories by Jean Stafford and J. D. Salinger, these three focus on social and class relationships, paying special attention to adolescents in conflict with adults. The sinister element common to many stories in *The Lottery* is absent, though the experiences related are characteristically unpleasant. "Janice," which dates to Jackson's sophomore year at Syracuse University, so impressed Hyman, her fellow student, that its appearance in *The Threshold*, a college magazine, led to their first meeting. Described by Hyman as "one of the shortest short stories on record" (*CAWM*, vii), "Janice," with its fast-paced dialogue, anticipates the narrative technique of "Colloquy." Reflecting Jackson's early interest in theater, the first-person narrator frequently introduces the dialogue with brief stage directions. For example, she indicates her friend Janice's tone in relating a recent suicide attempt: "Almost whimsical, indifferent: 'Locked myself in the garage and turned on the car motor'" (33). Janice seems to enjoy shocking the narrator and, later that day at a party, her other friends—much as the host's daughter in "The Intoxicated" delights in confounding a middle-aged guest. Indirectly, she blames her near-suicide on her mother, who has just told the girl she cannot afford to continue her college studies. The story ends with ellipses as Janice turns to a final listener: "Then, to Sally's incredulous stare: 'Nearly killed myself this afternoon, Sally . . .'" (34).

Another teenager draws incredulous stares in the second story, "Tootie in Peonage." Again, a peripherally involved narrator distances the reader from the central action. While Janice's friend conceals her possible annoyance with the suicidal young woman's repeated bids for attention, the older speaker in "Tootie in Peonage" makes no secret of her scorn for the lower-class girl who helps keep house for the narrator's friends, the Taylors. She ridicules Tootie's high hairdo, dangling arms, and glittering red fingernails, and is repelled by the girl's directness in commenting on the toilet habits of two-year-old Tommy Taylor. Both the narrator and Tommy's mother, Julie Taylor, shrink from Tootie's vulgar physicality:

> "She looked a little bit . . . backwoods New Hampshire, don't you think?" I asked, carefully regarding my cigarette.
> "Sort of . . . like an ape," Julie said tentatively. "And I got a look at her mate—this Bud. Gargantua." (36)

Tootie's laziness, sloppiness, and habit of asking the women for cigarettes make her an irritating addition to the household, but Tommy is charmed by her. Furthermore, the unplanned pregnancy that leads her to giggle in delight shows that she is resilient, if irresponsible. Forestalling Julie's speech of dismissal, Tootie announces she has broken up with Bud and is going home to her father.

The older women's disapproval of the unconventional Tootie resembles the harsh public response to Mrs. MacLane in "Flower Garden." As in "Trial by Combat" and "Afternoon in Linen," small-scale conflicts are portrayed against a background of world tension. Mr. Taylor works in a defense plant in Boston and comes to the New Hampshire summer house only on weekends. Tootie "brightly" reports that her father and Bud suspect the Taylors are German spies: "Maybe because you stay up so late, with the lights on, you know, and then you have so much money, and no husband" (39). In Jackson's later stories, such an innuendo would probably have ramifications, but here it is just one more reason for the narrator's and Julie's disdain.

Just as Tootie fails to meet Mrs. Taylor's criteria for what she calls a *"nice girl"* (35), a teenager who comes to the Garlands' house in "A Cauliflower in Her Hair" falls short of another mother's standards. One of Jackson's typically ineffectual husbands, Mr. Garland weakly responds to Mrs. Garland's concern that "she doesn't seem like an awfully *nice* girl, does she, this Millie?" (43). Although Mr. Garland jokes that Millie could wear cauliflower in her hair, Mrs. Garland resents that she has interrupted the evening meal to speak with their daughter Virginia. Equally disturbing to her is the girl's liberal use of mascara and lipstick. Mrs. Garland responds sharply when Millie assures Mr. Garland he is not an old man, no doubt sensitive that, at 41, she is two years older. After Mrs. Garland leaves the room, Mr. Garland boldly offers Millie a cigarette, but the older woman returns to urge the hesitant visitor to go to the store with Virginia, "like good children" (45).

These first three stories from *Come Along with Me* display a variety of narrative techniques. Ranging from first-person to third-person omniscient speakers, each relies heavily on dialogue to reveal character. Nuances and insinuations are important here, as they are in such *Lottery* stories as "After You, My Dear Alphonse" and "A Fine Old Firm." Jackson was a close social observer from the beginning, and the early stories have affinities with John Cheever's and John Updike's depictions of suburban manners. The 1940s are evoked by such details as Mr. Garland's perusal of the *Saturday Evening Post*, Mrs. Garland's leopard coat, and Virginia's 10¢ sodas. Tootie reads *True Confessions* and sings "I Found a Million Dollar Baby in a Five and Ten Cent Store," and Bud replaces his "Chevvy that would do fifty" with a Ford. A cigarette haze fills these living rooms, but Jackson cuts through the smokescreens of the women who will only allow nice girls through the door.

"I Know Who I Love" treats a similar tension in a more complex fashion. Written in 1946, this fourth story is among Jackson's first extensive experiments with limited third-person point of view, a technique she adopted for some of the best stories in *The Lottery*—"The Daemon Lover," "Flower Garden," "Pillar of Salt," and "The Tooth." Jackson originally planned to write a novel about her protagonist, Catharine Vincent, and several passages of outline and plot summary remain among her incomplete manuscripts at the Library of Congress (SJP, Box 29). The short story roughly corresponds to the action of the first part of the novel, which, Jackson wrote, would describe Catharine's "early life with a narrow and strict mother and father, her first awkward love affair, and her constant humiliations at school and at home." Jackson's strategy for relating these formative events in the novel is also relevant to the short story: "The first section, on Catharine's early life, is written without chronological order, but with related events together, because it is the way Catharine remembers it. It is merely an attempt to sketch out some of the various threads which led Catharine to her later conflict."

"I Know Who I Love" is unusual among Jackson's short stories because of these shifts in time, though two other stories in *Come Along with Me* use a similar technique for different reasons. In "Island" spatiotemporal dislocations juxtapose the senile Mrs. Montague's rich fantasy world with her dull reality. And in the closing story, "The Bus," the main character's sensation of being caught in a time warp underscores the surreal quality of her night journey. By inserting scenes from childhood, adolescence, and young womanhood into a frame story of Catharine Vincent at 23, Jackson shows the process by which the girl grew into an adult who reacts insensitively to her dying mother's need for sympathy.

A major development from the first three stories in *Come Along with Me*—which are fairly typical of Jackson's fiction through the early 1940s—is the reader's access to the protagonists' deepest emotions. Thus as Catharine Vincent opens her dead mother's trunk and "set[s] her mind dutifully to thinking of her parents," we are quickly introduced to childhood scenes: "For a minute or two her parents' memory would be centered in a flood of other memories, the thin teacher who snatched the drawing out of Catharine's hand and snarled, 'I should have known better than to assign this to a stupid half-wit.' Coming upon a boy named Freddie frantically rubbing out an inscription in chalk on a fence and, when Freddie ran away, reading with hollow empty sympathy words he had been so anxiously erasing: 'Catharine loves Freddie.' And then her father: 'Catharine, do the girls and boys in your school talk to each other about bad things?'" (48). Other painful episodes from the past are interspersed with confrontations between Catharine and the dying Mrs. Vincent: an awkward evening of ushering at *The Mikado* during her junior year of high school, Catharine's miserable twelfth birthday, and the uncomfortable meeting between her parents and her boyfriend from business school. In each case, the Vincents fail to comprehend their daughter's embarrassment and humiliation.

As a failed artist, Catharine resembles the one-time dancer Hilda Clarence of "The Villager" and the unsuccessful writer Elizabeth Styles of "Elizabeth," both of which were written at about the same time as "I Know Who I Love"; "Elizabeth" in particular shares many other similarities. The witch-trial framework on which Jackson had planned to construct a novel about Elizabeth Style has a parallel in the novel outline of Catharine's later life. Rejecting the God and the conventions of her husband and her dead father, Catharine was to associate freedom with the devil and a new group of friends, but in the end she would discover the impossibility of liberation. In both cases, the references to witchcraft and devil worship almost disappear from the short-story accounts. Catharine's boyfriend, Aaron, however, fits the demon lover prototype more closely than does the James Harris character in "Elizabeth":

> He smiled more than anyone Catharine had ever known, and she thought once that he looked satanic; she told him so and he smiled at her, smoke in his eyes.
> "The devil is the only true god," he said. (55)

Had Jackson incorporated the story into *The Lottery* as she once intended, she would certainly have changed Aaron's name to James Harris and possibly his yellow sweater to a blue suit. Aaron's mockery identifies him with Jamie of "The Daemon Lover"; he suggests that Catharine introduce him to her family as a thief and murderer who rapes young women. At other times, he affects a poetic diction much like that of Jim in "The Tooth": "Aaron said smoothly, 'Look at Cara's hands, Mrs. Vincent. They're like white waves on a white shore. They touch her face like moths'" (56). The narrator's early reference to Catharine's one note from Aaron foreshadows the end of the story, where the young woman turns from her mother's open trunk to the small cedar box that holds such "secret treasures" as that single letter. Catharine imagines Aaron sitting at "chromium bars," walking past "bright stores," smiling "with his quick sudden amusement, saying, 'Catharine? I once cared for a girl named Catharine'" (57).

While Catharine seems to accept her rejection by Aaron, she is clearly a victim of male power. The emphasis on Aaron's desertion at the end balances the story's opening emphasis on Catharine's father, William Vincent. A man who believes his large mustache makes him look "more the master of his house," he becomes a minister before his marriage to express his certainty of "being right, and virtuous, and easily sure of his authority"

(46). God is "practically the only person he felt really close to," and Mr. Vincent often threatens Catharine with twofold patriarchal disapproval by repeating, "Do you think you are satisfactory, in God's sight or mine?" (47). Despite her interest in art, Catharine goes to business school because her father needs help with "his numerous notes and the books of sermons he might write someday" (49). In contrast to the physically heavy and emotionally repressive Mr. Vincent, the slim and graceful Aaron seems to embody a fineness to which Catharine aspires. Although, at 23, she has "nearly forgotten her father" (46), the title of the story implies that Catharine still loves Aaron, who apparently left her a few years earlier, at about the time Mr. Vincent died.

The strangers who abruptly enter women's lives in three other *Come Along with Me* stories are even more closely akin than Aaron to the James Harris archetype. Like "The Daemon Lover" and "The Tooth," "The Beautiful Stranger" (ca. 1946), "A Visit" (1950), and "The Rock" (ca. 1951) build to disturbing conclusions in which a mysterious male brings the protagonist to her doom. In contrast to the pathetic Catharine Vincent, who believes "the romance and the glory of her life" are "waiting still" (51), these other female victims are left with no comforting illusions.

"The Beautiful Stranger" is among Jackson's most disconcerting stories about doubles. Margaret, an unhappy housewife, is delighted when she realizes the man she and her two children bring home from the train station is not her husband, John, but the beautiful stranger of the title:

> Who? she wondered suddenly; is he taller? That is not my husband.
> She laughed, and they turned to her, Smalljohn curious, and her husband with a quick bright recognition; she thought, why it is *not* my husband, and he knows that I have seen it. (60)

Although Margaret never discusses the substitution with him, she several times reassures herself that the man is indeed a stranger. While he sits next to her at dinner, John had always faced her from the other end of the table. When he says he will build a shelf to fill with "symbols," Margaret sees "his hands were stronger; this man would build whatever he decided he wanted built" (62). In contrast to the fear and pain she suffered in John's presence, the stranger brings "pure joy," ridding her of "any residue of suspicion and hatred" (61). Thus the ending is especially shocking. When Margaret returns late from shopping for a gift for the stranger, she cannot find her home. Somewhere among the many rows of houses is *her* house,

Margaret thinks, "with the beautiful stranger inside, and she lost out here" (65).

Lenemaja Friedman believes that, though Jackson "keeps her audience guessing" throughout, the conclusion proves Margaret has "lost touch with reality" and is, in fact, insane (Friedman, 46–47). Jackson's revisions of an earlier version, however, tend to strengthen the story's ambiguities. Especially significant is the cutting of three scenes from "Document of Loneliness," as Jackson entitled her draft (SJP, Box 15). In one scene Margaret perceives that the tablecloth that was green in the morning is yellow as she sets the table for lunch. She is troubled but, she reasons, may have been so happy with the beautiful stranger that "the identities of all things had slipped slightly." In the second excised scene Margaret notices the order of all the encyclopedias in the bookcase is unaccountably reversed. Finally, her mother-in-law phones and mentions John has just stopped by. Margaret insists "someone who is not John" arrived on the train from Boston, and asks, "How did he know where you lived?" before hanging up.

Besides eliminating episodes highly suggestive of mental disorder, Jackson also revised the stranger's longing for a tiny blue, purple, and gold ship model to his desire for a "little creature" to place on the shelf he will build. He saw one once, he tells Margaret: "Like a tiny little man, only colored all purple and blue and gold" (62). "Much later," adds the narrator—looking beyond the story's closing events—Margaret tells herself John could not have said such a thing. But the exotic stranger of "The Tooth" could well have expressed a similar craving. Adding to the possibility that the man in Margaret's house may be a demon lover is his sudden observation that someone heard he was dead in Boston; perhaps he is John's ghost or another supernatural visitor. Because the story is related from a third-person viewpoint limited to Margaret's perceptions, the reader can be no more certain than the reader of "The Tooth" whether the protagonist is mad or sane. In both stories repressed marital tension seems to be the source of each woman's delight in a charming male whose imaginative fantasies distinguish him from the husband to whom she has been monotonously, even painfully, bound for years.

The beautiful stranger in "A Visit," first published in *New World Writing* as "The Lovely House," does not displace a husband. The victim of his charm is another Margaret, however—a young woman who spends a school vacation at the remarkable home of her friend Carla Rhodes. Hyman notes in the preface to *Come Along with Me* that "A Visit" was Jackson's original title, and he also restores her dedication of this long and noteworthy story to Dylan Thomas. On his first lecture tour of the United States in 1950, Thomas attended a party at Jackson's house. According to Oppenheimer, not only did her stories impress him, but he was "the man who fitted her conception of the Demon Lover almost completely" (Oppenheimer, 150). The title may refer, then, to Thomas's visit as well as Margaret's. It also applies to the ghostly visitation of the attractive Paul, who arrives at the Rhodes mansion a week after Margaret in the company of Carla's eagerly awaited brother. In the confusion of welcomes, Margaret mistakes the more assertive Paul for the brother; she does not seem to notice that she and an old woman, also named Margaret, are the only members of the household who speak to Paul. At the end of the story, when the two young men are leaving, she finally realizes the dark-haired captain is the son of the family: *"and Paul: who was Paul?"* (111).

Paul appears to be the guardian of the Rhodes mansion, a beautiful but curious structure that rivals the Gothic houses of Jackson's last three novels: *The Sundial* (1958), *The Haunting of Hill House* (1959), and *We Have Always Lived in the Castle* (1962). Even as Margaret calls his attention to the worn carpet beneath their feet, Paul denies the building and its furnishings are subject to change: "'Nonsense,' he said violently. 'Don't you think I'd know my own house? I care for it constantly, even when *they* forget; without this house I could not exist; do you think it would begin to crack while I am here?'" (111). The elderly namesake whom Margaret meets in the rain-swept tower of the mansion is not pleased to learn that Paul is back: "'I say,' said the old lady, turning to look at Margaret, 'he should have come and gone already, and we'd be well out of it by now'" (104). But when the old Margaret and Paul speak gallantly to each other at the Rhodeses' ball, they laugh, and young Margaret is struck by the "strong resemblance between them" (107). The old woman remarks that Paul has not aged noticeably and probably never will. These hints of his ghostly nature—and the old woman's—are reinforced when the dark captain approaches the trio and tells young Margaret he will seize the opportunity of finding her alone to invite her to dance.

Carla and her mother also act unaware of Paul and the elderly Margaret. At a picnic, Carla virtually repeats Paul's description of a nearby river to young Margaret and then, as Margaret rises to investigate with him, accuses the girl of always wandering off. Mrs. Rhodes tells Margaret that she saw her "try the door of the ruined tower" (112), as if Margaret had not pulled the door open easily and ascended the steps effortlessly to visit the old woman Paul vaguely describes as "an aunt, or a great-aunt, or perhaps even a great-great-great-aunt" (101). Because Margaret is somewhat timid and clearly in awe of the mansion, the reader may speculate on her mental state. But Margaret has little in common with the suffering women of stories like "The Beautiful Stranger," and it is even more difficult to question her sanity than theirs. Moreover, the Rhodeses act as agitated over small signs of decay as Paul does, suggesting the house wields an inexplicable power over all of its inhabitants, human as well as inhuman, much like the less lovely house in *The Haunting of Hill House.*

Although Jackson is frequently categorized as a Gothic writer, "A Visit" is among her few short stories to adhere closely to such conventions as the haunted mansion. A stone faun by the front door and bronze fauns in the hall woodwork introduce a fanciful decorating scheme worthy of Poe. A prominent feature is the series of tapestries that rival any of the rich wall hangings in his stories. Tapestries in the gold room are edged in gilded frames and portray the house in sunlight; silver-framed tapestries of the house in moonlight hang in the silver room. The Gothic obsession with doubles is even more extravagantly incorporated into a mirrored room where Carla and Margaret watch themselves "diminishing and reflecting" in an endless succession of doorways (93). A nest of tables supports a nest of wooden bowls, and tapestries picture the house reflected in the lake, "and the tapestries themselves were reflected, in and out, among the mirrors on the wall, with the house in the tapestries reflected in the lake" (93–94). The confusion of inside and outside, reflection and substance, so overcomes Margaret that she withdraws in fright.

Strangest of all the pairings in the house are the alternate versions of Margaret. When she meets the old woman in the tower, the girl searches for an appropriate response to the coincidence of names, then smiles "uncertainly" and makes no comment (104). The narrator does not record Margaret's reaction when she eagerly reads an inscription in the room of tiles beneath a portrait of a pretty girl who stares "blindly from the floor": "'Here was Margaret,' it said, 'who died for love'" (97). Mrs. Rhodes and Carla, who have a special affection for the picture, seem intent on observing its effect on Margaret: "'I was wondering what Margaret would say when she saw it,' said Carla, smiling also [like her mother]" (97). Near the end of the story, Carla's brother reports that, among new signs of decay, a tile is missing from this portrait. (The signs also include a "crack in the solid stone" over the conservatory window [109], a likely allusion to Poe's ominous fissure in "The Fall of the House of Usher.") Young Margaret hurries to the room of tiles to verify the loss and discovers "the broken spot looked like a tear" (110).

After Paul and the captain leave, Mrs. Rhodes ignores Margaret's reference to the end of her own visit and turns to her embroidery to create a final Margaret; she asks the girl to sit with Carla on the lawn near the river so she can fill in the foreground and complete the latest tapestry of the house. "We shall be models of stillness," Carla laughs as she invites Margaret to join her outside (112). Earlier that same day Margaret speculated that the figures in the dining room tapestries "might remember, secretly, an imagined process of dressing themselves and coming with laughter and light voices to sit on the lawn where they were woven" (109). When Margaret arrived at the Rhodeses' house, she felt she had "come home"; the conclusion suggests she is so linked with the substance of the mansion she will never leave, and may always have been there. The house claims her, not as violently as Hill House claims Eleanor Vance at the end of *The Haunting of Hill House*, but just as surely.

The most obviously demonic of the charismatic strangers in *Come Along with Me* appears in "The Rock," a story Hyman found untitled, in early draft form (*CAWM*, vii). Like the more intricate "A Visit," "The Rock" is unusual among Jackson's short fiction for its Gothicism. In both stories, a young unmarried woman vacations at a unique house and meets a man mysteriously connected with the remote location. The inn that rises from the black surface of Rock Island is reminiscent of old Margaret's bleak tower, and Paula Ellison's growing attachment to her fellow guest is as disturbing as young Margaret's love for Paul.

Paula's first view of the island from the water is nightmarish; it stretches "impossibly large over her head," backlit by a red sunset: "a great black jagged rock, without signs of humanity or sympathy, with only dreadful reaching black rocks and sharp incredible outlines against the sunset" (115). By calling the young man who pilots the small boat a ferryman, the narrator adds to the impression that Paula, her sister-in-law, and her convalescent brother Charles are bound on a mythic journey to the underworld. The "great fire" that gives the only light in the huge living room of the guest house is appropriately hellish, flickering against walls made of rock (117). Paula tries to analyze the "great despair and impulsive dislike" she feels toward both the building and the abrupt landlady, who assumes Paula would choose to domesticate the stark room with curtains and flowers.

The small man who greets her after breakfast the next day acts timid rather than devilish, but he looks at her with "a sort of hypnotized stare" that Paula "rudely" returns (121). His eyes, she thinks, "must be almost the color and texture of the rock itself." From this first meeting, when she experiences a "shock of recognition," the stranger exercises an unusual hold on Paula. Her sister-in-law and her exhausted brother spend their days inside, but Paula follows the little guest all over the island. At the end he seems "somehow taller" (129), and she is fully in his power. When the landlady uncharacteristically puts a sheltering arm around Paula, the man "sadly" smiles: "No use at all, you know."

The only other story from *Come Along with Me* that incorporates as many Gothic elements as "A Visit" and "The Rock" is "The Bus" (1965), one of Jackson's last works. Two drafts end with the protagonist's discovery that her frightening adventure at an unfamiliar roadstop is a bad dream; in both earlier versions, the old woman awakens "in the bus, which she had never left" (SJP, Box 19). But in the published text, the reassuring final clause is omitted and Miss Harper is again roughly deposited by the driver at the same isolated crossroads where her night of terror began.

Jackson's Gothicism again centers in a single woman's visit to an isolated house that entraps her. The once lovely building where Miss Harper finds shelter from the stormy night is now a bar and grill with a crooked sign. Though the garden has become a parking lot, Miss Harper feels a "warm stir of recognition" (186). She tells the crude bartender Belle that she once lived in a similar house, but Miss Harper is mistaken in her assumption that, as "a woman at least," Belle would be "someone who might understand and sympathize" (187).

Left to find her own way upstairs for the night, Miss Harper automatically turns to the front room on the left, the position of her girlhood bedroom. She realizes hundreds of houses must be built on the same square pattern, but the room is almost a double of the one she slept in as a child. The bed, however, frightens her with its "faint smell of dark couplings" (189). The explicit sexual reference is rare for Jackson, and, like her revision of "Mrs." Harper in an early draft to "Miss" Harper, it emphasizes the old woman's loneliness and possibly her aversion to sex. Reminiscent of the Freudian symbolism of "The Tooth," a wooden snake in the bedroom closet comes alive and disturbs Miss Harper's attempt to sleep with its clattering. Though she laughs when she recognizes it as her childhood toy, it fiercely throws itself at her ankles, joining several other playthings in an attack that sends Miss Harper screaming into the dark hallway. She awakes on the bus, only to be dropped off once more in the rain at Ricket's Landing. The driver's "This is as far as you go" (192) suggests that he, like Paula's ferryman in "The Rock," transports lonely women on one-way journeys to dark underworlds. "The Bus" is very much in the spirit of the popular contemporaneous television series "The Twilight Zone," with its weekly excursions into alarming realms of the imagination.

"The Summer People" (1949) and "The Little House" (1962) forego most of the Gothic trappings of the last three stories, but their endings are comparably disquieting. "The Summer People" is set in the same type of tradition-bound New England village as "The Lottery" and "Flower Garden." Like Tessie Hutchinson and Mrs. MacLane, the Allisons are "ordinary people" (66) who become victims of an extraordinary communal effort to preserve a customary way of life. Longtime summer residents, the couple violates the status quo when they decide to stay at the lake past Labor Day.

Early in the story Mrs. Allison attributes the grocer's "inconclusive" conversations to a "horrible" degeneration of old "Yankee stock" (68). The real horror lies in the formerly helpful villagers' active revenge on the unwelcome outsiders. Delivery of food and kerosene to the secluded cottage is cut off. The already poor telephone connection worsens and eventually goes dead. When a letter from their son finally arrives, the handwriting is familiar, but both parents sense a strangeness in the contents, as if Jerry did not write it at all. On the Friday after Labor Day, Mr. Allison quietly tells his wife their car has been tampered with. He takes her hand as a storm strikes the fragile house: "And then, while the lightning flashed outside, and the radio faded and sputtered, the two old people huddled together in their summer cottage and waited" (78).

In "Flower Garden" and "The Renegade" Jackson also developed a tension between country ways and city ways, but the conflict becomes deadly in "The Summer People." Her extensive reworking of the original conclusion produces an effect of shock equal to that of "The Lottery" (SJP, Box 18). The impending disaster at the lake is an autumnal parallel of the summer sacrifice of Tessie Hutchinson. An opening reference to the pleasant days of "midsummer" (66) recalls the first sentence of the earlier story, with its evocation of the solstice, and Mrs. Allison's mocking observation that rain would be "good for the crops" (71) parodies the farmers' concerns and Old Mr. Warner's proverb in "The Lottery." The comfortable domesticity of Mrs. Allison, who "lovingly" scrubs her baking dishes (70), is interrupted as fatally as is Mrs. Hutchinson's morning dishwashing.

In "The Little House" too an outsider from the city offends country sensibilities. Miss Amanda Dolson and her sister Caroline are insulted when they receive no offer of tea during their visit to a new neighbor in the village. "City ways," Miss Amanda sniffs, and Miss Caroline remarks that Elizabeth could at least have given them some "city cake" (178). James

Egan blames the Dolsons for Elizabeth's final state of panic in the inherited house she had envisioned as a sanctuary: "Her dream has been shattered by rudimentary human evil—the gossip and meddling of the Dolson sisters."[50] But even before Miss Caroline arrives with the news that "Aunt" did not die of natural causes, the young woman's joy of ownership is tempered by guilt that she was not attentive to the old lady, annoyance at the cluttered decor, and "a little chill touching the back of her neck" (173) when she reflects she is alone in the dimly lit house. Elizabeth's unpleasant encounter with the elderly sisters simply aggravates the "cynicism and melancholy and the wearying disappointments of many years" (172).

At the end of the story Miss Amanda and Miss Caroline return to their own cozy house, speculating that the newcomer might not stay. Elizabeth, who sees "only darkness" at the top of the stairs on her way to bed, retreats wildly to Aunt's lighted kitchen, articulating the despair of several of Jackson's isolated women: "Don't leave me here alone . . . please don't leave me here alone" (178). Like the ominous conclusion of "The Summer People," the dark ending of "The Little House" conveys a powerful sense of threat. The Allisons "waited" in the desolate cottage, and Elizabeth wonders, "What's waiting behind the [bedroom] door?" (178). In an earlier, untitled version of the story, Jackson showed exactly what was waiting. As Elizabeth, "humming happily," turns to the stairway, "the man who had been hidden in the shadows on the stairs came two steps forward and caught her. 'I thought you were gone away forever,' he said sadly, 'and now I got to do it all over again'" (SJP, Box 19). The revision skillfully heightens the suspense by leaving the protagonist—and the reader—to imagine the worst. Jackson's closing technique in *The Sundial* is similar; the identity of Mrs. Halloran's killer is left uncertain as the rest of the household boards up the family mansion to ride out the coming Apocalypse: "My," sighs a minor character. "It's going to be a long wait" (*Sundial*, 245).

While Elizabeth and the Allisons fail to establish a secure home, women in "A Day in the Jungle" (1952) and "Louisa, Please Come Home" (1960) deliberately turn their backs on domestic security. Elsa Dayton of "A Day in the Jungle" angrily flees what she perceives as her husband's dullness and neglect. Reminiscent of Margaret in "The Beautiful Stranger," she bitterly yearns for a drastic change in her life. The narrator's brief reference to Elsa's dead baby may suggest she is suffering from depression. In leaving the apartment, whose windows look as "blank and unexciting as always" (132), Elsa is leaving her marriage: "the humiliation of the wedding and the bad dreams of the long nights and the hideous unprivate months" (130). Although she signs her own name in the hotel register ("Elsa Masters

Dayton"), when she speaks with a man in the dining room she pretends to be visiting the city from Maine. The businessman is eager to return to his Chicago home, but Elsa has "a clear general impression of belonging in this scene of movement, of passage" (136). Anticipating the Doris Lessing character in "To Room Nineteen" who periodically seeks freedom from her family at a hotel, Elsa likes "the thought that she had a completely private place here" (137).

Elsa makes a dinner date with her husband after he tracks her down by phone, but she is determined to be independent. On her way to the restaurant, she realizes that "for the first time she moved knowingly and of choice through a free world" (139). Yet Elsa's exciting new world crumbles as abruptly as Margaret's did in "Pillar of Salt." Suddenly, a "nagging small feeling which she knew clearly now as fear and which had been following her cautiously for hours, perhaps for weeks or years stepped up . . . and walked along beside her" (139). Elsa is alarmed by neon lights whose dangling wires might electrocute her. She imagines herself a potential victim of an enemy, stranger, or madman who might threaten from a window or a car. She could be crushed by a swaying trolley or cut to death by a falling pane of glass. For three dizzying pages, Jackson relates fantasies of disaster. When the terrified Elsa arrives at the restaurant, her husband looks "so wonderfully safe and familiar" that she smiles in relief, thinking, "I have been alone for so long" (142). Once again—as in "The Daemon Lover," "The Tooth," "The Beautiful Stranger," and other stories—a discontent woman's venture into a freer life proves a dangerous, if heady, experience.

In the published version of "A Day in the Jungle," Jackson omitted her draft conclusion, which offered a curious look into the future: "This, then, was the end of the journey of Elsa Masters Dayton. Although she did not know it then, she was to die nearly fourteen years later of influenza and Don, who remained a loving husband to the last, remarried and always kept a snapshot of her, taken on their honeymoon, on his desk at the office" (SJP, Box 19). Given Elsa's opinion of the wedding as a "humiliation," the honeymoon snapshot probably recorded a very superficial happiness. In returning to Don, Elsa chooses a familiar trap over a frightening escape.

Louisa Tether of "Louisa, Please Come Home" has more luck than Elsa in making a permanent getaway, but she is a daughter, not a wife. Just as Elsa "always suspected" she might leave her husband (132), Louisa "always knew that I was going to run away sooner or later" (154). Two events motivate her to carry out her escape plans: her sister's wedding, which she seems pleased to disrupt, and her dismissal from a "little fancy" college, which she left "with nobody's blessing" (159). Louisa becomes so confident in her new identity as Lois Taylor, stationery shop clerk in a distant city, that she asks her landlady, Mrs. Peacock, whether she sees any similarity between Lois and the runaway girl whose photograph appears in the paper. The comfortable Mrs. Peacock—who has much in common with Angela Motorman's landlady, Mrs. Faun, in the incomplete novel "Come Along with Me"—seems to be all the family Louisa needs. They discuss the young woman's future and consider pooling their savings to buy a car or take a trip. "I was free," says Louisa, "and getting along fine" (165) when, three years after her flight, she runs into her old neighbor Paul, who insists on rushing her back to her family.

Louisa almost cries with homesickness when she sees the big white house again, but the front door is symbolically shut as she approaches with Paul—"Mrs. Peacock would have been halfway down the walk to meet us" (166). In a startling denouement, Louisa's sister, mother, and father all deny she is the missing girl. Louisa learns that Paul, hoping for a reward, has already presented the Tethers with two well-primed imposters; they refuse to be tricked again. "Maybe they were so used to looking for me by now that they would rather keep on looking than have me home," Louisa reasons; "maybe once my mother had looked in my face and seen there nothing of Louisa, but only the long careful concentration I had put into being Lois Taylor, there was never any chance of my looking like Louisa again" (168). Thus Louisa achieves the complete separation from her family she sought. But now she realizes "all I wanted was to stay" (168), and every year, on the anniversary of her flight, she listens to her mother's radio message: "Louisa, please come home" (170).

Recipient of the Edgar Allan Poe Award in 1961, "Louisa, Please Come Home" is one of Jackson's most thoroughly rewritten stories. Five versions exist, and all but the published form are entitled "Louisa (Hoax)" (SJP, Box 17). In one very different draft, Louisa secretly marries Paul while she is at college and then runs away with him after he steals money from her father. Paul refuses to let her go home until the two need financial help three years later. They pretend Louisa has had amnesia and that Paul came across her on a New York street. Their hoax is ruined when a mutual friend of Paul and Louisa follows them from New York and cruelly interrupts the family gathering by addressing Louisa as "Dottie." Paul and Louisa leave, but she writes a year later from Cairo to confess her original reason for running away and to explain that, despite the amnesia story, she really is Louisa. This version ends on the same note of estrangement as

"Louisa, Please Come Home" since the letter is never sent: "What would be the use?" Louisa concludes.

"Island" (1950) too is drastically reworked from its early, untitled draft form (SJP, Box 16). Jackson's most important revision in this account of the aging Mrs. Montague is the addition of a warm world of the imagination to which the widow with a wandering mind can escape. Mrs. Montague's escape is the most satisfactory of the many attempted flights in the *Lottery* and *Come Along with Me* stories; no one, including Mrs. Montague, is harmed by the adventure. Although the landscape of her fantasy resembles the vista that lures Clara Spencer from her family in "The Tooth," she does not journey in the company of a demon lover. Mrs. Montague's island provides the sensory stimulation lacking on the gray day in New York that she goes walking with her caretaker, Miss Oakes. The fantasy allows the old woman to break away from the "life of placid regularity" Miss Oakes so efficiently "engineer[s]" for her (79). Moreover, the island constitutes an alternative reality inaccessible to the matter-of-fact companion, who laughs when Mrs. Montague colors whole pages of her coloring book blue. "You don't know what things *are*, really," Mrs. Montague complains to Miss Oakes (83).

A two-and-a-half-page description of Mrs. Montague's idyllic retreat disrupts the narrative of the women's customary afternoon stroll. On one level Mrs. Montague obediently responds to Miss Oakes's tug on her arm, but on another "she opened her eyes suddenly and was aware that she saw" (85). Much of what she sees is a fanciful rearrangement of details from her own life. The "unbelievably" blue sky is straight out of her coloring book. An "ugly red and yellow parrot" (86) recalls a plastic bird in a shop window Mrs. Montague saw on her walk, but also Miss *Polly* Oakes, whose budget dresses are typically "garish reds and yellows" (80). Earlier, Mrs. Montague nostalgically had told Miss Oakes, "Once when we were children we used to take off all our clothes and run out in the rain" (82). In her fantasy she "slip[s] easily out of the straps and buttons and catches of many garments, which she remembered as difficult to put on" (86), and buries the whole pile in the sand.

On the island Mrs. Montague recovers long-lost appetites and abilities. The idea of food comes to mind, "for a minute unpleasant and as though it meant a disagreeable sensation, and then glowingly happy" (86). She dines on purple grapes, cheese, and "rich little cakes" (87), a sensuous contrast to her usual evening meal of prune juice and oatmeal. Mrs. Montague's legs are now so strong that she runs: "it was impossible to move slowly on the island, with the clear hot air all around her, the ocean stirring constantly"

(86). In the imaginary world Mrs. Montague is able to deal with her frustrations. She laughingly draws a picture of her dutiful son in the sand, then grinds it away with a bare foot. She also pushes her fist through her rough drawing of a doorway, perhaps a rendering of her confining apartment door. The island is so real to Mrs. Montague that her hat, which Miss Oakes angled carefully for their walk, becomes "offensive" to her, with its "patently unreal roses" (86). The sand turns cooler and grayer, and Mrs. Montague finds herself passing the bakery with Miss Oakes, but the closing scene suggests Mrs. Montague has the power to re-create her escape. Back at the apartment, while Miss Oakes goes through the usual routine of calling room service for dinner, Mrs. Montague—who says she has "had enough" (89)—bends over her coloring book to insert "a red and yellow blot far up in the blue trees" (90).

The semi-autobiographical "Pajama Party" differs in many ways from the other 13 stories of *Come Along with Me*. Like "Charles" "Pajama Party" is a humorous family fiction, not a tale of a misunderstood, threatened, or alienated woman. In contrast to the single or unhappily married females of most *Come Along with Me* stories, the narrator of "Pajama Party" is a wife and mother who seems wholly absorbed in planning her daughter's birthday party. Carol Cleveland describes the subsequent confusion as "domestic frenzy" and remarks that Jackson's family memoirs are "early and admirable examples of an American literary subgenre: the diary of the mad housewife" (Cleveland, 199). It is the narrator's final inability to contain the chaos that relates her to many of Jackson's more desperate protagonists.

Her son Laurie, grown from the kindergartener of "Charles" to a teenager, says she is mad (144), and a neighbor calls her crazy (145), but the unnamed mother has obviously not "lost her mind" in the same way Mrs. Montague of "Island" has (79). Events, however, conspire against her orderly arrangements. The woman borrows cots and empties her linen closet of sheets to accommodate the four 11-year-old visitors in Jannie's bedroom, but, after arguing and making up, they fall asleep crowded together in the guest-room bed. Jannie's mother has a penchant for routine, much like Miss Oakes in "Island," but the party guests resist regulation as stubbornly as Mrs. Montague does. Ignoring the narrator's request for quiet, the girls play raucously with fortune-telling cards, creating plots worthy of a James Harris story: "I could hear someone calling on a tall dark man and someone else remarking bitterly upon jealousy from a friend" (150). The final disruption comes at 3:17 A.M., when Jannie awakens her exhausted mother with the news that Kate feels sick and needs to be taken home.

Like "The Night We All Had Grippe," which follows a Jackson lecture in *Come Along with Me*, "Pajama Party" is in the vein of James Thurber's prose sketches and cartoons of riotous domesticity. The detailed bed switches in these family stories are particularly Thurberesque, and the slapstick action of "The Night We All Had Grippe" so strongly evokes Thurber's "The Night the Bed Fell" that Jackson may have intended it as a parody. Both authors wrote for the *New Yorker* during the 1940s and 1950s, and they exchanged letters on the exceptional response to "The Lottery." During the 1940s Jackson drew a series of unpublished family cartoons along Thurber's spare lines (SJP, Box 36); Stanley Edgar Hyman is recognizable by his beard, and Jackson always appears in a long gown with the hairstyle of a Medusa.

There is, in fact, a hint of Medusa's glare in much of Jackson's comedy. The narrator of "Pajama Party" reaches "wearily" for the coffee pot and "sullenly" refutes her husband's opinion that one party guest would be enough (145). Jannie and her girlfriends listen to Elvis Presley's "Heartbreak Hotel" at top volume. Such details are important to feminist critics like Nancy A. Walker, who emphasizes the "subtext of anguish" in the humorous writings of Jackson, Dorothy Parker, Betty MacDonald, and other American women.[51] As James Egan points out, however, through "selective perception" Jackson is able to exclude "the ominous and melancholy" from the family stories to a great extent, thus producing a "vision of a nurturing domestic world" (Egan, 16, 23). Jackson knew this vision would sell well, of course, but the image of a welcoming home also holds strong appeal for many characters in what she considered her more serious fiction, including such *Come Along with Me* women as Margaret ("The Beautiful Stranger"), Elizabeth ("The Little House"), and Louisa Tether ("Louisa, Please Come Home"). To the destruction or the redemption of the protagonists, it is an appeal that becomes obsessive in *The Sundial*, *The Haunting of Hill House*, and *We Have Always Lived in the Castle*.

# The Uncollected Stories:
# Seeking the Self

The week Shirley Jackson's first novel, *The Road through the Wall*, appeared, a phone call from the local society columnist interrupted her preparations for a publicity trip to New York. Jackson describes the purported conversation in "Fame," a humorous essay printed by *The Writer* in the momentous summer of 1948, two months after the *New Yorker* published "The Lottery." The caller's abrupt "Hello, who's this?" is "a common enough Vermont greeting," according to Jackson, but it precipitates an uncommon dialogue:

> "This is Shirley Jackson," I said, a little soothed because my name reminded me of my book.
> "Well," she said vaguely. "Is Mrs. Stanley Hyman there, please?"
> I waited for a minute and then, "This is Mrs. Hyman," I said reluctantly.
> Her voice brightened. "Mrs. Hyman," she said, pleased. "This is Mrs. Sheila Lang of the newspaper. I've been trying to get in touch with you for *days*."[52]

Soliciting announcements for "North Village Notes," Mrs. Lang is more interested in Jackson's house and children than in the author's attempts to discuss her book and the publication party hosted by Farrar & Straus. In the next day's column, among items on town meetings and illnesses, Jackson reads: "Mrs. Stanley Hyman has moved into the old Thatcher place on Prospect Street. She and her family are visiting Mr. and Mrs. Farrarstraus of New York City this week" (266).

Despite its brevity, "Fame" embodies in essay form many of the themes of Jackson's short stories. In treating the Hymans—three-year residents—as newcomers to the village, Mrs. Lang anticipates the city–country tension of "Flower Garden" and "The Summer People." The conflict between the "sweet old lady's" domineering voice (265) and the suppressed voice of the young respondent parallels the generational clashes of women in "Trial by Combat" and "The Little House." In her futile effort to assert her personal worth, the narrator resembles female protagonists in "The Daemon Lover" and "Elizabeth." The doubleness of the writer-housewife is echoed not only in the strange doubles of "The Beautiful Stranger" and "A Visit" but in Jackson's career-long fascination with the complexities of personality. As Lenemaja Friedman observes, Jackson's characters are often absorbed in "establishing their own identity" (Friedman, 158); this focus—evident in stories as varied as "Charles," "The Tooth," and "Louisa, Please Come Home"—often helps to explain the high level of anxiety in Jackson's fiction. Few of the uncollected stories match the achievement of the *Lottery* and *Come Along with Me* volumes, but many are intriguing explorations of the divided self, usually the female self.

The works I discuss include some of the best treatments of this theme in the uncollected stories, among them a few of the semi-autobiographical pieces Jackson subsequently integrated into the family memoirs, *Life among the Savages* and *Raising Demons*. Following Hyman's example in the preface to *Come Along with Me*, I have made the selections with quality and diversity in mind.

One of Jackson's most memorable family stories, "The Third Baby's the Easiest" (1949), develops the same identity crisis described in "Fame." Although the anonymous narrator (ostensibly Jackson herself) asserts her readiness for the third baby's arrival, she refuses to limit her self-definition to wife and mother. She admits to reacting "nervously" when "the frightful moment" comes and she jumps out of bed "at two in the morning as though there had been a pea under the mattress."[53] Her uneasiness is not relieved when she must unexpectedly prove herself to the hospital receptionist:

> "Name?" the desk clerk said to me politely, her pencil posed.
> "Name," I said vaguely. I remembered, and told her.
> "Age?" she asked. "Sex? Occupation?"
> "Writer," I said.
> "Housewife," she said.
> "Writer," I said.
> "I'll just put down housewife," she said. "Doctor? How many children?" (61)

Nancy Walker cites this scene three times to suggest the "double message" of women's humor (Walker, 33). A "subversive subtext" created by such verbal exchanges exposes women's "subjugation" (Walker, 66) and "trivialization" (Walker, 145).

Her husband and the doctor try to calm her down as she awaits delivery, but the narrator persists in making unconventional responses that upset both men: "I've changed my mind, I don't want any baby, I want to go home and forget the whole thing" (62). When the doctor sympathetically tries to identify with her—"I know *just* how you feel"—she utters "a word which certainly I knew that I *knew*, although I had never honestly expected to hear it spoken in my own ladylike voice" (62–63). Her husband "urgently" but futilely asks her to "stop yelling" (63). The final stage of the narrator's distancing herself from her maternal role comes en route to the operating room, as she identifies with a hero under attack: "'She loved me for the dangers I had passed,' I said to the doctor, 'and I loved her that she did pity them'" (63). The physician twice advises her to hold her breath, perhaps fearing hysteria. He probably does not realize she is quoting Othello's response to the Duke of Venice, who cannot believe the beautiful Desdemona would willingly marry a Moor. To the feminist subtext uncovered by Nancy Walker, we might add a related subtext of the self struggling to declare its value, despite appearances that blind the viewer—especially the viewer in a position of authority—to the individual's hidden worth. A black man can be a lover and a military champion, and a pregnant housewife can indeed be a writer.

Several years and one baby later, the still nameless narrator of Jackson's family stories explains how her husband's profession as a teacher at a women's college further threatens her sense of self. "On Being a Faculty Wife" (1956) appeared originally in the Bennington College alumnae magazine, was slightly expanded for *Mademoiselle*, and finally was incorporated into *Raising Demons*.[54] Denying her anger at being treated as a drab escort for her brilliant husband, the speaker humorously recommends that young men who plan to be professors should wear "a large kind of identifying badge" to protect "innocent young girls who might in that case go on to be the contented wives of disc jockeys or even car salesmen" (116).

The faculty wife, says Jackson, probably had "a face and a personality of her own" at one time, "but if she has it still she is expected to keep it decently to herself" (116). The narrator depicts herself standing "moodily" in the hall while her husband is enthusiastically welcomed to a student party (117). She retreats to a corner with other faculty wives, whose main topic of conversation is their children. Approached by a student-hostess in a strapless pink dress, she sarcastically reacts to praise of the great man's vitality: "Absolutely nothing but boyish vitality and youthful charm all over the place. He's positively faunlike. Why, I could tell you things—" (136). In contrast to her assertiveness with the desk clerk in "The Third

Baby's the Easiest," the woman denies she has an identity apart from her husband and children. When the hostess insensitively asks, "How come you just ended up doing housework and stuff? Couldn't you get a job?" the narrator does not mention her writing. "I have a job," she says. "I cook and sew and clean and shop and make beds and drive people places and—" (136). The pastimes of a faculty wife are, after all, "conducted in a respectably anonymous and furtive manner" (116).

Shirley Jackson wrote more than 30 family stories, and many besides "Third Baby" and "Faculty Wife" demonstrate the impossibility of providing a simple answer to Mrs. Lang's challenge in "Fame": "Who's this?" In "Aunt Gertrude" a visit to an elderly relative disorients the narrator, who discovers "with a kind of bewilderment, that I had to bend my head to come onto the porch," though her children pass easily under the rose-framed doorway.[55] Aunt Gertrude's voice so strongly recalls the past "it seemed like my mother pulling me instead of me pulling Jannie" (52). Another kind of identity confusion occurs in "Mother Is a Fortune Hunter." The narrator approaches a policeman who is trying to persuade four unattended children to put a coin in their expired meter: "'Here, officer,' I said, stepping forward generously. 'See? I'm putting a penny in the parking meter and now the little girl's nice mommy won't be arrested.'"[56] One child says, "Thank you, lady," and another assures the youngest of the group, "Mommy will be coming real soon now" (77). The narrator *is* Mommy, too embarrassed to claim the overparked car; her children easily accept temporary roles as another woman's family.

Jannie develops her own act in "*So* Late on Sunday Morning" when she interrupts a breakfast conversation to ask where she is and who she is. She thinks she fell from the woodpile during a game of pirates with her friends: "Betty was the captain and Johnnie was the mate and I was the shrew—."[57] "Crew," her mother corrects her, and Sally charges Jannie with stealing the amnesia plot from a television show (48). Even as a four-year-old, Jannie played many parts. In "All the Girls Were Dancing" the narrator describes the "desperately important" issue of establishing her daughter's name: "Her brother calls her honey, sis and dopey, her baby sister calls her Nannie, and she calls herself, variously, Jean, Jane, Anne, Linda, Barbara, Estelle, Josephine, Marilyn, Susan, and—frequently—Mrs. Ellenoy. The second Mrs. Ellenoy."[58] The mother, who herself uses "two names, a professional and a married name," complains of "a constant bewildering shifting of names around our house" (36). Worse than the confusion of names, a "bitter matter of identification" occasionally arises. Although Jannie is larger than Sally, for example, "there is an uncanny shifting of identity there, since the smaller is now wearing the clothes the larger wore last year, and they both have blond curls and blue eyes."

Several women from Jackson's more obviously fictional stories are as divided as the narrator of the family sketches. In two humorous pieces, "The Strangers" (1952) and "Journey with a Lady" (1952), conventional characters suddenly admit the urge to live a radically freer life—a theme Jackson treats more seriously in *The Lottery* and *Come Along with Me*. In the first story Mrs. Webster's small-town conformity is contrasted to the adventurous spirit of her urban sister Barbara, who curiously pulls at the Websters' curtain to watch new neighbors move in. Mrs. Webster advises Barbara to replace her scarlet high-heels with "some respectable shoes," adopting "the strong moral tone which comes easily to mothers of daughters."⁵⁹ Her teenage daughter Babs resembles Barbara in personality as well as name. Mrs. Webster complains that the two "rush to extremes" (68), and she hesitates to let the girl visit Barbara in her New York apartment, fearing the influence of "your clothes and your theaters and your cocktail parties" (24).

Both sisters are about 40, but the unmarried woman seems several years younger. She suspects "people would all say I was an old maid" (24) if she took a job in the Websters' town, and she confesses to having lunch in New York with "idle men," as Mrs. Webster calls them. Unlike the typical single woman in stories from *The Lottery* and *Come Along with Me*, Barbara finds her unmarried state liberating. When Mrs. Webster is amazed at all the housework her sister helps perform in one day—along with the more self-indulgent tasks of doing her nails, setting her hair, and knitting part of a sweater—Barbara remarks, "I suppose it's because I don't have the responsibility for everything" (69).

The new family of strangers across the street acts as a catalyst for Mrs. Webster's well-hidden discontent. From what Babs and her brother Michael report, the Halloran household runs with surprising efficiency and good humor. Mrs. Webster cannot understand how Mrs. Halloran keeps seven children as "clean" and "nice" as hers seem to be. Compounding his wife's frustration in struggling to meet her own high standards, Mr. Webster comments on Mrs. Halloran's striking good looks; the next day he says that at second glance her looks are not outstanding, but her voice is noteworthy. Fearing to measure herself against an attractive woman who just laughs pleasantly when one of her sons spills a drink on the living room rug, Mrs. Webster avoids making a courtesy call for days. Finally, Mr. Webster announces at dinner that Mr. Halloran has been caught for bigamy, and not simply with two wives but three, all of whom live across the street with their shared offspring. Mrs. Webster reacts "faintly," as the reader might anticipate. "I'm so glad I didn't run over," she says with dignity (71).

In the final paragraph, though, Mrs. Webster astonishes her family by laughing loudly, her usually neat hair "coming unpinned" (71). They know her so well they could never guess the proper mother has just had a remarkable epiphany, "her first faint glimpse of a bright new world, a world where perhaps the mild Mr. Websters buried themselves at their offices and the Mrs. Websters, in groups of two or three, sat peacefully over their afternoon tea, their mutual housework done, their common children fed and clothed, their long and comfortable hours spent in unending leisure." The illegal sisterhood is a comic solution to the plight of Jackson's overburdened, emotionally undernourished wives, a comfortable alternative to the thrilling liaisons with mysterious males in "The Tooth" and "The Beautiful Stranger." Free from masculine interference, these peaceful little groups of women anticipate the harmonious household of the two Blackwood sisters in Jackson's final book, *We Have Always Lived in the Castle*, a harmony also achieved only through defiance of the law.

"Journey with a Lady" similarly suggests a woman may have to break the rules to attain her selfhood. Another humorous treatment of nonconformity, this story, like "The Strangers," contrasts married and unmarried women of about the same age. Mrs. Wilson is even more of a stereotype than Mrs. Webster; coincidentally, both are named Helen, but the narrator invariably refers to them as "Mrs." Uneasy as her nine-year-old boards the train alone to visit his grandparents, Mrs. Wilson is full of warnings and advice. While Mr. Wilson tells the boy to have a good time, the mother nervously twists her fingers and repeats her caution to "be careful."[60]

The fearful Mrs. Wilson is the opposite of the fearless single woman who becomes a surrogate mother for Joe on the train. Rejoicing in the journey, the boy resents the intrusion when "his paradise" is "invaded by some woman" who takes the seat beside him (77), but he is impressed she can identify a uniformed man in their car as a policeman: "he knew perfectly well that most women cannot tell the difference between a policeman and a mailman" (78). Then he is astounded at the exchange between the policeman and his companion:

"Name?" he said sternly to the woman.

"Mrs. John Aldridge, officer," said the woman promptly. "And this is my little boy Joseph."

The woman grins as she tells Joe she stole $2,000 from her "old tightwad" employer (79), and Joe grins back, fascinated by her "outlaw glory" (78). She realizes she can escape only briefly—"For one thing, I always knew I had to come home again" (79)—but she has spent a wonderful two weeks buying clothes and watching movies.

The enthralled boy collaborates with the fugitive, offering her one of his adventure comics. When the sharp-eyed policeman again passes through the car, Joe loudly asks, "How is your book, Ma?" and the laughing woman answers, "Fine, fine" (79). Accompanying her to the dining car, the boy "triumphantly" thinks how amazed the other passengers would be if they knew "this innocent-looking woman and her son were outsmarting the cops every step they took." "Blissfully," Joe accepts her invitation to choose from the menu; he stares when she suggests he might prefer a few desserts to a hamburger or spaghetti. Five minutes before they arrive at Joe's stop, he wonders if his substitute mother could avoid punishment by apologizing: "'Wouldn't do at all,' said the woman. 'I really had a fine time'" (80).

The final scene recalls the opening of the story. Joining his grandfather on the station platform, Joe remembers his promise to phone his worried mother. He waves "violently" as the policeman escorts the woman from the train, and she responds with a wave and a "So long, Joe" (81). The amused grandfather says Joe has been reading too many comics when the boy regrets the police caught her; Joe just answers "Yeah" to the old man's speculation that the officer is the woman's brother. Loyally keeping her secret, the boy reacts to his grandfather's questions about the trip by mentioning a boy he saw sitting on a fence. "I didn't wave to him, though," he concludes, indirectly affirming his solidarity not with the ordinary child but with the exceptional woman.

A young Andy Warhol illustrated "Journey with a Lady" for *Harper's*. Three of his four line drawings are of Joe; the final picture shows the woman standing beside the officer. Only the eyes and lips are sketched on the figures, but the man's features are serious and the woman's seem to glow, even in captivity (80). She had told Joe, "You sort of build up all your life for one real good time like this, and then you can take your punishment and not mind it so much" (79). Few of Jackson's women act out their fantasies, but many dutiful mothers and career women in her fiction share the outlaw souls of Mrs. Webster and the lady on the train.

Another type of incongruity between appearance and disposition is evident in "Behold the Child among His Newborn Blisses" (1944) and "A Great Voice Stilled" (1960). Published more than 15 years apart, the two stories expose the hypocrisy of characters whose presence in medical waiting rooms is symbolic of the need for a healing of their cruel spirits. (Flannery O'Connor chose a similar setting for the same reason in the frequently anthologized "Revelation.") In both works characters first appear solicitous of others' well-being but ultimately display a callousness that reverses the reader's original impression. "Behold the Child" alludes to the child in Wordsworth's "Intimations of Immortality" ode who, even at six, is forgetting the glories of his heavenly pre-existence and growing accustomed to the "shades of the prison-house" of earthly existence. Wordsworth calls the child a "little Actor" who proudly learns new parts, "As if his whole vocation / Were endless imitation."[61]

The title applies most obviously to five-year-old Thomas, who observes his mother's confusing transformation when they encounter a retarded child at the doctor's office. The woman's heartless reference to the other boy as an "idiot" teaches the son a harsh lesson in prejudice. To reinforce the lesson, she unexpectedly slaps Thomas on the face, and the story ends as he begins to cry. The gesture is especially brutal in light of her earlier boast that Thomas never cries, "except when he's hurt, of course."[62]

This final savagery is a shocking contrast to the sympathy the mother displays early in the story when another woman's baby girl develops hiccups. The camaraderie is interrupted when an "enormous middle-aged woman" slowly enters with 10-year-old Girlie, a retarded boy frightened because he has never been to the doctor (293). The first two mothers are incredulous that the boy, whose hand is bandaged, has missed innoculations and check-ups, and they become angry when he roughly charges into Thomas and makes him cry. They do not acknowledge that Thomas unwittingly provokes the attack by twice asking whether the newcomer is a girl.

With Girlie's unsuitable name, Jackson implies a connection between his mental handicap and the female sex. A minor revision of the manuscript, which she entitled "Girlie," suggests the identification has to do with the child's inarticulateness. Jackson's original explanation for the name was the boy's appearance. In the first of two drafts Girlie's mother says, "When he was born his old man took one look at him and said, 'He looks to me more like a girl than a boy,' and so that's why we call him Girlie" (SJP, Box 15). The printed version, however, emphasizes the baby's stillness: "'I'll tell you,' she said, 'when he was born he didn't cry a sound, and his old man said he couldn't be a real man, so quiet, and so that's why we call him Girlie'" (294). Jackson stresses the gender confusion by having Girlie's mother add that the child "doesn't know himself, sometimes" whether he is a girl or a boy (295).

Sexual difference is one of the most basic means of defining a person, and the first two mothers are intent on differentiating. They themselves are several times distinguished by the narrator as "the little boy's mother" and "the little girl's mother." When a woman enters the waiting room from the doctor's inner office with a screaming baby, the mother of the little girl commiserates. She quickly identifies the baby as one who has just received an injection and asks, "Boy or girl?" (298). Her own daughter is appropriately outfitted in a ruffled pink dress. Thomas's mother will not even grant Girlie the distinction of gender: "'Thomas,' the little boy's mother said softly, 'do you know what you were playing with? Do you know what Mother had to sit here and watch you playing with? Do you know that boy was an idiot?'" (297). Thomas's name means "twin," but his mother refuses to see the shared humanity of the two boys. In denying Girlie's personhood, she limits her own.

At one time intended for the *Lottery* collection, "Behold the Child" appeared instead in *Cross-Section: A Collection of New American Writing*, in the company of works by Brendan Gill, Langston Hughes, Jane Bowles, Richard Wright, Arthur Miller, Norman Mailer, and others.[63] Judy Oppenheimer observes that Stanley Edgar Hyman persuaded his friend Ralph Ellison to submit a story ("Flying Home"), Ellison's first hardcover publication (Oppenheimer, 103). Hyman's own contribution is an essay, "The New *War and Peace*: A Speculation," which discusses war literature in general and the literature of World War II in particular. The editor, Edwin Seaver, said many of the 1,000 submissions treated racial injustice, especially the "Negro problem"; he found it curious that hardly any dealt with the "Jewish problem" (*Cross-Section*, viii). Jackson herself depicted both forms of racial injustice in stories from the 1940s: the mistreatment of blacks in "After You, My Dear Alphonse" and "Flower Garden," and the subtle discrimination against Jews in "A Fine Old Firm." All three stories resemble "Behold the Child" in disclosing the intolerant hearts of kind-faced women.

Jackson describes another display of hypocrisy in "A Great Voice Stilled," whose publication in *Playboy*, a new market for Jackson, greatly distressed her mother (undated letter from Geraldine Jackson to Shirley Jackson [SJP, Box 2]). While Mr. Jones, a world-famous author, lies dying in a hospital bed, his friends, former lovers, and reviewers gather in the waiting room. The group includes a tall man in a blue suit; his name is Arthur B. Arthur, though his appearance is that of James Harris in the *Lot-*

*tery* stories. A woman named Joan sobs inconsolably, but she has competition from Katherine Ashton, whose escort, the academic Martin, "flatly" confronts Joan: "Katherine knew him exactly as well as you did."[64] Reminiscent of the egotistical professors in "On Being a Faculty Wife" and in Jackson's college novel, *Hangsaman*, Martin says Jones would not have "the *gall* to live" after the activity inspired by his recent heart attack: "Here Angell is flying down from Boston. And practically the whole staff of *Dormant Review* up all night working on obituaries and remembrances and his American publisher already getting together a *Festschrift*, and the wife flying in from Majorca if they weren't able to stop her. And Weasel calling every major literary critic from here to California to get them here in time" (57). Much of the story is composed of similarly self-revelatory dialogue.

The acquaintances in the waiting room feign concern, but their selfishness is apparent even after a nurse announces Jones has just died. Deprived of hearing his last words, they sententiously compete in pronouncing epitaphs:

"A great voice has been stilled," Weasel said reverently.
"My only, truest love," Joan mourned.
"He writes now with a golden pen."
"A great writer is a great man writing." (91)

Like the protagonist's lawyer colleagues in Tolstoy's "The Death of Ivan Ilych," they consider how they might benefit from the death. Martin hopes to replace Jones in a lecture series (he can expound on Jones's works), and Weasel comments "vaguely" on "the responsibility of the intellectual" before "patter[ing]" away (91). The story ends with Katherine's sarcastic echo of Joan's "My only, truest love" and her laughing request that Martin accompany her to dinner at a "nice little place where they make sweetbreads."

Two of Jackson's better-known stories, "The Possibility of Evil" (1965) and "One Ordinary Day, with Peanuts" (1955), so exaggerate conflicting aspects of the main character's personality that a Jekyll-Hyde effect, far beyond simple hypocrisy, results. In contrast to the realism of "Behold the Child" and "A Great Voice Stilled," these two stories strain the reader's credulity, though the narrator's voice is no less matter of fact. John G. Parks discusses "The Possibility of Evil," which appeared posthumously in *Saturday Evening Post*, as a "key" to much of Jackson's fiction: "It contains many of the elements basic to her work, including a sensitive but narrow female protagonist, a gothic house, economy of language, intimations of something 'other' or 'more,' a free-floating sense of depravity, experiences of dissociation, and a final turn about in events or a judgment."[65] According to Parks, Miss Adela Strangeworth, the self-righteous central character, wrongly believes evil is something *"out there"*; rather, as she may begin to realize at the conclusion, "evil is a component within us all that can be transcended only through its recognition and acceptance" (Parks, 322).

Blindness to her own evil produces a split between Miss Strangeworth's public and private identities. As she walks down Main Street in the small town she thinks of as her own, she stops to greet people and ask about their health. In the grocery store, customers turn from their shopping to salute her. She reassures a young mother who seems worried about her baby's development and wonders why several other neighbors act distracted or grim. Alone at her desk, however, Miss Strangeworth has been composing anonymous letters for a year, to warn the townspeople of "possible evil lurking nearby."[66] She rejects her grandfather's quill pen and her father's fountain pen to print childishly with a dull pencil stub such messages as "DIDN'T YOU EVER SEE AN IDIOT CHILD BEFORE? SOME PEOPLE JUST SHOULDN'T HAVE CHILDREN, SHOULD THEY?" (64).

Miss Strangeworth is conscious of the contrast between her public image and her secret writings. She sends the letters unsigned because "her name, Adela Strangeworth, a name honored in the town for so many years, did not belong on such trash" (68). The crude notes are out of place in the otherwise neat and well-ordered world of her trim house on Pleasant Street and her beautiful rose garden. Judy Oppenheimer sees "The Possibility of Evil" as a "nakedly revealing" story about Jackson's determination to preserve a "proper lady" image while sending her own "terrible messages to the world" in her fiction (Oppenheimer, 271–72). But Miss Strangeworth seems less akin to Jackson than to the malicious old women of "Trial by Combat" and "Flower Garden," as well as the manipulative Mrs. Halloran of *The Sundial*, published in 1958, the same year the manuscript of "The Possibility of Evil" is dated (SJP, Box 17).

She also has an antecedent in Faulkner's secretive Miss Emily Grierson, who kills her Yankee lover in "A Rose for Emily." Among Jackson's papers at the Library of Congress is a three-page parody, "Go Down, Faulkner (In the throes of William Faulkner's 'Go Down, Moses')," along with a two-page untitled essay or journal entry in which she mentions her "good meaty bout with sex and Faulkner" (SJP, Box 19).[67] Though no direct evidence exists for Faulkner's influence on "The Possibility of Evil," Jackson's original title—"Miss Strangeworth and Her Roses"—evokes "A Rose for Emily." Both protagonists are proud septuagenarian spinsters whose ancestors were civic leaders for generations. While the town of Jefferson has a Civil War cemetery, Jackson's northern village pays tribute to an earlier war with its statue of Ethan Allen, hero of the Revolution. Miss Emily's house looks like a decayed version of Miss Strangeworth's family home; both women are legendary figures whose small towns follow their movements with special interest. Jefferson protects Miss Emily to her death, but Miss Strangeworth's fellow citizens finally turn against her. Discovering the author of the poisonous letters, they send her one in return: "LOOK OUT AT WHAT USED TO BE YOUR ROSES" (69).

The protagonist's name in "One Ordinary Day, with Peanuts," John Philip Johnson, is even more indicative of doubleness than Adela Strangeworth's name. Pleased with the feel of his resoled shoes, Mr. Johnson steps out into a bright morning that mirrors his good cheer. He bestows candy, peanuts, money, and advice on many needy strangers: a nervous single mother and her son, a young woman and a young man whom he brings together, a beggar, and a cab driver, among others. The narrator stresses Mr. Johnson's sincerity. When he offers to pay a woman after making her late for work, his "flat statement, obviously innocent of irony, could not be, coming from Mr. Johnson, anything but the statement of a responsible and truthful and respectable man."[68]

Only at the end of the day does his benevolence take a bizarre turn. "Horrified" that his taxi driver plans to bet on a horse named Vulcan on a Wednesday, Mr. Johnson gives the man $10 to bet Thursday on any horse whose name indicates " . . . well, grain. Or any growing food," particularly a horse "whose name includes the letters C, R, L" (60). The excited cabbie wonders if Tall Corn will do, and Mr. Johnson says, "Absolutely." Jackson may be playfully alluding to "The Lottery," where references to myth, game, and ritual also lead to an unexpected conclusion. At home, Mr. Johnson, like Miss Strangeworth, reveals just how limited the public perception of his character has been. In an uncanny reversal, he offers to "change over tomorrow," trading places with his smiling but tired wife, who has spent the day deliberately making people miserable (161). Somehow Miss Strangeworth and Mr. Johnson accommodate conflicting selves with full awareness. The effect on the reader, however, is as jarring as Elizabeth Richmond's discovery of her four-way personality split in Jackson's *The Bird's Nest.*

Jackson's opinion of "One Ordinary Day, with Peanuts" was not high. "It's a terrible story," she wrote to her parents on learning it would be included in *Best American Short Stories, 1956* (letter to Leslie and Geraldine Jackson, 4 October 1956 [SJP, Box 3]). She exaggerated the circumstances of original publication by explaining the story "was written for (golly) *Fantasy and Science Fiction*, for which I was paid by a lifetime subscription to the magazine, since at their usual rate I would have gotten something like $18 for it." An earlier letter to Jackson from her agent, Bernice Baumgarten, said *Fantasy and Science Fiction* would pay $150 for the piece, which Baumgarten had been trying to place since 1951 (letter of 25 November 1953 [SJP, Box 4]). Jackson may have confused the details of payment, since Baumgarten had sold "Bulletin," a very short story on time travel, to the same magazine during the same period for a life subscription and $54, twice the standard rate of three cents a word (Baumgarten's letters to Jackson, 2 September, 2 October, and 8 October 1953 [SJP, Box 4]).

Despite her sarcastic comment on *Fantasy and Science Fiction*, Jackson subsequently published two other stories in the magazine. Scenes from both reproduce the astonishing moment in "One Ordinary Day, with Peanuts" when identity loses all fixedness to become as changeable as the soles on Mr. Johnson's shoes. In "The Omen" a distracted Edith Webster gets on the wrong bus, picks up another woman's lost shopping list as she leaves, and is asked by several strangers whether her name is Miss Murrain. One persistent man wonders if she is positive in her denial: "Edith stared. 'I'm not the lady you are looking for,' she said as firmly as she could. (Am I? she wondered suddenly.)"[69] A stout woman grabs her arm, and a crowd collects nightmarishly around her, but Edith recovers when several children shriek that the "real" Miss Murrain has already been found in a treasure hunt sponsored by Murrain Brothers coffee.

A more desperate situation occurs in "The Missing Girl," a tale about a 13-year-old whose roommate reports her disappearance to authorities at the summer camp she is attending. The Camp Mother can tell the incompetent police chief very little about the missing girl, and the photograph on her application record is "so blurred that it resembled a hundred other girls in the camp."[70] The painting counselor says, "If I remember this girl, she did sort of vague stuff, almost *unwilling*. Rejection, almost—if I can find a picture you'll see what I mean" (47). Other counselors have even less substantial memories of Martha Alexander. When a search of several days is unsuccessful, the girl's uncle and the Camp Mother meet with Chief Hook. For no clear reason, the uncle—who had offered a reward—says Mrs. Alexander is quite sure her daughter decided against enrolling at the camp. The Camp Mother does not object to this virtual denial of the girl's existence; in fact, she now recalls Martha's application was put into the "possibly undesirable" file. The narrator adds that a body "which might have been Martha Alexander's was found, of course, something over a year later," stuffed among bushes the searchers had passed by (52). Martha's roommate, Betsy, and the Camp Mother are drawn to the unidentified person's grave, haunted by the memory of the missing girl.

A more literal haunting transforms an outsider to a townswoman in "Home" (1965), the last story Shirley Jackson published before her death. Ethel Sloane's move to the lovely old Sanderson place in the country leaves her with an insecure identity. She tells her husband the villagers make her feel at home, but her new raincoat and boots mark her as a stranger, and she wishes the storekeepers would "show a little more alacrity in remembering her name."[71] Her very speech separates her from her neighbors: "Briefly she wondered whether she might not say 'for a spell' instead of 'for a while,' and then decided that sooner or later it would come naturally" (116). Misinterpreting a hardware clerk's caution against using the river road in rainy weather, she fears she has offended rural sensibilities by boasting of her ability to maneuver through the mud. "I can manage; I'm country now," she reassures herself.

Ethel Sloane becomes truly country only after she twice gives two local ghosts a ride along the dangerous road. The first time she picks up the old woman and the crying barefoot boy, she has so much trouble handling the car on the hill that she exchanges few words with her passengers. Finally asking directions to their house, she turns to find the back seat empty. At home, her husband, Jim, hesitantly tells Ethel the story of a little Sanderson boy who was "stolen or lost or something" 60 years ago; a "crazy old woman" was suspected of kidnapping him (118). Surprisingly, Ethel is thrilled to hear about "our very own ghosts." She can't wait to go to town the next day to boast about the encounter and "find out all I can."

Jim's attempts to stop her from confronting the villagers are useless, but the ghosts themselves succeed in chilling her happy mood. Reappearing after Ethel has seated herself in the car, the old woman complains that she could not take the boy home because of strangers in the house. Jackson describes the impact of the visitation in much the same language she uses in *The Haunting of Hill House*: "The skin on the back of Ethel's neck crawled as though some wet thing walked there; the child stared past her, and the old woman's eyes were flat and dead" (118). Ethel is reduced to whispers and babbling, but she promises to take the two back where she met them. As the car skids toward the high creek, the boy laughs wildly. Alone again, the terrified Ethel wrenches the vehicle back toward the road.

When Ethel Sloane arrives at the hardware store, the clerk notices her distress and greets her by name. In contrast to her loquaciousness of the day before, she responds with typical village reticence by speaking briefly about the accident and censoring the supernatural details of her near-death. The appreciative clerk repeats his earlier vague warning about the river road and asks if the Sloanes will be coming to the PTA social. "We certainly will," Edith answers. The ending is a happy one for a Shirley Jackson story. Ethel has achieved insider status and an appropriate humbling.

Ironically, however, the upbeat scene reverses Jackson's original conclusion by sparing the woman's life. The crossed-out final paragraph in the manuscript describes Ethel Sloane pulling in vain at the steering wheel, the child's "horrible laughter" in her ears as "the car turned by itself and crashed, almost soundlessly, into the churning, sucking waters below" (SJP, Box 16). Not only does Ethel remain an outsider, but her husband will presumably leave the unlucky house, allowing the boy to return home under the guidance of the maligned old woman, who seems to be a protector rather than a kidnapper.

The triumph of the ghostly villagers did not appeal to the editorial staff of *Ladies Home Journal*, however. Negotiating the sale of the story, Carol Brandt told Jackson the magazine's fiction department was shocked and disappointed by the final catastrophe; they asked Jackson to end not with a death but with Ethel's quick maturing and identification with the townspeople (letter from Brandt to Jackson, 26 January 1965 [SJP, Box 6]). Subsequent letters informed Jackson her revisions were approved and the magazine would pay $2,000 for the story (Brandt to Jackson, 6 April and 19 April 1965 [SJP, Box 6]).

Maybe Jackson rescued Ethel Sloane because she wanted to make a quick sale, or maybe she decided she would be repeating herself by dooming another urban protagonist. The original ending is very close to the stormy finales of "Flower Garden" and especially "The Summer People," for example. On the other hand, as a survivor Ethel Sloane resembles Angela Motorman, the heroine of "Come Along with Me," Jackson's novel-in-progress at her death. Names and a strong sense of self are important to both women. In contrast to almost all the other married females in Jackson's short stories, Ethel is neither anonymous (like the narrator of the family stories) nor routinely called "Mrs." Even in the manuscript, the narrator refers to her as either Ethel or Ethel Sloane, although her husband is a writer and she seems to have no job outside the house.

Had Ethel gone to her death, "Home" would still be a very fitting last story. James Egan traces the "search for an acceptable familial and domestic environment" through Jackson's large body of work (Egan, 21). Ethel and Jim Sloane are as intent on establishing a new home as the drowned boy and old woman are in recovering a long-lost one. For Ethel, the lure of home is related to an even larger concern of Jackson's fiction: the urge to define and affirm one's identity. After two days in the village, she reflects, "We're the kind of people, Jim and I, who fit in a place like this; we wouldn't belong in the suburbs or some kind of a colony; we're real people" (116). The ghosts, though, view the Sloanes as "strangers," and the resulting conflict is one of the most desperate struggles to assert the self since Tessie Hutchinson's in "The Lottery."

As Stanley Edgar Hyman predicted, Shirley Jackson's "powerful visions of suffering and inhumanity" have become "increasingly significant and meaningful" (*MSJ*, ix). She is an eloquent voice of the Age of Anxiety. Her characters walk the same slippery plank Emily Dickinson described at the start of the modern era. Many of the women in Jackson's fiction lead narrow lives, circumscribed by the walls of house or office, yet they are even more susceptible than the men and children to huge losses: of love, identity, and existence itself. The comic chatter of the family stories cannot fill the silences of the numb protagonists in her more serious works. From the earliest pieces in the *Lottery* and *Come Along with Me* collections through her last uncollected stories, Jackson expresses the vulnerability of the powerless. Whether the threat is James Harris, the community, or their own families, the central figures of Jackson's most memorable stories stand precariously on the rim of an abyss.

# Notes to Part 1

1. *Cross-Section: A Collection of New American Writing*, ed. Edwin Seaver (New York: L. B. Fischer, 1944), 555. Jackson's "Behold the Child among His Newborn Blisses" appears in *Cross-Section*, 292–98.

2. Shirley Jackson Papers, Box 16, Library of Congress, Washington, D.C.; hereafter cited in text as SJP. This essential collection for research on Jackson contains 41 archival boxes of letters, drafts, proofs, sketches, early diaries, and other material. Boxes 15–19 hold the manuscripts of about 190 stories and other short pieces, many unpublished. The preliminary pages for the "Intoxicated" volume are in a Library of Congress folder with drafts of the story "The Intoxicated," first published in *The Lottery*. Several *Lottery* stories not listed in the contents for "The Intoxicated" appeared in magazines in 1948 and 1949.

3. *The Lottery* (New York: Fawcett Popular Library, 1975).

4. See Susan Garland Mann, *The Short Story Cycle: A Genre Companion and Reference Guide* (Westport, Conn.: Greenwood Press, 1989).

5. A Mr. Harris figures importantly in "The Daemon Lover," "Like Mother Used to Make," "The Villager," "Elizabeth," "Seven Types of Ambiguity," and "Of Course." The name Harris is briefly mentioned in "The Renegade," "Flower Garden," and "A Fine Old Firm." A mysterious Jim in "The Tooth" and a letter writer in "Got a Letter from Jimmy" are further variations on the name.

6. *The Lottery and Other Stories* (New York: Farrar, Straus & Giroux, 1982), 8, 15; hereafter cited in text.

7. "The Renegade," *Harper's*, November 1948, 40.

8. "A Fine Old Firm," *New Yorker*, 4 March 1944, 67.

9. "The Tooth," *Hudson Review* 1, no. 4 (1949): 508 and passim.

10. Stanley Edgar Hyman, "The Child Ballad in America: Some Aesthetic Criteria," in *The Promised End: Essays and Reviews 1942–1962* (Cleveland: World Publishing, 1963), 264; hereafter cited in text.

11. Donald Barr, "A Talent for Irony," *New York Times Book Review*, 17 April 1949, 4; hereafter cited in text.

12. Judy Oppenheimer, *Private Demons: The Life of Shirley Jackson* (New York: G. P. Putnam's Sons, 1988), 171; hereafter cited in text.

13. *The Road through the Wall* (New York: Farrar, Straus, 1948), 134–35.

14. Sharon O'Brien, *Willa Cather: The Emerging Voice* (New York: Oxford University Press, 1987), 372.

15. See Harvey Breit, "Talk with Miss Jackson," *New York Times Book Review*, 26 June 1949, 15; hereafter cited in text. Also, "On an Author," *Herald Tribune Book Review*, 5 July 1953, 2.

16. Lenemaja Friedman says the Glanvill references may have been suggested by the publisher to make *The Lottery* look "mysterious and, therefore, salable" (*Shirley Jackson* [Boston: Twayne Publishers, 1975], 67–68; hereafter cited in text). On the other hand, the Shirley Jackson Papers contains a folder (Box 20) with two pages of material typed by Jackson from the Glanvill book, including the first of the four passages cited in *The Lottery*. There Jackson spells Glanvill as "Glanvil" and the first word of his title as "*Sadducismus*," misspellings that are incorporated into *The Lottery*.

17. The passage is omitted from the 1982 paperback edition cited in this study, and it does not appear in the first American edition of 1949, but Jackson apparently saw that it was included in the first British edition of 1950. See Joseph Glanvill, *Saducismus Triumphatus; or, Full and Plain Evidence Concerning Witches and Apparitions*, facsimile ed., introduction by Coleman O. Parsons (1689; Gainesville, Fla.: Scholars Facsimiles and Reprints, 1966), 360–61; hereafter cited in text. The other three passages from Glanvill are on pp. 61, 143, and 227 of *The Lottery*; see Glanvill, 88, 466–67, and 90–91.

18. *The Witchcraft of Salem Village* (New York: Random House, 1956), 146.

19. Compare Eileen's vision to Aunt Fanny's prediction in Jackson's *The Sundial* of an imminent catastrophe whose survivors will be "a kind of chosen people" (*The Sundial* [New York: Farrar, Straus & Cudahy, 1958], 43; hereafter cited in text). "Harrison for President," an unpublished story in SJP, Box 16, closely resembles "The Intoxicated" in pitting a college-age daughter against a male friend of the family who frowns at her rude remarks during a Christmas party in her home.

20. See "The Phantom Lover," *Woman's Home Companion*, February 1949, 24–25, 95–98, 100. Friedman contrasts the two versions, arguing that James Harris "appears to be an actual man" in the *Woman's Home Companion* version but is either imaginary or a phantom in "The Daemon Lover" (51–52). Two other critics who think James Harris may be an illusion are Mary Kittredge ("The Other Side of Magic: A Few Remarks about Shirley Jackson," in *Discovering Modern Horror Fiction*, vol. 1, ed. Darrell Schweitzer [Mercer Island, Wash.: Starmont, 1985], 10) and Steven K. Hoffman ("Individuation and Character Development in the Fiction of Shirley Jackson," *Hartford Studies in Literature* 8 [1976]: 201).

21. Elizabeth Bowen, preface to *Ivy Gripped the Steps and Other Stories* (New York: Knopf, 1946), ix.

22. See "The Villager," *American Mercury*, August 1944, 186–90.

23. "My Life with R. H. Macy," *New Republic*, 22 December 1941, 862.

24. Robert L. Kelly, "Jackson's 'The Witch': A Satanic Gem," *English Journal* 60 (1971): 1204.

25. M. Thomas Inge, *Comics as Culture* (Jackson: University of Mississippi Press, 1990), 97. Frederick Burr Opper, better known for "Happy Hooligan" and "Maude the Mule," drew "Alphonse and Gaston" for Sunday newspapers from 1902 to 1904. Several early silent films were based on the comic strip (Inge, 143). "Alphonse and Gaston" also appeared in newspaper ads for a short period in the 1940s (see Bill

Blackbeard, "Alphonse and Gaston," *The World Encyclopedia of Comics*, ed. Maurice Horn [New York: Chelsea House, 1976], 78).

26. Carol Cleveland, "Shirley Jackson," in *And Then There Were Nine . . . More Women of Mystery*, ed. Jane S. Bakerman (Bowling Green, Ohio: Bowling Green State University Popular Press, 1985), 201; hereafter cited in text.

27. Shirley Jackson wrote an updated version of the fairy tale in her one-act play, *The Bad Children*, music by Allan Jay Friedman (Chicago: Dramatic Publishing, 1959). The musical was Jackson's gift to her children, inspired by her daughter Joanne's need for a school play (Oppenheimer, 222).

28. See "Charles," *Mademoiselle*, July 1948, 87, 114, and *Life among the Savages* in *The Magic of Shirley Jackson*, ed. Stanley Edgar Hyman (New York: Farrar, Straus & Giroux, 1966), 398–403; hereafter cited in text as *MSJ*.

29. Linda Trichter Metcalf, "Shirley Jackson in Her Fiction: A Rhetorical Search for the Implied Author," Ph.D. diss., New York University, 1987, 126.

30. See SJP, Box 29, for Jackson's notes for the novel. The short story "Elizabeth" develops about half of the plot outline for the book-length project. In the short-story manuscript (SJP, Box 15) James Harris is Mr. Vining, a name Jackson borrowed from the same section of *Saducismus Triumphatus* that provided names for Elizabeth Style, Miss Hill, and Robert Hunt (Glanvill, 361). Shax, a devil's name, was also the name of one of Jackson's many cats (Oppenheimer, 116).

31. Scott Elledge (*E. B. White: A Biography* [New York: W. W. Norton, 1984], 182) thus characterizes the "new writing" promoted by Katherine White at the *New Yorker*. White recommended that editor Harold Ross publish Vladimir Nabokov, James Thurber, John Updike, John Cheever, and Mary McCarthy, among many others.

32. Charlotte Margolis Goodman, *Jean Stafford: The Savage Heart* (Austin: University of Texas Press, 1990), 188.

33. Cullen Murphy, "Hey, Let Me Outta Here!," *Atlantic*, August 1989, 66. Murphy's brief history of ventriloquism points out links with magic and the supernatural. He quotes a practicing ventriloquist on "the schizophrenic aspect of ventriloquism, the tension between illusion and reality, that both attracts and repels" (71).

34. Dennis Welch, "Manipulation in Shirley Jackson's 'Seven Types of Ambiguity,'" *Studies in Short Fiction* 18 (Winter 1981): 27.

35. Stanley Edgar Hyman, *The Armed Vision* (New York: Knopf, 1948), 277. In his acknowledgments Hyman particularly thanks Jackson, "who did everything for me that one writer can conceivably do for another and whose patience and kindness in regard to it are worthy of a far better work" (xiv). *The Armed Vision* is dedicated to Jackson as "a critic of critics of critics."

36. See William Butler Yeats, "I Am of Ireland," in *Selected Poems and Three Plays of William Butler Yeats*, ed. M. L. Rosenthal, 3d ed. (New York: Macmillan, 1986), 153; other poems from this collection cited in text.

37. Among the miscellaneous papers in SJP, Box 41, is a typed page on which Jackson copied the account of Abraham's bargaining with God over the fate of

Sodom and Gomorrah from Genesis 18:20ff. The transcription ends with the heading "Chapter 19," a reference to the episode in which Lot's wife becomes a pillar of salt.

38. Richard Pascal, "'Farther than Samarkand': The Escape Theme in Shirley Jackson's 'The Tooth,'" *Studies in Short Fiction* 19 (Spring 1982): 139, 138. Metcalf similarly comments on Clara's "psychological collapse" (92).

39. Toni Reed, *Demon-Lovers and Their Victims in British Fiction* (Lexington: University Press of Kentucky, 1988), viii, 113.

40. Stanley Edgar Hyman, *The Tangled Bank* (New York: Atheneum, 1962), esp. 233–69. Jackson's University of Rochester library check-out card for *The Golden Bough* is inserted in a five-year diary for 1933–37 in SJP, Box 1, file 2. An entry in a separate 1935 diary in the same file says Jackson "Got 'Golden Bough'" on 12 November 1935.

41. Helen E. Nebeker, "'The Lottery': Symbolic Tour de Force," *American Literature* 46 (March 1974): 106; hereafter cited in text. An early folkloristic reading of "The Lottery" is Seymour Lainoff's "Jackson's 'The Lottery,'" *Explicator* 12 (March 1954): item 34. James M. Gibson summarizes several critics' responses to "The Lottery" in the introductory paragraphs of "An Old Testament Analogue for 'The Lottery,'" *Journal of Modern Literature* 11 (March 1984): 193.

42. "Biography of a Story," in *Come Along with Me: Part of a Novel, Sixteen Stories, and Three Lectures*, ed. Stanley Edgar Hyman (New York: Viking, 1968), 214; hereafter cited in text as "Biography."

43. Peter Kosenko, "A Marxist/Feminist Reading of Shirley Jackson's 'The Lottery,'" *New Orleans Review* 12, no. 1 (Spring 1985): 30; hereafter cited in text.

44. Joseph Church, "Getting Taken in 'The Lottery,'" *Notes on Contemporary Literature* 18, no. 1 (September 1988): 10; hereafter cited in text.

45. Fritz Oehlschlaeger, "The Stoning of Mistress Hutchinson: Meaning and Context in 'The Lottery,'" *Essays in Literature* 15 (Fall 1988): 259; hereafter cited in text. Gayle Whittier's provocative essay "'The Lottery' as Misogynist Parable" (*Women's Studies* 18, no. 4 [1991]: 353–66) appeared too late for me to incorporate her discussion of "male dominance" (356), which is more detailed than those of Kosenko and Oehlschlaeger.

46. In SJP, Box 17. This scrap, like Jackson's typical typed drafts, is written all in lowercase letters, which I have capitalized where needed. Hyman's second wife, Phoebe Pettingell, told Judy Oppenheimer that Hyman contributed the proverbial rhyme to "The Lottery" (Oppenheimer, 130, and note on this source, 288).

47. Barbara Allen, "A Folkloristic Look at Shirley Jackson's 'The Lottery,'" *Tennessee Folklore Society Bulletin* 46, no. 4 (December 1980): 121.

48. Preface to *Come Along with Me*, vii; hereafter cited in text as *CAWM*.

49. See Jackson's contents page for the planned "Intoxicated" collection (SJP, Box 16).

50. James Egan, "Sanctuary: Shirley Jackson's Domestic and Fantastic Parables," *Studies in Weird Fiction* 6 (1989): 17; hereafter cited in text.

51. Nancy A. Walker, preface to *A Very Serious Thing: Women's Humor and American Culture* (Minneapolis: University of Minnesota Press, 1988), xii. Contrast Oppenheimer, who sees "no dark side" (169) in the family stories.

52. "Fame," *Writer*, August 1948, 265; hereafter cited in text.

53. "The Third Baby's the Easiest," *Harper's*, May 1949, 59; hereafter cited in text. See also *Life among the Savages* in *MSJ*, 420–30.

54. My page references are to "On Being a Faculty Wife," *Mademoiselle*, December 1956, 116–17 and 135–36; hereafter cited in text. The story was incorporated into *Raising Demons*, in *MSJ*, 638–43.

55. "Aunt Gertrude," *Harper's*, April 1954, 51; hereafter cited in text.

56. "Mother Is a Fortune Hunter," *Woman's Home Companion*, May 1954, 77; hereafter cited in text.

57. "*So* Late on Sunday Morning," *Woman's Home Companion*, September 1953, 48; hereafter cited in text.

58. "All the Girls Were Dancing," *Collier's*, 11 November 1950, 36; hereafter cited in text.

59. "The Strangers," *Collier's*, 10 May 1952, 24; hereafter cited in text.

60. "Journey with a Lady," *Harper's*, July 1952, 76; hereafter cited in text. S. T. Joshi has located a reprint of this story under the title "This Is the Life" in *Ellery Queen's Mystery Magazine*, June 1958.

61. The title phrase is the first line of stanza 7, "Ode: Intimations of Immortality from Recollections of Early Childhood," in Wordsworth's *Selected Poems and Prefaces*, ed. Jack Stillinger (Boston: Houghton Mifflin, 1965), 188. Also relevant to Jackson's story is Wordsworth's sentimental treatment of the child in "The Idiot Boy," pp. 58–69 in Stillinger's edition.

62. "Behold the Child among His Newborn Blisses," in *Cross-Section*, 296; hereafter cited in text.

63. The story is listed as "Girlie" in the contents page of the "Intoxicated" collection (SJP, Box 16).

64. "A Great Voice Stilled," *Playboy*, March 1960, 58; hereafter cited in text.

65. John G. Parks, "The Possibility of Evil: A Key to Shirley Jackson's Fiction," *Studies in Short Fiction* 15, no. 3 (1978): 320; hereafter cited in text.

66. "The Possibility of Evil," *Saturday Evening Post*, 18 December 1965, 64; hereafter cited in text.

67. Intrigued by Oppenheimer's reference to the journal entry (*Private Demons*, 94), I searched the SJP for the parody and discovered "Go Down, Faulkner." Faulkner scholar Doreen Fowler and I called the article to the attention of Dean Faulkner Wells, who was collecting material for a book of Faulkner parodies. Jackson's piece was subsequently published for the first time in *The Best of Bad Faulkner*, ed. Dean Faulkner Wells (San Diego: Harcourt Brace Jovanovich, 1991), 129–32. See also Jackson's reference to Popeye, from Faulkner's *Sanctuary*, in my Part 2 selection "Notes on an Unfashionable Writer."

68. "One Ordinary Day, with Peanuts," *Magazine of Fantasy and Science Fiction,* January 1955, 56; hereafter cited in text.

69. "The Omen," *Magazine of Fantasy and Science Fiction,* March 1958, 125.

70. "The Missing Girl," *Magazine of Fantasy and Science Fiction,* December 1957, 48; hereafter cited in text.

71. "Home," *Ladies Home Journal,* August 1965, 65; hereafter cited in text.

*Part 2*

# THE WRITER

# Introduction

In his preface to *The Magic of Shirley Jackson*, Stanley Edgar Hyman writes, "After the first years, when several interviews and radio appearances failed to satisfy her, [Jackson] consistently refused to be interviewed, to explain or promote her work in any fashion, or to take public stands and be a pundit of the Sunday supplements. She believed that her books would speak for her clearly enough over the years, and I share her belief."[1] Jackson explained in a 7 March 1955 letter to her parents that recent offers to speak at a writers' conference in Salt Lake City and to appear on a television quiz show in New York held "no temptations whatsoever. Actually since *Bird's Nest* [her 1954 novel] was published I have made it a rule—officially on file at my agent's and my publisher's—that I will involve myself in absolutely no personal publicity under any circumstances, which includes everything from interviews and photographs to that cute biographical information ('She writes with a turkey feather dipped in rainwater') everyone is crazy about. I just refer everyone to *Who's Who in America*, with great satisfaction."[2]

Reviewers and editors often paraphrased the brief biographical narratives composed by Hyman and Jackson in the late 1940s, here reprinted in full for the first time from manuscripts in the Shirley Jackson Papers at the Library of Congress. Jackson's comments, written late in 1948 while *The Lottery; or, The Adventures of James Harris* was in press, seem to draw on Hyman's "Notes on Shirley Jackson," compiled about a year earlier to introduce Jackson to readers of her first book, *The Road through the Wall* (1948). Irritated by Farrar and Straus's emphasis on the demonic element of *The Lottery* in its advertising campaign, Jackson omitted from her autobiographical sketch the references to her interest in witchcraft and magic that Hyman had included in his observations on her home life and hobbies.

The most detailed account of one of Jackson's infrequent interviews is Harvey Breit's "Talk with Miss Jackson" for the *New York Times Book Review*, reprinted in this section. Breit's column, which followed on the successful publication of *The Lottery*, stresses Jackson's interest in the short-story form and reports her opinions of several other authors, from Fanny Burney to André Gide. Like Hyman's and Jackson's press releases, the *New*

*York Times* essay makes special reference to the works of Samuel Richardson. Jackson explains the appeal of the eighteenth-century writer at length in her "Notes on an Unfashionable Novelist," an essay found in draft and final versions at the Library of Congress but apparently never before published. Dr. John Montague, the pompous anthropologist of Jackson's *The Haunting of Hill House*, reads Richardson to induce sleep, but Jackson finds several attributes in Richardson's work that are absent from much twentieth-century literature. Also reprinted in this section from the Shirley Jackson Papers is "The Unloved Reader," Jackson's critical review of books by her contemporaries Donald Barthelme and Alfred Chester. Although Jackson provided an alternative conclusion that softens her original negative emphasis, there is no evidence that the review, probably composed in 1964, the year the two books were published, ever saw print.

The speeches reprinted by Hyman in *Come Along with Me: Part of a Novel, Sixteen Stories, and Three Lectures* (1968) are essential texts for understanding Jackson's perception of the writer's task. Two years earlier, in his preface to *The Magic of Shirley Jackson*, Hyman said that Jackson's sole exception to her "vow of silence" on discussing her work was "a willingness, even an eagerness, to lecture about the craft of fiction at colleges and writers' conferences, where she could assume an audience with some serious interest in such matters" (*MSJ*, ix). Hyman believed these talks contained "some of the few sensible and useful words I know on that impossible subject—what fiction is and how it gets made" (*MSJ*, ix). Breadloaf and the Marlboro School of Writing were Jackson's most famous sponsors, but she also spoke at several colleges, including Syracuse University, her alma mater. In a letter to her parents in May 1964, about a year before her death, she remarked that she had accepted lecture dates through the summer and winter into the next spring. She added that she and Hyman each had "three prepared lectures and they have to be carefully calculated not to overlap"; she could not, for example, give the same presentation at Columbia and New York University (SJP, Box 3).

The first of the three speeches in *Come Along with Me*, "Experience and Fiction," is accompanied by the autobiographical story, "The Night We All Had Grippe." This section reprints the balance of the talk, including Jackson's extended critique of "the most perfect nonstory" she ever read,[3] but omits the story, along with a few pages of the lecture in which she describes the writing of *The Haunting of Hill House*. Her comments on the origins of fiction in human experience, the importance of capturing the reader's interest, and the creation of distinctive characters are clearly directed toward aspiring authors. The second lecture, "Biography of a

Story," records the astonishing impact of Jackson's most famous story, "The Lottery," which she usually read in conjunction with the speech. The reprinted text here omits most of the passages she quotes from her readers' letters to focus instead on Jackson's own somewhat bewildered response to her instant fame.

Jackson presents her third lecture, "Notes for a Young Writer," as an incomplete commentary on short-story writing, initially composed for her daughter Sarah and later offered to a larger audience. She describes a story as "an uneasy bargain with your reader" (*CAWM*, 234) and states the need for a "surface tension" in the narrative (235). I omit Jackson's prohibitions against "small graceless movements" (235) and part of her advice on creating conversations and using "coloring words" (239) and other tools of language. Jackson briefly taught short-story writing at Bennington College, and this final lecture reads like a summary of many of the guidelines she must have suggested to her students. Like "Experience and Fiction," "Notes for a Young Writer" emphasizes not themes and theories but writing as a craft.

The four letters from which I publish excerpts are found in the Library of Congress's large file of Jackson's correspondence with her parents, Leslie and Geraldine Jackson. Jackson's long, single-spaced, typed letters are typically full of domestic events. Only in this group from late 1948 and 1949 does she comment in detail on her writing, and most of these details concern publication matters, especially for *The Lottery*. I standardize Jackson's style to add the capital letters that are typically missing from her informal letters, as well as her story drafts. Jackson corresponded regularly with her family, and hundreds of these documents are in the Shirley Jackson Papers, but, regrettably, very few of Jackson's letters to non–family members are available at the Library of Congress or in any published form. Letters to Jackson among the Shirley Jackson Papers from James Thurber, Bernard Malamud, Roald Dahl, Isaac Bashevis Singer, and many other literary figures of her time support Hyman's assertion that her "fellow craftsmen" knew and valued her work (*MSJ*, ix).

The section's final two selections come from a file of incomplete literary manuscripts in Box 29 of the Shirley Jackson Papers. Both are novel-treatment outlines for works that took final form as two short stories I discuss in Part 1: "Elizabeth" from *The Lottery* and "I Know Who I Love" from *Come Along with Me*. The précis headed "I Know Who I Love" accompanies several pages of narrative on Catharine—the protagonist of the short story and the abandoned novel—and a long outline that traces Catharine's movements from Buffalo to New York to New Hampshire to a small room, which evidently becomes consumed by fire. The references to literal and figurative witchcraft in both novel outlines disappear from the short-story versions, though demon-lover figures make appearances in the published stories. These outlines provide valuable histories of two of Jackson's more important stories; they also contain some of her most dramatic portrayals of tormented women.

## Notes

1. *The Magic of Shirley Jackson* (New York: Farrar, Straus & Giroux, 1966), ix; hereafter cited in text as *MSJ*.

2. Shirley Jackson Papers, Box 3, Library of Congress, Washington, D.C.; hereafter cited in text as *SJP*.

3. *Come Along with Me: Part of a Novel, Sixteen Stories, and Three Lectures*, ed. Stanley Edgar Hyman (New York: Viking, 1968), 196; hereafter cited in text as *CAWM*.

# Notes on Shirley Jackson

*Stanley Edgar Hyman*

She will be twenty-eight this December. She was born in San Francisco and grew up in Burlingame, California, which is, presumably, the setting for her novel, *The Road through the Wall*. When she was in high school, her family moved to Rochester, New York, where she lived until her marriage. After a brief flurry with the University of Rochester, she attended Syracuse University, with no great academic distinction, but managed to get a degree. She wrote everything there was to write in college, including what I believe is excellent poetry, which she has never attempted to publish, and in her senior year founded, edited, and wrote most of a wild mimeographed literary magazine named *Spectre* (of which her present husband was managing editor) which shocked the college, was an enormous success, made a whopping profit for its frightened backers, the English honorary society, and still survives, under another name, limping along sedately.

Shortly after graduation, she married, and held a succession of unpleasant and badly paid jobs, each for a very brief period: wrote continuity for a radio station devoted to racing results, read proof for a printer who specialized in small type and columns of figures, sold Modern Library books in Macy's, wrote advertising and stalled off creditors for a crooked advertising agency, etc. After a year of this sort of thing she got fed up with working, decided she never would again, and never has. She and her husband moved to New Hampshire, where they lived in the woods for a year in a shack without plumbing or electricity, writing. Up there she sold her first story, a comic reminiscence entitled "My Life with R. H. Macy," to *The New Republic* for $25. From that day on she was a professional short-story writer, and has since sold stories to *The New Yorker* (many), *Mademoiselle, Charm, House and Garden* (never printed), the first *Cross-Section, The American Mercury, Story, The Yale Review*, and other magazines too dreadful to name. They have been printed in *Best Stories of 1944, Primer for White Folks, The Price of Liberty*, etc.

Manuscript dated 22 September 1947 from the Shirley Jackson Papers, Library of Congress. Used by permission of Phoebe Pettingell Hyman.

She is married to Stanley Edgar Hyman, a staff writer for *The New Yorker*, whose first book, a study of modern literary criticism, will be published by Knopf in the spring. They have two children, Laurence Jackson, a boy of 5, and Joanne Leslie, a girl of two. After New Hampshire, they lived in New York until the spring of 1945, when Mr. H. got a job teaching literature at Bennington College and they moved to Bennington, Vt. When he retired from teaching a year ago, they continued living there, because Miss Jackson likes the town, the people, and rounding up contributed apple pies for PTA suppers.

At present, she is working on several long short stories and her second novel, which will probably have a college background. In addition, she plays the guitar and sings five hundred folk songs (none of them lifted from Burl Ives records) as well as playing the piano and the zither. She also paints, draws, embroiders, makes things out of seashells, plays chess, and takes care of the house and children, cooking, cleaning, laundry, etc. She believes no artist was ever ruined by housework (or helped by it either). She is an authority on witchcraft and magic, and has a remarkable private library of works in English on the subject, and is perhaps the only contemporary writer who is a practicing amateur witch, specializing in small-scale black magic and fortune-telling with a Tarot deck. She hopes sometime in the future to write on the subject. She is passionately addicted to cats, and at the moment has six, all coal black, as well as a dog that has been raised as a cat and for all anyone knows, believes he is a cat.

She reads prodigiously, almost entirely fiction, and has just about exhausted the English novel, from John Lyly to Sylvia Townsend Warner, and has moved over into the French. Ahead of her lie the Russian, Scandinavian, etc. Her favorite period is the eighteenth century, her favorite novelists are Fanny Burney, Samuel Richardson, and Jane Austen. She does not much like the sort of neurotic modern fiction she herself writes, the Joyce and Kafka schools, and in fact except for a few sports like Forster and Miss Warner, does not really like any fiction since Thackeray. She wishes she could write things as leisurely and placid as Richardson's, but doesn't think she ever will. She likes to believe this is the world's fault, not her own.

# Biographical Material
## Shirley Jackson

I will be twenty-nine this December. When I look back on twenty-nine years from this end of it, it seems a very short and perplexing space of time; when I start at the beginning and try to work up to now, it turns into novels. Starting from this end, then, I am pleased to think that this is only my second book and I have many more ahead of me. I have one more children than books, although I hope eventually to have more books than children. The children lead by virtue of my latest daughter, Sarah Geraldine, four months old. The next oldest is a daughter named Joanne Leslie; she is three. My oldest is a son, Laurence Jackson, who is six. My youngest book is named *Lottery; The Adventures of James Harris,* and my older book is *The Road through the Wall;* it is one.

I live in a place called North Bennington, Vermont. I live here because my husband, who is Stanley Edgar Hyman, author of *The Armed Vision,* taught odds and ends at Bennington College for a while and when he decided to give up teaching we just kept on living here, because the house is big (fourteen rooms) and it's a nice town for children to grow up in, and I'm on the Entertainment Committee for the PTA and write the programs for the Home Talent Show.

Before we came here we lived in New York City and I wouldn't like to live there again. When we first moved here I used to be anxious to go down to New York for a couple weeks about every three months, and now if I go down once a year it's reluctantly and for no more than a day or so. I like it better here.

I don't like housework, but I do it because no one else will. My older daughter and I are practically learning to cook together. I write in the evenings mostly, I guess, although sometimes I let the children help me write in the mornings. They are all very sympathetic about my writing, and my son no longer tries to justify me to his friends; I read him one story I had written about him, and he was tolerant but not very much amused.

Manuscript from the Shirley Jackson Papers, Library of Congress. Used by permission of Sarah H. Stewart.

I like to play the guitar and I like to play poker and bridge and I like to listen to people talking. I don't like laundry but I do that too.

I do not much like modern novels. I like Samuel Richardson and Jane Austen and Fanny Burney and Mrs. Ferrier. Modern novels seem very vague and inconclusive after someone like Richardson. Writers like Richardson and Fanny Burney give no sense of being hurried or pressed for unique ideas; they are peaceful and gracious and write with an infinite sense of leisure that I envy greatly.

I graduated from college and got married in 1940, and I sold my first story in 1941. Laurence was born in 1942, and since then I have been writing a great deal, novels and stories and PTA programs.

I like cats and dogs and children and books. I wish I didn't have to write this.

# "Talk with Miss Jackson"
## Harvey Breit

Magic is the word that has been woven around the literary personality of
Shirley Jackson, the latest to join the select corps of triumphant women
short-story writers who apparently flourish in America. Of the stories that
make up her surprisingly high-selling collection—entitled *The Lottery*—critics have said they signaled a return to an era of witchcraft and
magic, the supernatural and some sort of devil worship. One critic went so
far as to say that Miss Jackson wrote not with a pen but with a broomstick.

This, as the phrase commonly goes, may or may not be. To the uncos-
mological eye, Miss Jackson *qua* Miss Jackson looks not only wholesome
but very much on the day-side. She is neat, detached and impersonally
warm. She subtly radiates an atmosphere of coziness and comfort, and
appears to be of a tranquil disposition. All in all, Miss Jackson looks like a
mother. And she is, in fact, mother to a good many things—though she is
in her mere twenties—having under her protective sway three children,
two dogs, six cats and one husband. She does indeed use a broomstick, but
for household chores rather than as a means of transportation.

True, Miss Jackson believes in magic. She says it works for her, both the
black and white varieties. But she also says it's a silly thing to talk about.
Obviously, Miss Jackson was able to be natural even about the supernatural. Having cleared the air of ghosts, Miss Jackson settled back to talk of
more tangible matters—literature, for instance.

Writing in general, she says, short stories in particular are perhaps nearest and dearest to her heart. But it is as a mother—and not as a witch—that
she approaches the heart of the matter. "I can't persuade myself," Miss
Jackson said, "that writing is honest work. It is a very personal reaction,
but 50 per cent of my life is spent washing and dressing the children,
cooking, washing dishes and clothes, and mending. After I get it all to bed,
I turn around to my typewriter and try to—well, to create concrete things
again. It's great fun, and I love it. But it doesn't tie any shoes."

Unlike Thomas Mann, for example, who feels writing to be a burden,

Miss Jackson can't see writing as work at all. "It's as much fun," she reiterated, "as sending the children off to school. My husband [the critic Stanley Edgar Hyman] fights writing; it is work for him, at least he calls it work. I find it relaxing. For one thing," she continued laughingly, "it's the only way I can get to sit down. There is delight in seeing a story grow; it's so deeply satisfying—like having a winning streak in poker."

When she was asked, unfairly, what she was trying to do in her stories, Miss Jackson didn't quite know. "I keep trying to think how I do it," she said. "That would explain it. I get a couple of ideas that go together and they are very exciting. 'Daemon Lover' started that way. Someone told me an anecdote, just a few sentences. (Sort of like Henry James, you know.) I like thinking about it, turning it around, thinking of ways to use a situation like that in order to get a haunting note. It gets quite real. I think of what other thing it will go with, while I'm washing the dishes. But I do it because it's fun, because I like it."

Miss Jackson's critical attitudes are consistent with her creative ways. She doesn't like the nineteenth century much, but for her own personal, logical reasons. "I think of poor Dickens," she said. "He slaved and worked; he didn't enjoy himself. The nineteenth century is moody and touchy and it broods too much. I like the eighteenth-century novels, Richardson and Fanny Burney. Everyone should be made to read *Pamela*. Richardson—nobody believes me—but there's a tremendous sense of leisure and peace in him, and he wrote just for the love of it. He just took a really rich, deep pleasure in doing it."

She thought, hesitated, conceded. "I guess I do like the Brontës in the nineteenth century. But I really think they wrote for pleasure. And, of course, today there is Ivy Compton-Burnett. Who will deny that she is an eighteenth-century writer?"

The best writers in her genre, she thinks, are Katherine Anne Porter and Elizabeth Bowen. "For sensitivity to words and subtlety of meaning you can't find anyone better than Miss Porter. Miss Bowen's 'Look at All Those Roses' is a lovely, very beautiful story."

Among male writers Miss Jackson takes André Gide and E. M. Forster. "I think," she said, "Gide is one of the great writers alive today. He is one of those profitable people. Both Forster and Gide are faultless. They have that absolute instinct."

An unerring sense was what Miss Jackson was talking about—and Miss Jackson wants it for herself. She is in the middle of a novel, working very slowly at it. "I'm going twice as carefully," she said carefully, "as I ever did before. I *have* to get it right."

# Notes on an Unfashionable Novelist
## Shirley Jackson

It is difficult today to suggest seriously that any thinking, responsible person sit down and read a book; the glorified comic magazine we call the "modern" novel has taken too firm a hold on our racing, bewildered minds. It is too easy to read a thin volume where everything is said only once, and seven or eight words suffice for a sentence, just as seven or eight pat phrases suffice for an idea; why read anything "long," or, worse still, "old"? Why, for instance, read a stuffy old character like Samuel Richardson, who looms only very vaguely back there beyond Henry James and past Thackeray and is more than obscured by Jane Austen; why read Richardson, who was certainly very moral and extremely long, and, not to put too fine a point on it, dull?

I can think of, offhand, three reasons. I can find in someone like Richardson three attributes somehow lost today, and intensely, humanly, valuable. Peace, principle, kindness. All three as emphatically stuffy and old-fashioned as your grandmother's wedding gown, and as emphatically lost from general circulation.

Peace would come first today, I should think. Out of a time when things moved slowly, when nerves were sensibilities and conversation was formal and, if you like, stilted, and when a man could, if he chose, write a book a million words long and expect people to have time for it, Richardson made three books; they move along like molasses, no small action is consummated in less than ten pages, they line up, volume after volume, of solid, meaningful words, and they are leisurely, relaxed, gracious. Richardson was a fat little man who ran a fine printing business and worked hard at it; he sat daily at tea with groups of admiring ladies; he liked his cat and he liked his garden and he liked gossip about high life, and he had plenty of time. With all his interests and all his busy concerns—and he stayed fat; he liked his food—he wrote three novels, *Pamela*, *Clarissa Harlowe*, and *Sir Charles Grandison*, which, placed end to end, would fill up two mystery-story shelves in a modern circulating library.

Manuscript from the Shirley Jackson Papers, Library of Congress. Used by permission of Sarah H. Stewart.

## Part 2

Page after page, volume after volume, of intimate letters go into these novels, letters back and forth from one character to another, describing events, commenting on the descriptions, reflecting on the moral implications of several courses of action, requesting more comments, all taking plenty of time, nobody hurrying. In any dramatic crisis the heroine has time for a polysyllabic remonstrance, which she reports faithfully in her letters, the villain has time for a lengthy insincere apology, which *he* reports faithfully in *his* letters, and both explain their actions minutely, and ask for comments from their correspondents, which they get, along with recapitulations of what *might* have been done under the circumstances, and comments on *that*. And in it all, a vast sense of leisure to reflect, to choose, to be graceful. Peace—the opportunity to have time to think.

Principle is a good reason, too. Sir Charles Grandison (who may be the perfect man) cannot marry the woman he loves, or even let her suspect that he loves her, because he feels himself responsible to another woman who is devoted to him. Clarissa Harlowe is abducted and seduced, but she cannot marry her repentant seducer, although offered riches, a title, the forgiveness of her family and perfect respect from all her friends, because her conception of herself as honorable has been destroyed. Pamela is kidnapped, besieged, commanded, bribed, tormented, and deceived, but cannot bring herself to yield to the irresponsible Mr. B until she is offered a genuine wedding ring. It all sounds like the most outrageous nonsense, and yet what is it but an exaggerated notion of honor? And is it possible that honor, however exaggerated, can be quite so ridiculous? Pride of self, dignity, respect, still exist today, one hopes, and although Pamela and Clarissa and dear Sir Charles put their values in an area once removed from the area in which our values lie today, are they quite so foolish? Is a sinful man the less sinful because his crimes are against a standard more rarified than ours? Lovelace, who ruined Clarissa, is not perhaps so *bad* a man as *Sanctuary*'s Popeye, but Lovelace is certainly as real a sinner in his sphere; moreover, he had more time to be bad and to be subtle about it than Popeye. The goodness of Richardson's good characters—and they are very sharply divided, half to the devils, half to the angels, and not the less meaningful for it—is in the same terms as the badness; that is, they are good in the sense that, translated into terms we know fully, comes out as things we like and admire and would like to be ourselves. There are, after all, things wholesome and things defiantly unpalatable; stretch them as far as you like and at one point they become Lovelace and Clarissa; at another they become Mario and the magician, or Preacher Casey and the deputies.

Kindness, the third attribute, is an outlandish word to use about a writer, or about writing, or about anything except people and the way they feel. And yet kindness is a strong quality in Richardson, the sort of kindness which comes out in a tremendous tenderness the man himself must have felt and tossed about embarrassingly on everyone who came his way. His characters, for instance, are nice to each other. One of them may abhor another; some of them, again like Lovelace, outrage every precious tenet of a rigid morality and bring this outrage to bear on others; frequently these precise, lazy people are cross with one another, and stirred to anger: Harriet Byron was completely out of patience along about volume eight, when Sir Charles was sedately making absolutely *sure* that no conceivable shred of formality had been inadvertently overlooked. Nevertheless implicit in every word, every comment upon a comment, is the deep conviction of sympathy: not "we are all from the same mind, Richardson's," but "we are all from the same people, the mortal." That is a valuable thing to record, and perhaps it takes ten volumes to put it across.

There is very little humor in Richardson, and, to be honest, some of the books are pretty heavy going—Pamela's reflections on the education of her children, or some of the long stretches in *Grandison* where everyone takes a breather from the burning question (is it honorable or is it not?) and they just sit back and write long letters scrutinizing themselves—but without every word of it you couldn't really be satisfied that Sir Charles ought to propose or that Pamela deserves her husband. The richness of it is in those long muddy sections, the dark background of the bright tapestry. Disrespectfully, after Pamela's prolonged musings on children, we are delighted to see Mr. B contemplate an elopement with a designing widow. It takes a long time to read Richardson, and, even so, he's only the stuffy little man a long way back beyond even Thackeray down the length of years that is Fielding standing in front of him—but peace, principle, and kindness are the qualities that may even survive our own distempered time.

# The Unloved Reader

*Shirley Jackson*

A short story—in common, of course, with all other written work—is of no use whatsoever without a reader. The act of writing is after all a two-way process, one of communication rather than complacent self-expression. The function of the story, most simply, is to be read. A good story must engage its reader, persuade him that he wants to belong in the story for as long as it lasts, so that he will participate eagerly in the act of communication which the author has initiated. There are no set rules, really, for the writing of stories, and no single point at which a story stops being a story and becomes something else, but surely a story which does not so engage the reader must be considered a failure.

What is there to say, then, about a kind of story which sets out actively to bewilder and antagonize the reader? I suppose the polite answer would be to call it a story-of-the-absurd, and to say that at least in Mr. Barthelme's case the method seems completely successful; if Mr. Barthelme intends his reader to *enjoy* his stories, perhaps he has not succeeded so completely. Mr. Barthelme obscures his pages with odd—and frequently uninteresting—items of irrelevant information, and uses the *non sequitur* and nonsense phrase almost past endurance; even though this does make his stories considerably longer the total effect is frankly very hard on the reader. In one story he lists twenty-eight comic doctor names (Dr. No, Dr. Fu Manchu, Dr. Pepper) who are holding a meeting in a drug store; in another story a "huge man wearing the Double Eagle of St. Puce" rattles off (with no relevance) a list of sixty-seven unrelated subjects beginning with the letter S. One of Mr. Barthelme's heroes has a radio station, on which he plays *The Star-Spangled Banner* "60 times between 6 and 10 A.M., 120 times between 12 noon and 7 P.M., and the whole night long except when, as was sometimes the case, he was talking." When he talks, he repeats one word over and over in a monotonous voice. "Nevertheless," he says, "nevertheless, nevertheless, nevertheless. . . ."

Unpublished review of *Come Back, Dr. Caligari*, by Donald Barthelme, and *Behold Goliath*, by Alfred Chester, from the Shirley Jackson Papers, Library of Congress. Used by permission of Sarah H. Stewart.

113

*Part 2*

Mr. Barthelme can alternate his fast shotgun delivery with a slow style:

> The mailman (Rosemarie's mailman) persisted in his irritating habit of doing the other side of the street before he did her side of the street. Rosemarie ate a bowl of Three-Minute Oats.
> Eric cut his nails with one of those 25¢ nail cutters.
> The bomb Henry Jackson threw at his father failed to detonate. Why did you throw this Schlitz can at me Henry? Henry's father asked, and why is it ticking like a bomb?
> Hilda appeared in Paul's cellar. Paul, she asked, can I borrow an axe? Or a saw?

On the jacket of this book, the publishers discuss Mr. Barthelme's way with his form: he baits it, they say, insults it, turns it inside out. Well, yes. That's just about the way it reads. I am prepared to concede that Mr. Barthelme's baiting-and-insulting is thorough and complete, probably does exactly what he intends it to do, and even sometimes creates an odd mosaic effect, but I do not for a moment maintain that it is a pleasure to read. Here I do think that Mr. Barthelme is mistaken; it is all very well, perhaps admirable, to bait and insult an established form, but unless the end product is something more than the form outraged, nothing is really gained, and what is lost, at least in this case, is the reader.

As far as style is concerned, Mr. Chester is surely more conventional. ("Goliath thought back to his dream of walking naked and soundless, holding himself in his hands like opaque water, and he thought back beyond that to where the water cleared and to where it was not—the where being there because the water was not—until for an instant his mind fell into a hole the size of the cosmos which was because everything was not.") His characters are driven by the persistent notion that they are ghosts, that they have no existence, that they are only emptiness, and I suspect that behind this lurks Mr. Chester's own feeling that his characters *are* ghosts. This is a deep evasion of responsibility; here is a writer who does not feel that he need make his characters "real" because they are, admittedly, *not* real. They are almost invisible, as a matter of fact, against their several backgrounds. A woman murders her illegitimate baby, the richest young woman in the world lies dying alone, a child is terrified into running away from home, and none of it matters in the slightest. Not one of these people has enough dimension to catch the reader; they are all ghosts. The reader cannot commit himself even for the space of the story, because there is nothing there.

I have not given any adequate notion of Mr. Chester's subject matter. "In Praise of Vespasian," for instance, is a guided tour through the public urinals of several large cities, led by Joaquin, who is in search of homosexual adventure. "Ismael" is the story of the narrator's broken love affair with a young Puerto Rican boy ("After all, I've never had a Puerto Rican before"). The title story follows the meanderings of Goliath, who wanders the city, full of nothingness, seeks out and destroys his mother, visits an old man who lives in an empty room, goes to a dreary party, and finally keeps an assignation with a teen-age boy in a pergola.

Again, as with Mr. Barthelme, if this is what Mr. Chester wants, he has certainly got it. A book about a collection of ghosts performing a collection of unlovely acts is not necessarily a failed or even a poor book, but again I must return to the essential reader; is this what he deserves?

✦

[Jackson appended this alternative final paragraph to her review.]

Mr. Chester is capable of surprising the reader into attention, however, as in the last story in the book, when with an absolutely sure hand he creates a character who, while still ghostlike, is truly haunting. In this, "The Head of a Sad Angel," Mr. Chester is also writing about music, an area where he is wholly convincing. Perhaps because she has the music to make her more tangible, the Countess is a poignant and moving character, with authority in her voice and a true pain in her loneliness. When Mr. Chester writes a good story, with something concrete to work with, he writes it very well indeed.

# "Experience and Fiction"

*Shirley Jackson*

It is most agreeable to be a writer of fiction for several reasons—one of the most important being, of course, that you can persuade people that it is really work if you look haggard enough—but perhaps the most useful thing about being a writer of fiction is that nothing is ever wasted; all experience is good for something; you tend to see everything as a potential structure of words. One of my daughters made this abruptly clear to me when she came not long ago into the kitchen where I was trying to get the door of our terrible old refrigerator open; it always stuck when the weather was wet, and one of the delights of a cold rainy day was opening the refrigerator door. My daughter watched me wrestling with it for a minute and then she said that I was foolish to bang on the refrigerator door like that; why not use magic to open it? I thought about this. I poured myself another cup of coffee and lighted a cigarette and sat down for a while and thought about it; and then decided that she was right. I left the refrigerator where it was and went in to my typewriter and wrote a story about not being able to open the refrigerator door and getting the children to open it with magic. When a magazine bought the story I bought a new refrigerator. That is what I would like to talk about now—the practical application of magic, or where do stories come from?

People are always asking me—and every other writer I know—where story ideas come from. Where *do* you get your ideas, they ask; how do you ever manage to think them up? It's certainly the hardest question in the world to answer, since stories originate in everyday happenings and emotions, and any writer who tried to answer such a question would find himself telling over, in some detail, the story of his life. Fiction uses so many small items, so many little gestures and remembered incidents and unforgettable faces, that trying to isolate any one inspiration for any one story is

From *Come Along with Me: Part of a Novel, Sixteen Stories, and Three Lectures*, ed. Stanley Edgar Hyman (New York: Viking, 1968), 195–204. Copyright 1952 by Shirley Jackson. Used by permission of Viking Penguin, a division of Penguin Books USA Inc. Jackson wrote this essay in 1958; Viking uses the copyright date (1952) of the accompanying story.

incredibly difficult, but basically, of course, the genesis of any fictional work has to be human experience. This translation of experience into fiction is not a mystic one. It is, I think, part recognition and part analysis. A bald description of an incident is hardly fiction, but the same incident, carefully taken apart, examined as to emotional and balanced structure, and then as carefully reassembled in the most effective form, slanted and polished and weighed, may very well be a short story. Let me try an example.

I have lifted this from a story written several years ago by a college student I knew; it has always stayed in my mind as the most perfect nonstory I ever read. This is how the plot goes: In a small town the people are having a church fair, the high point of which is the raffling off of a particularly beautiful quilt made by one of the local ladies; the quilt has been the talk of the town for weeks, and the admiration and envy of all the women; all of them want it badly. The raffle is held, and the quilt is won by a summer visitor, a wealthy woman who has no use for the quilt and no desire for it. She sends her chauffeur over to the platform to pick up the quilt and bring it back to her car.

Now, this story written straight, as I just read it, is almost meaningless. It is a simple anecdote, and carries only the statement that the women in the small town resent the summer visitor, and dislike having her win the quilt; its only actual impact is the ironic point that the quilt should have been won by the only woman attending the raffle who really did not want it. Now, suppose this were taken apart and reassembled. We would then have to examine more particularly four or five people most concerned—the summer visitor, the chauffeur, the woman who made the quilt, the minister who raffled it off, and perhaps the one village woman—I believe there always *is* one—who was most open and loud in her disapproval; as things stand now, these people have no faces, only parts to play. Suppose we were to give them personalities, sketch in people, lightly at first, experimentally; suppose the summer visitor is actually a shy, friendly person who very much wants to be liked, and thinks that accepting the quilt will endear her to the villagers; suppose she is foolish enough to try to give the quilt back again afterward? Suppose the minister had intended this church fair as an attempt to make peace among the quarreling women in the village, and now sees their quarrels ended when they unite in hatred of the outsider? Then consider the chauffeur; as the story stands now he has the most agonizing two or three minutes of all—the walk from the car, through the people of the village, to the platform to take up the quilt and carry it back; if the chauffeur came from a small town himself, and knew what such people were like, how would he feel during those few minutes? Suppose the chauffeur were a boy from that town, hired for the summer to drive the wealthy visitor's car? And, beyond all else, how do the *men* in the village feel at the feuding over the quilt?

If the story is going to be a short one, it is of course only necessary to focus on one of these characters—I like the chauffeur, myself—and follow this character from beginning to end; in a short story the time would of course be limited to the actual moments of the raffle, with the background sketched in through conversation and small incidents—the way the village women look at the fancy car, perhaps, or the minister's nervousness when he comes to draw the number; the point of the story might be indicated early, telegraphed, as it were, if the story opened with the summer visitor buying a cake at one of the stands, while the village women watch her and make their private comments; I keep calling them "village women," by the way; I do not mean by that that they are primitive, or uneducated, or unsophisticated; I think of them only as a tightly knit group, interested in their own concerns, and as resentful of outsiders as any of us.

If it were going to be a longer story, these people would be examined in more detail, and there would have to be more incidents, all paralleling the final one, the characters would have to be more firmly drawn, and the scene of the fair made more vivid as a background. The longer story might open with the village ladies decorating the fair grounds in the morning, with their bickering and arguing over whose booth was going to have the best location, and the woman who made the quilt would have to be there, set in with a definite character—perhaps they all hate her, but will defend her and her quilt because the summer visitor is the outsider?

It is almost silly to say that no one will read a story which does not interest him. Yet many writers forget it. They write a story which interests *them*, forgetting that the particular emotional investment they brought to the incident has never been communicated to the reader because, writing the story, they wrote down only what happened and not what was felt. In our story of the quilt, the girl who originally wrote it had been, as a daughter of the woman who made the quilt, very much involved in both the excitement and the indignation, but there was nothing of that in the story. She only wrote down what happened when an outsider won a quilt at a church fair. She said she didn't want the story to be autobiographical, and so she had kept herself entirely out of it. She had kept herself out of it so successfully, in fact, that the story was hopelessly dull; it had nothing in it except its one small ironic point; the rest of the story was waste, and padding. The village ladies were named Mrs. Smith and Mrs. Jones and it

119

was not possible to tell one from another. Even the minister merged into the general flat landscape, recognizable only by his name. She pointed out that these were real people, and if she described them any more clearly they might read the story and be offended. And she couldn't change any of it because that was the way it had really *happened*. What was the purpose, she thought, of changing the events when this ironic little incident *had* really happened, she had been there and seen it, and had always wanted, she said, to write it down because it seemed just perfect material for a story.

Now there are three elements here, three mistaken conceptions, which would keep this anecdote from ever turning into a story. I think it cannot be too firmly emphasized that in the writing of any kind of fiction no scene and no character can be allowed to wander off by itself; there must be some furthering of the story in every sentence, and even the most fleeting background characters must partake of the story in some way; they must be characters peculiar to *this* story and no other. A boy who climbs an apple tree to watch the raffling off of the quilt only wastes time and attention if that is *all* he does; the reader's mind is taken away from the story while he watches that boy climb the tree. But if the boy climbs the tree directly over the visitor's fancy car, and amuses himself by dropping green apples down onto the roof of the car and snickering, he is still a background character but he has added to the story by reinforcing the village attitude toward the outsider. The reader has, presumably, seen small boys climb apple trees before, but this boy exists nowhere else in the world than in this story and this village, and it must be made clear that that is where he belongs.

The second point I want to emphasize is that people in stories are called characters because that is what they are. They are not real people. It is, of course, possible to choose a character and describe him so completely that the reader sees him as a whole personality, rounded and recognizable. The only trouble with that is that it takes several thousand pages of solid description, including a lot of very dull reading. Most of us have enough trouble understanding ourselves and our families and friends without wanting to know *everything* about a fictional character. A person in a story is identified through small things—little gestures, turns of speech, automatic reactions; suppose one of the women in our quilt story is excessively and foolishly modest; suppose that when someone praises her cakes she answers that they're really not very good, actually she made *much* better cakes for the church fair last year; she just wishes that no one would even *taste* a piece of this year's cake, because it's really not any good at all; or if someone else remarks on how delicate her embroidery is, she will say that it's really nowhere near as good as everyone else's, and she could do much better if she had more time, although of *course* nothing she ever made could *begin* to be as good as Mrs. Smith's, although of course if she had as much time to spend doing embroidery as Mrs. Smith she might be able to do even *half* as well. That woman is identified for the reader permanently. If the reader comes to a conversation later, and he reads the remark: "Oh, it's not really anything good at *all*; anyone could have done better, really; I just get embarrassed if anyone even *looks* at my poor work"—he knows at once who is talking. It is not necessary to describe the woman any further; everyone has heard people who talk like that, and any reader will know at once exactly what she is like. Any minor character may be spotlighted in the background in this manner and major characters will of course take on new depths of personality by being so clearly identified; suppose the minister in our story has a nervous or tired gesture that he makes over and over without thinking—suppose he covers his eyes wearily with his hand when he is worried—a small gesture like that will do more to describe him than a biography.

Further, let me stop briefly to quarrel with the statement that this event cannot be improved upon because that is the way it really happened. The only way to turn something that really happened into something that happens on paper is to attack it in the beginning the way a puppy attacks an old shoe. Shake it, snarl at it, sneak up on it from various angles. Perhaps the simple little incident you are dying to turn into fiction may carry a wholly new punch if you wrote it upside down or inside out or starting at the end; many stories that just won't work out as straightforward accounts go smoothly and neatly if you start from the end; I mean, tell the ending first and then let the story unfold, giving the explanations which make the story plausible. In our quilt story, of course, the entire setup would fall apart if we tried writing it from the end—unless the end is really the girl who wrote the story in the first place, and would not put in real people because she was one of them. See what happens to the story then; it becomes a story about conflicting loyalties, the story of a girl who loves her home town and yet, having left it behind, finds also in herself a certain sympathy with the outsider, the wistful woman who does not belong anywhere. If we do what I call turning the story inside out, we can abandon the church fair and the raffle temporarily, give the summer visitor two small children, put the two small children on the outskirts of the crowd—say down by the brook, playing with some of the village children, and let their amiable play stand in the foreground against the raffle in the background, contrasting the children playing with the suspicion and hatred building up among the grownups. Or suppose we want to turn the story outside in—how about making the summer visitor a fairly stupid woman, who is determined to win the quilt, and puts through some high-handed maneuvering to make sure she wins it? By changing the emphasis and angle on this little plot we can make it say almost anything we like. There is certainly no need to worry about whether any of this is true, or actually happened; it is as true as you make it. The important thing is that it be true in the story, and actually happen *there*. . . .

It is much easier, I find, to write a story than to cope competently with the millions of daily trials and irritations that turn up in an ordinary house, and it helps a good deal—particularly with children around—if you can see them through a flattering veil of fiction. It has always been a comfort to me to make stories out of things that happen, things like moving, and kittens, and Christmas concerts at the grade school, and broken bicycles; it is easier, as Sally said, to magic the refrigerator than it is to wrench at the door. And it is certainly easier to sit there taking notes while everyone else is running around packing the suitcases and giving last-minute instructions to the moving men. I remember that once the income-tax people were making one of their spot checks in our locality, and, to our intense dismay, one of the spots they decided to check was us. Nothing can protect you at a time like that; no matter how conscientious you have been about your income tax, guilt overwhelms you when that man walks in. He was only at our house for about an hour, and all the time he was in the study with my husband, studying canceled checks and mortgage receipts, and I could hear my husband yelling "Depreciation, depreciation," I was in the dining room with my typewriter, defending myself. I had started to compose an impassioned letter to the United States Government about unjustifiable tyranny over honest law-abiding citizens, but I could not resist a few words of description of the way our family had received the news that the man was coming, and by the time the conference in the study was over I was well along in a story about a quietly lunatic tax investigation—and guess who was going to be the villain. When the income-tax man was ready to leave he came through the dining room with my husband and stopped to say, oh yes; he gathered that I was a writer. Say, he went on, he had often wondered—where did writing people get the ideas for the stuff they wrote? Huh? He picked up one page of my manuscript and I barely got it away from him in time. I really don't know what would have happened to our tax returns if he had read it.

I would like, if I may, to finish with a story which is the most direct translation of experience into fiction that I have ever done. For one thing, I had a high fever the whole time I was writing it. For another thing, I was interrupted constantly with requests to take upstairs trays of orange juice or chicken soup or aspirin or ginger ale or dry sheets or boxes of crayons. For another thing, while I was writing it, my husband was lying on the couch with a hot-water bottle saying that writing stories was all very well, but suppose he died right then and there—was there anyone to care? I may even have whined a little myself, carrying trays and getting hotter hot-water bottles and telling everyone that they were just pretty lucky that they had me at least, to wait on them and take care of them in spite of the fact that I was every bit as sick as they were, and only the purest spirit of self-sacrifice kept me going at all, and they should be grateful. Actually, my husband and two of our children had the grippe, and I was only just catching it; only the fact that I had to finish the story kept me from abandoning them and going someplace quiet to lie down. We had only three children then, by the way—we didn't know when we were well off—and the one referred to variously as Sally, or Baby, is now of an age to read, and repudiate, an accurate accounting of her own behavior. The story was published as "The Night We All Had Grippe," and I got a letter about it from a lady in Indiana. I would like to make a little extra money writing, she wrote to me in this letter. Tell me, where do you get ideas for stories? I can never make up anything good.

# "Biography of a Story"

*Shirley Jackson*

On the morning of June 28, 1948, I walked down to the post office in our little Vermont town to pick up the mail. I was quite casual about it, as I recall—I opened the box, took out a couple of bills and a letter or two, talked to the postmaster for a few minutes, and left, never supposing that it was the last time for months that I was to pick up the mail without an active feeling of panic. By the next week I had had to change my mailbox to the largest one in the post office, and casual conversation with the postmaster was out of the question, because he wasn't speaking to me. June 28, 1948 was the day *The New Yorker* came out with a story of mine in it [cover date was 26 June]. It was not my first published story, nor my last, but I have been assured over and over that if it had been the only story I ever wrote or published, there would be people who would not forget my name.

I had written the story three weeks before, on a bright June morning when summer seemed to have come at last, with blue skies and warm sun and no heavenly signs to warn me that my morning's work was anything but just another story. The idea had come to me while I was pushing my daughter up the hill in her stroller—it was, as I say, a warm morning, and the hill was steep, and beside my daughter the stroller held the day's groceries—and perhaps the effort of that last fifty yards up the hill put an edge to the story; at any rate, I had the idea fairly clearly in my mind when I put my daughter in her playpen and the frozen vegetables in the refrigerator, and, writing the story, I found that it went quickly and easily, moving from beginning to end without pause. As a matter of fact, when I read it over later I decided that except for one or two minor corrections, it needed no changes, and the story I finally typed up and sent off to my agent the next day was almost word for word the original draft. This, as any writer of stories can tell you, is not a usual thing. All I know is that when I came to read the story over I felt strongly that I didn't want to fuss with it. I didn't think it was perfect, but I didn't want to fuss with it. It was, I thought, a serious, straightforward story, and I was pleased and a little surprised at the ease with which it had been written; I was reasonably proud of it, and hoped that my agent would sell it to some magazine and I would have the gratification of seeing it in print.

My agent did not care for the story, but—as she said in her note at the time—her job was to sell it, not to like it. She sent it at once to *The New Yorker*, and about a week after the story had been written I received a telephone call from the fiction editor of *The New Yorker*; it was quite clear that he did not really care for the story either, but *The New Yorker* was going to buy it. He asked for one change—that the date mentioned in the story be changed to coincide with the date of the issue of the magazine in which the story would appear, and I said of course. He then asked, hesitantly, if I had any particular interpretation of my own for the story; Mr. Harold Ross, then the editor of *The New Yorker*, was not altogether sure that he understood the story, and wondered if I cared to enlarge upon its meaning. I said no. Mr. Ross, he said, thought that the story might be puzzling to some people, and in case anyone telephoned the magazine, as sometimes happened, or wrote in asking about the story, was there anything in particular I wanted them to say? No, I said, nothing in particular; it was just a story I wrote.

I had no more preparation than that. I went on picking up the mail every morning, pushing my daughter up and down the hill in her stroller, anticipating pleasurably the check from *The New Yorker*, and shopping for groceries. The weather stayed nice and it looked as though it was going to be a good summer. Then, on June 28, *The New Yorker* came out with my story.

Things began mildly enough with a note from a friend at *The New Yorker*: "Your story has kicked up quite a fuss around the office," he wrote. I was flattered; it's nice to think that your friends notice what you write. Later that day there was a call from one of the magazine's editors; they had had a couple of people phone in about my story, he said, and was there anything I particularly wanted him to say if there were any more calls? No, I said, nothing particular; anything he chose to say was perfectly all right with me; it was just a story.

I was further puzzled by a cryptic note from another friend: "Heard a man talking about a story of yours on the bus this morning," she wrote. "Very exciting. I wanted to tell him I knew the author, but after I heard what he was saying I decided I'd better not."

One of the most terrifying aspects of publishing stories and books is the realization that they are going to be read, and read by strangers. I had never fully realized this before, although I had of course in my imagination dwelt lovingly upon the thought of the millions and millions of people who were going to be uplifted and enriched and delighted by the stories I wrote. It had simply never occurred to me that these millions and millions of people might be so far from being uplifted that they would sit down and write me letters I was downright scared to open; of the three-hundred-odd letters that I received that summer I can count only thirteen that spoke kindly to me, and they were mostly from friends. Even my mother scolded me: "Dad and I did not care at all for your story in *The New Yorker,*" she wrote sternly; "it does seem, dear, that this gloomy kind of story is what all you young people think about these days. Why don't you write something to cheer people up?"

By mid-July I had begun to perceive that I was very lucky indeed to be safely in Vermont, where no one in our small town had ever heard of *The New Yorker,* much less read my story. Millions of people, and my mother, had taken a pronounced dislike to me.

The magazine kept no track of telephone calls, but all letters addressed to me care of the magazine were forwarded directly to me for answering, and all letters addressed to the magazine—some of them addressed to Harold Ross personally; these were the most vehement—were answered at the magazine and then the letters were sent to me in great batches, along with carbons of the answers written at the magazine. I have all the letters still, and if they could be considered to give any accurate cross section of the reading public, or the reading public of *The New Yorker,* or even the reading public of one issue of *The New Yorker,* I would stop writing now.

Judging from these letters, people who read stories are gullible, rude, frequently illiterate, and horribly afraid of being laughed at. Many of the writers were positive that *The New Yorker* was going to ridicule them in print, and the most cautious letters were headed, in capital letters: NOT FOR PUBLICATION or PLEASE DO NOT PRINT THIS LETTER, or, at best, THIS LETTER MAY BE PUBLISHED AT YOUR USUAL RATES OF PAYMENT. Anonymous letters, of which there were a few, were destroyed. *The New Yorker* never published any comment of any kind about the story in the magazine, but did issue one publicity release saying that the story had received more mail than any piece of fiction they had ever published; this was after the newspapers had gotten into the act, in midsummer, with a front-page story in the San Francisco *Chronicle* begging to know what the story meant, and a series of columns in New York and Chicago papers pointing out that *New Yorker* subscriptions were being canceled right and left.

Curiously, there are three main themes which dominate the letters of that first summer—three themes which might be identified as bewilderment, speculation, and plain old-fashioned abuse. In the years since then, during which the story has been anthologized, dramatized, televised, and even—in one completely mystifying transformation—made into a ballet, the tenor of letters I receive has changed. I am addressed more politely, as a rule, and the letters largely confine themselves to questions like what does this story mean? The general tone of the early letters, however, was a kind of wide-eyed, shocked innocence. People at first were not so much concerned with what the story meant; what they wanted to know was where these lotteries were held, and whether they could go there and watch. . . .

✤

I have frequently wondered if this last letter is a practical joke; it is certainly not impossible, although I hope not, because it is quite my favorite letter of all "Lottery" correspondence. It was mailed to *The New Yorker*, from Los Angeles, of course, and written in pencil, on a sheet of lined paper torn from a pad; the spelling is atrocious.

Dear Sir:
The June 26 copy of your magazine fell into my hands in the Los Angeles railroad station yesterday. Although I donnot read your magazine very often I took this copy home to my folks and they had to agree with me that you speak straitforward to your readers.

My Aunt Ellise before she became priestess of the Exalted Rollers used to tell us a story just like "The Lottery" by Shirley Jackson. I don't know if Miss Jackson is a member of the Exhalted Rollers but with her round stones sure ought to be. There is a few points in her prophecy on which Aunt Ellise and me don't agree.

The Exalted Rollers donnot believe in the ballot box but believe that the true gospel of the redeeming light will become accepted by all when the prophecy comes true. It does seem likely to me that our sins will bring us punishment though a great scouraging war with the devil's toy (the atomic bomb). I don't think we will have to sacrifice humin beings fore atonement.

Our brothers feel that Miss Jackson is a true prophet and disciple of the true gospel of the redeeming light. When will the next revelations be published?
Yours in the spirit.

Of all the questions ever asked me about "Lottery," I feel that there is only one which I can answer fearlessly and honestly, and that is the question which closes this gentleman's letter. When will the next revelations be published, he wants to know, and I answer roundly, never. I am out of the lottery business for good.

# "Notes for a Young Writer"

## Shirley Jackson

These are some notes, not necessarily complete, on the writing of short stories; they were originally written as a stimulus to my daughter Sally, who wants to be a writer.

In the country of the story the writer is king. He makes all the rules, with only the reservation that he must not ask more than a reader can reasonably grant. Remember, the reader is a very tough customer indeed, stubborn, dragging his feet, easily irritated. He will willingly agree to suspend disbelief for a time: he will go along with you if it is necessary for your story that you both assume temporarily that there really is a Land of Oz, but he will not suspend reason, he will not agree, for any story ever written, that he can see the Land of Oz from his window. As a matter of fact, you would do well to picture your typical reader as someone lying in a hammock on a soft summer day, with children playing loudly nearby, a television set and a radio both going at once, a sound truck blaring past in the street, birds singing and dogs barking; this fellow has a cool drink and a pillow for his head, and all you have to do with your story is catch his attention and hold it. Remember, your story is an uneasy bargain with your reader. Your end of the bargain is to play fair, and keep him interested, his end of the bargain is to keep reading. It is just terribly terribly easy to put a story down half-read and go off and do something else. Nevertheless, for as long as the story does go on you are the boss. You have the right to assume that the reader will accept the story on your own terms. You have the right to assume that the reader, however lazy, will exert some small intelligence while he is reading. Suppose you are writing a story about a castle. You do not need to describe every tower, every man at arms, every stone; your reader must bring his own complement of men at arms and towers; you need only describe one gardener to imply that the castle is well stocked with servants. In your stories, then, set your own

From *Come Along with Me: Part of a Novel, Sixteen Stories, and Three Lectures*, ed. Stanley Edgar Hyman (New York: Viking, 1968), 234–43. © 1960 by Shirley Jackson. Used by permission of Viking Penguin, a division of Penguin Books USA Inc. Jackson wrote this essay in 1962.

landscape with its own horizons, put your characters in where you think they belong, and move them as you please.

Your story must have a surface tension, which can be considerably stretched but not shattered; you cannot break your story into pieces with jagged odds and ends that do not belong. You cannot begin a story in one time and place, say, and then intrude a major flashback or a little sermon or a shift in emphasis to another scene or another character, without seriously marring the story, and turning the reader dizzy with trying to keep up. Consider simple movement from one place to another; if some movement is necessary and inevitable—as of course it is in most stories—then let the reader come along with you; do not jolt him abruptly from one place to another; in other words, let your story move as naturally and easily as possible, without side trips into unnecessary spots of beauty. Suppose you are writing a story about a boy and a girl meeting on a corner; your reader wants to go to that very corner and listen in; if, instead, you start your boy and girl toward the corner and then go off into a long description of the streetcar tracks and a little discussion of the background of these two characters and perhaps a paragraph or so about the town improvement which is going to remove the streetcar tracks they are crossing, and the girl's father's long-time aversion to any form of wheeled traffic—you will lose your reader and your story will fall apart. Always, always, make the duller parts of your story work *for* you; the necessary passage of time, the necessary movement must not stop the story dead, but must push it forward. . . .

. . . Try to remember with description that you must never just let it lie there; nothing in your story should ever be static unless you have a very good reason indeed for keeping your reader still; the essence of the story is motion. Do not let your chair be "a straight chair, with no arms and a hard wooden seat." Let your heroine go over and take a firm hold of the back of a straight wooden chair, because at the moment it is stronger than she. Naturally it is assumed that you are not going to try to describe anything you don't need to describe. If it is a sunny day let the sun make a pattern through the fence rail; if you don't care what the weather is don't bother your reader with it. Inanimate objects are best described in use or motion: "Because his cigarette lighter was platinum he had taken to smoking far too much." "The battered chimney seemed eager to hurl down bricks on anyone passing." Also, if your heroine's hair is golden, call it yellow.

Conversation is clearly one of the most difficult parts of the story. It is not enough to let your characters talk as people usually talk because the way people usually talk is extremely dull. Your characters are not going to stammer, or fumble for words, or forget what they are saying, or stop to clear their throats, at least not unless you want them to. Your problem is to make your characters sound as though they were real people talking (or, more accurately, that this is "real" conversation being read by a reader; look at some written conversation that seems perfectly smooth and plausible and natural on the page, and then try reading it aloud; what looks right on the page frequently sounds very literary indeed when read aloud; remember that you are writing to be read silently). Now the sounds and cadences of spoken speech are perfectly familiar to you; you have been talking and listening all your life. You know, for instance, that most people speak in short sentences, tending to overuse certain words. You know that whenever anyone gets the floor and a chance to tell a story or describe an incident he will almost always speak in a series of short sentences joined by "and"; this is of course a device to insure that his audience will have no chance to break in before he has finished his story. You know that in a conversation people do say the same things over and over; there is very little economy in spoken speech. There is a great deal of economy in written speech. Your characters will use short sentences, and will tell long stories only under exceptional circumstances, and even then only in the most carefully stylized and rhythmic language; nothing can dissolve a short story quite so effectively as some bore who takes up the middle of it with a long account of something that amuses him and no one else. A bore is a bore, on the page or off it. . . .

Now look at this device: "'I hate fresh asparagus,' she said to her kitchen clock, and found herself saying it again ten minutes later to Mrs. Butler in the grocery; 'I hate fresh asparagus,' she said, 'it always takes so long to cook.'" You are, at this moment, well into a conversation with Mrs. Butler; your reader, being a common-sense type, no doubt assumes that before the remark about asparagus your heroine and Mrs. Butler said good morning my aren't you out early and isn't that a charming hat. Your reader may also assume, if he is perceptive, that your heroine in some fashion turned away from her kitchen clock, got her hat and coat on, picked up her pocketbook, forgot her shopping list, and in some fashion either walked or drove or bicycled to the store. She is there, she is in the middle of a conversation with Mrs. Butler; not ten words ago she was at home talking to the clock. The transition has been relatively painless; your reader has been required to read only one sentence and get around one semicolon, and the asparagus remark has been repeated simply to tie together the two halves of the sentence.

Your characters in the story, surely, are going to be separate and widely differing people, even though they are not necessarily described to the reader. You yourself have some idea of what they are like and how they differ; there is, for instance, in almost everyone's mind, an essential difference between the hero and the heroine. They don't look alike, even if you are the only one who knows it; your reader will assume it; after all, he has seen people before. They don't dress alike, they don't sound alike. They have small individualities of speech, arising naturally out of their actions and their personalities and their work in the story. Suppose you are using three little girls talking together; you *could* distinguish them by saying that one wore a blue dress, the second had curly hair, and the third was on roller skates, but wouldn't it be simply better writing to identify them by their positions in the group of three; that is, making their actions and their conversations more meaningful because the girls are related to one another at once? They form a hierarchy: first there is a leader who does most of the talking, makes the plans, and provokes the action. The second must be subordinate, but not too much so; she does not initiate, but by following the leader encourages the leader into further action; she will disagree and perhaps even rebel up to a point. The third is of course the tagalong, the one left out when three is a crowd, and her actions and conversation are echoing and imitative of the other two, particularly the leader. The third character will throw her support to whichever of the other two seems stronger at the moment, and can thus, although a very minor character indeed, bring force to bear and influence action. Once three such characters are determined, the entire course of their conversation, no matter how trivial it might be in the story, is predetermined and strong. Once again: people in stories tend to talk in patterns. If your heroine is prepared to be so violent about fresh asparagus it would be reasonable to suppose that her conversation and opinions would generally be a little more emphatic than another character's. She would "adore that silly hat," for instance, or "die if that noise doesn't stop." She will carry out this positive manner in her actions; she will put out a cigarette, for instance, with forceful little poundings, she will set the table carelessly and noisily, but quickly, there will be no nonsense about her likes and dislikes. You might oppose to her a character who is uncertain, who lets cigarettes burn out in the ash tray, who rarely finishes a sentence or who will substitute a phrase like "*you* know" for a finished thought: "I usually carry an umbrella but sometimes . . . *you* know." "I guess it's time I left. I guess you're pretty busy?" Your character, remember, must not talk one way and act another, and can only outrage this consistency for a reason; a character who breaks out of a pattern is shocking and generally insane. . . .

✦

Now I want to say something about words artificially weighted; you can, and frequently must, make a word carry several meanings or messages in your story if you use the word right. This is a kind of shorthand. I once had occasion to send a heroine on a long journey during which she expressed her loneliness and lack of a home by imagining dream lives in various places she passed; this daydream is climaxed when at lunch she hears a little girl at a nearby table ask for her milk in a cup of stars; the lonely girl thinks that what she too is asking for is a cup of stars, and when she finally finds her home she will drink from a cup of stars. Later, when other characters are talking of their own comfort and security the lonely girl announces proudly that *she* has a cup of stars; this is by then not only recognizable as an outright lie, but a pathetic attempt to pretend that she is neither lonely nor defenseless. "Cup of stars" has become a shorthand phrase for all her daydreams. Notice, however, that once such a word or phrase has been given a weighting you cannot afford to use the word or phrase *without* the weighting; my lonely girl cannot refer idly to cups of stars anywhere else, because those words are carrying an extra meaning which must not be dissipated.

If you announce early in your story that your lady with the aversion to asparagus is wearing a diamond-and-ruby wrist watch your reader will be intrigued: here is a detail apparently not essential to the story and yet you thought it worthwhile to put it in; the reader will be watching to see what you are going to do with it. If you then turn up another character who is wearing a solid-gold wrist watch your reader will begin to wonder whether you are just queer for watches or whether this is going to amount to something in the story. You must satisfy his curiosity. If you then remark that the diamond-and-ruby wrist watch was a gift from an old boy friend of the lady's, the watch is then carrying something extra, and when at the end of the story she throws the watch at her husband's head she is throwing her old boy friend too. The reader is also going to have to know who gave the other fellow the solid-gold wrist watch and whose head *that* one is going to hit; nothing can be left suspended in mid-air, abandoned. If you start your story on a small boy going home to pick up his football so he can get into the game in the corner lot, and then let him fall into one adventure after another until the end of the story, your reader is going to come out of that story fighting mad unless he is told whether or not the boy got his football and whether he ever got back to the game.

*Part 2*

Now about this business of the beginning implying the ending, something which all the textbooks insist upon. You will actually find that if you keep your story tight, with no swerving from the proper path, it will curl up quite naturally at the end, provided you stop when you have finished what you have to say. One device, of course, is beginning and ending on what is essentially the same image, so that a story beginning, say, "It was a beautiful sunny day," might end, "The sun continued to beat down on the empty street." This is not a bad policy, although it can be limiting. There is no question but that the taut stretched quality of the good short story is pulled even tighter by such a construction. You can tie your story together, however, with similar devices—how about a story which opens on a lady feeding her cat, and ends on a family sitting down to dinner? Or a story which opens on your heroine crying and closes on her laughing? The beginning and ending should of course belong together; the ending must be implicit in the beginning, although there have been stories which were defeated because the author thought of a wonderful last line and then tried to write a story to go with it; this is not wrong, just almost impossible. I am not going to try to tell you how to set up a plot. Just remember that primarily, in the story and out of it, you are living in a world of people. A story must have characters in it; work with concrete rather than abstract nouns, and always dress your ideas immediately. Suppose you want to write a story about what you might vaguely think of as "magic." You will be hopelessly lost, wandering around formlessly in notions of magic and incantations; you will never make any forward progress at all until you turn your idea, "magic," into a person, someone who wants to do or make or change or act in some way. Once who have your first character you will of course need another to put into opposition, a person in some sense "anti-magic"; when both are working at their separate intentions, dragging in other characters as needed, you are well into your story. All you have to do then is write it, paying attention, please, to grammar and punctuation.

# Letters from Shirley Jackson
# to Leslie and Geraldine Jackson

## [ca. 18 December 1948]

My book of stories [*The Lottery*] is all wrong; they set it up in type all mixed up, and as a result of fixing that, the book will be delayed until April; they put through the copy for the jacket blurbs without consulting me, and made two serious errors and a number of embarrassing statements about me, which I am trying to have taken out now, and which will probably delay the book still further, and their advertising campaign, which they told me about proudly, is so excruciating that I will never show my face out of Vermont again. They are playing up *Lottery* as the most terrifying piece of literature ever printed, which is bad enough, and they have a long statement from Christopher Morley saying that *Lottery* scared him to death and will give ulcers to anyone who reads it, and they are working on things that say "Do you *dare* read this book" and except for "Lottery" it's a harmless little book of short stories. I feel like a fool. And the two stories I had at the *Woman's Home Companion* and *Mademoiselle*—they were both being considered, and looked very promising—both came back with glowing statements about how they were the best stories these people had ever read but of course they couldn't buy them. Which leaves me high and dry till the stories get to another magazine. And Stanley, who is marketing his new book, got offered a contract with a thousand dollar advance, by a fine publisher. The only catch is that they don't want to sign for six months or a year, until he's got more of it written. Which leaves us high and dry again, and which also brings me to the uncomfortable part of my letter, which is your asking how we stood financially. I was going to answer you

Shirley Jackson dated the letters from which these excerpts are taken simply with the day of the week and, in one case, the day of the month. The finder's guide to the Shirley Jackson Papers at the Library of Congress supplies the dates. I provide standard capitalization throughout, along with quotation marks and italics for titles. Used by permission of Sarah H. Stewart.

saying thank you and that we were doing fine, because Stanley was getting his advance and I was selling at least one story, but now that everything has bounced at once things are a little grim, and I would like to ask you if you can lend us a couple of hundred dollars; we will be all clear again in the spring (those stories have got to sell *some*where, even to a literary magazine for fifty bucks; Stanley is bound to get his advance *some*time) and some money now would make it possible to clear up everything that can't be postponed, and would also enable us to keep Mrs. Nadeau, who is our main luxury right now, and will of course be the first to go when things are tough. I can't fire her for a while and then get her back again, and I'd like to keep her for a while to see if I can't make it till some money comes through. Also I can't bear to fire the poor old thing, especially right before Christmas; if only she'd let us pay her in books! We suddenly find ourselves living very bohemian-ly, something we haven't done in quite a while—I charged all my Christmas presents at Gimbel's and got out fast, Stanley just barely managed to get money to the bank to cover the check we gave the hotel, and so on. We always manage to spend more than we've got, because money seems to come so easily, for stories and articles, and then suddenly something like this happens, and we realize that we live too well, and I think we both get scared. At any rate—not to prolong my tale of woe—if you *can* find it possible, we'd be terribly grateful, and if not—just before Christmas is a fine time, isn't it?—please don't worry about it. Everything always manages to come out all right somehow.

I am writing frantically, partly to have enough stuff out so that *some*thing will sell, and partly because in the last six months I have been saving most of the stuff I wanted to write until after Sally was born. So I am spending most of my time writing, and not doing much else.

## [11 April 1949]*

Dearest Mother and Pop,

Although there are a million things I want to ask you—like how you are, for instance— and whether you are all recovered and feeling fine again, and so on—I am so excited by my book that I've got to tell you about that even before anything else! You know, it comes out this Wednesday, the thirteenth, and by now, two days before publication, they've sold more copies than they did of the novel, and are talking seriously about passing any records so far for short story sales. They've had a second printing

---

* Finder's guide gives date as March 1949, but internal evidence suggests this date.

before publication, have two English publishers competing for the English rights, have featured reviews in the *Times* and *Tribune*, including an extra one in the *Times*, daily as well as Sunday, and an Associated Press review that says I am author of the week and that *Lottery* is a work of genius and the publishing event of the year! There has been a lot of publicity about it, mainly because of the story "Lottery," so that featuring it in the book was probably very wise of them, although I opposed it. They've turned down three or four requests to reprint the story itself, because they are very optimistic about having the whole book reprinted as a pocketbook before the end of the year. Their publicity plan, which is smart although acutely embarrassing, got me down to New York for one day last week to be interviewed by a very nice man from the Associated Press, who said that he understood I was a specialist in black magic and would I please tell him all about it. Fortunately he had just bought me two drinks, so I was able to tell him, very fluently indeed, about black magic and incantations and the practical application of witchcraft to everyday life, most of which I remembered out of various mystery stories. He kept telling me I was the greatest writer in the world and I kept giving him this sick smile and saying thank you very much may I have another drink please. I kept thinking what a fool I was making of myself and then when he got up to go I said very politely that I hoped his newspaper would like the interview and he said if it worked out right it ought to hit about two hundred newspapers. All I can think of is some of my idiotic statements in two hundred newspapers.

Also, the government—*don't* ask me why—has bought fifteen hundred copies to put in all the army and navy libraries. Joseph Henry Jackson in San Francisco, who is for some reason working his head off for me, is apparently holding bookstores up at the point of a gun and making them order thousands of copies. I think he thinks we're related. I have already passed the point in sales where the advance is paid off, and all this is gravy. From two thousand copies on I've been making money. They have six thousand in print now, with their two printings, and calmly expect to sell them all, although the novel only sold about three thousand. Moreover, they expect to get rid of those odd thousands of copies of the novel now; they've had two requests from reviewers for it, saying they missed it before and *Lottery* has gotten them interested in it. The publishers haven't put a cent into it yet; all this is honest free publicity, although after it is published they are going to put a thousand dollars into preliminary advertising, and then more if it looks like the book is going well.

You can imagine how I feel, in the middle of all this. Sort of small, and scared, and desperately anxious to go up and tap J. H. Jackson on the shoulder and say listen, mister, the book is terrible, honest. Because it is, of course. I read it a few days ago and it's flashy and sensational and all fixed up to sell. And every advance review we've seen is favorable, although they keep referring to Saki, and Truman Capote, and John Collier, none of them writers I admire particularly, as people of whom the stories are reminiscent. And they're all cashing in quite shamelessly on the press the devil has been getting recently, including half a dozen respectable books, mostly novels, which have come out in the last six months, and which use the devil as a character. Also, there have been several odd witchcraft cases in the papers, and it all mounts up into a general interest in magic and such, which Farrar and Straus are exploiting, with me in the middle.

## [13 June 1949]

The things that have been happening start with *Lottery*'s being quite a success; it's sold five thousand copies, which beats all books of short stories for just ever so long, thanks to people like J. H. Jackson—are you *sure* he isn't a cousin?—who keep plugging it and mentioning it and building sales in California, although I expect you and Pop are accounting for a few hundred a week. Anyway I've been lined up for interviews and photographs in everything from *Time* on—wasn't that picture a stinker, though? That was the one he wanted to take in the lobby of the Algonquin hotel, and I balked. I've been interviewed by the *Times* and the *Tribune* and the Associated Press, and all the nonsense I told you about, that the publishers made up, is turning out to be wonderful stuff because the book is selling, so I have to tell people all this nonsense all over again, because the publicity man from the publishers is sitting over me if I say any of it wrong.

Anyway on the strength of *Lottery* I sold three stories in a row to *Good Housekeeping* and we paid all our bills including the income tax. And we bought a television set which was the silliest thing we ever did, and the children love it and so do all our friends, just like the ads say. And there is a man who wants to make "Lottery" into an opera, and the *Reader's Digest* has picked up my "Third Baby" thing, and something called *Omnibook* wants "Lottery," and the *Best Short Stories of 1949* does too. The agent turned down two people who wanted to make it into a play, and accepted the offer of an English publisher to bring it out in London this fall, followed, if there is any interest, by the novel next spring. If Joseph Henry Jackson writes two more articles about it Farrar and Straus will put it into a third edition. The silliest thing of all is that my agent's asking price is now a thousand bucks a story for me, and then she keeps me so busy with interviews I don't have time to write. Except the *New York Times* asked me very politely to review a book for them and I said sure. Naturally, I'm having a wonderful time being fussed over, and I love it, but I feel like an awful fool most of the time.

Except for one other thing, that can wind up the literary news for today. The one other thing is that surprisingly enough, Stanley is not teaching but I am. Stanley turned down the college offer of a job because they wanted him on a five year contract and he only wants to teach alternate years, and the next week there was a grand fight—completely unconnected!—in the literature division and two of the faculty quit in the middle of the year. One of them was the short story man, and they asked me to fill in for him for a month, so again I said sure, and here I am teaching short story, and I love that, too. I have two classes a week and the girls and I talk very seriously about the Art of Writing and then they ask me very timidly where they can sell their stories and I tell them there's nothing to it. I took the job with two conditions—one, a hundred bucks a week, and the other, that the college president learn to square dance. If he doesn't learn by this coming Saturday I quit.

## [ca. 9 November 1949]

I quite agree with you about the recent stories. They are written simply for money, and the reason they sound so bad is that those magazines won't buy good ones, but deliberately seek out bad stuff because they say their audiences want it. I simply figure that at a thousand bucks a story, I can't afford to try to change the state of popular fiction today, and since they will buy as much of it as I write, I do one story a month, and spend the rest of the time working on my new novel or on other stories. Stuff like the "Son and Bully" story turns out like that because I won't write love stories or junk about gay young married couples, and they won't take ordinary children stories, and this sort of thing is a compromise between their notions and mine, and is unusual enough so that I am the only person I know of who is doing it. That's why I can sell them. In addition, the fan mail on such stories is going up, and I am now getting long letters asking for advice on bringing up children, letters which I answer with the statement that if I knew enough to give advice my children would be better than they are. As a result, it's keeping a name for me, building up a following, opening new markets with plenty of money, and helping support us while I take my time with the novel. I haven't done much writing this summer—excluding one popular story a month—but am back at work on the novel [*Hangsaman*] now that the ball season is over. *Road through the Wall* comes out in a twenty-five cent edition in January, advertised, I am afraid, the way the reprint people are advertising all the legitimate novels they reprint—changing the name, putting a lurid cover on the book, and playing it up as some fantastic love-among-the-haystacks routine. They've done it to everyone, and I notice that they insisted on having the final say on cover design and advertising with mine, so I suppose I'll be having the same thing. They expect a sale of seventy-five thousand, which seems fantastic. The stories you repudiate are selling at a furious rate abroad, two of the *Good Housekeeping* ones having turned up in England, and one other in Sweden. None of this means much money now, of course, and the sixty pounds my English publisher still owes me has stopped looking like as much as it did, but still the things are building up to what will eventually be a regular reprint income.

# Shirley Jackson's Outlines for Stories

## ["Elizabeth"]

The novel is the story of one climactic day in the life of a woman who has figuratively leagued herself with the devil, and her figurative destruction. The story parallels in detail the discovery and condemnation of a witch, and the parallel will be stated in the title and chapter headings of texts from witchcraft cases at each stage.

Elizabeth is in her early thirties, from a small upstate [New York] village, her mother recently dead. For the last ten years [she] has been having an affair with her employer, having "made a pact with the devil," and has raised herself to a prominent job in his small vanity publishing company, which specializes in gypping ambitious young authors. Her witchcraft thus gives her a certain power over others, through the publishing, and a precarious security through her relationship with her employer. Both of these are threatened suddenly with the appearance of a new employee, a young girl who has attracted the interest of [Elizabeth's] employer. In one day, proceeding partly from an inevitable sequence of events and partly from Elizabeth's own sense of guilt and ominous significance of events growing through the day, her witchcraft is discovered and she is destroyed.

CHAPTER 1: HER NEIGHBORS THREATEN AND ACCUSE HER: Her landlady makes a crack about a man's cigar ashes in her room; the sodajerk in the drug store talks of his writing, she suggests her publication, and he says he has heard it is a gyp; someone on the bus makes a scene exposing her as a domineering woman.

CHAPTER 2: SHE IS LEFT TO BE WATCHED: Her morning in the office, with her ineffectual campaign against her rival, the new girl.

Shirley Jackson gave both outlines the heading "novel"; the summary of "Elizabeth" has no title in Jackson's manuscript, although she titled the other manuscript "I Know Who I Love." Both outlines are in the Shirley Jackson Papers, Library of Congress. Used by permission of Sarah H. Stewart.

143

CHAPTER 3: SHE APPEALS TO THE DEVIL FOR ASSISTANCE: Lunch with her boss, unpleasant tension and nagging.

CHAPTER 4: THE SUMMONS: Back in her office, she receives a message from a couple from her home town, old friends of her family. She calls them, they ask her to meet them after theatre that night, and, to impress them, she names the back room of a literary bar.

CHAPTER 5: SHE PRESENTS HERSELF TO HER TORTURERS: She has the early evening to kill and calls another old home town friend, a boy she had known in high school, who is now a successful writer, and takes him up on a standing dinner invitation. He says that his kid sister is in from college to be entertained, she forces herself in on the party.

CHAPTER 6: SHE IS HEMMED IN: Afternoon at the office: she attempts to consolidate her position in order to be able to face her old friend as a successful and happy business woman.

CHAPTER 7: MEETING WITH THE TORTURERS: She goes home, dresses, and her friend and his kid sister arrive to pick her up; they have a preliminary drink and everything goes badly.

CHAPTER 8: THE TORTURE BEGINS: They go to a big Broadway night club. Everything that happens is humiliating and unbearable; she has a severe headache.

CHAPTER 9: DISCOVERY OF THE WITCH'S MARK: In the powder room while she is washing the kid sister sees the entwined initials inside her ring.

CHAPTER 10: THE TORTURE GOES ON: The kid dissatisfied, they go to a jazz club. The headache is worse, the young cheerfulness unbearable. She has to leave to get to her appointment, leaves them there having a good time and glad to see her go, taxis to the bar where she is to meet her other friends.

CHAPTER 11: THE TRIAL: She meets the middle-aged home town couple, has a friendly talk with them that exposes her complete failure. They get serious, propose that she go back to the home town to keep house for her father. She refuses.

[CHAPTER] 12[:] Aaron [This inserted note is undeveloped.]

CHAPTER 13: THE DEVIL FORSAKES HER: She gets the idea that she can salvage everything, decides that she will plead with her boss to make his publication legitimate, get a divorce and marry her, etc. She goes out to the phone to call her boss for a conversation late that evening. On the way to the phone she sees him at the bar with the office rival; he says that they worked late, stopped in for a drink. She talks to them for a moment, then goes back to the old couple.

CHAPTER 14: CONFESSION AND SENTENCE: She admits total failure, and tells her friends she will go back and keep house for her father.

CHAPTER 15: DEATH IN PRISON: She knows it is for good.

## "I Know Who I Love"

This is to be the story of a strangely haunted woman, whose life becomes a cheap tragedy because of her anxiety to be an artist in the sense in which she sees art, as irresponsibility and lack of discipline. The first section of the book describes her in the light of her early life with a narrow and strict mother and father, her first awkward love affair, and her constant humiliations at school and at home. The second, longest section of the novel, set in a New England farming community where she is living with her husband, takes her through the inevitable conflict between her dream life and its reality, which ends in her complete defeat, and the last section, which is to be only about ten pages long, runs quickly through the rest of her life.

The conflict of Catharine, the main character, can be expressed in several different ways. On one hand, it is the disagreement between her desire to live outside a conventional world (because she has been unhappy in it) and her inability to live constructively without a set of conventions; or, in another aspect, it is the conflict between the unexciting, dreary God of her father's religion, and the devil, which becomes everything her father disapproves of. Finally, in her New England home, God and the conventions become associated with her husband and his farming friends, and freedom and the devil with several people whom Catharine gathers around her, the most important being a boy from a neighboring farm whom Catharine sees as her solution. She attempts finally to resolve her difficulty by destroying the enemy, with the unconscious assistance of the farm boy, but fails and is forced to resign herself to the complete impossibility of freedom.

Oscar, Catharine's husband, is the second important character; he is allied with all that his wife is against, the work of the farm, the neighbors, the quiet, hard-working life, and he likes being allied with it. He and his idol, the most important farmer in the district, are the instruments of Catharine's defeat.

Other characters will be the boy, Jimmie, who is going to grow up to be just like Oscar, but still has vague ideas of something better; Oscar's friend, the important farmer, whose love for his land and particularly his timber is the greatest force in his life, leading him to the tolerance and understanding which confuse Catharine; and the countryside which Catharine is bucking, the lean, slightly uninspired New Hampshire farms, with their set ways and regular crops, and the men and women who disliked Catharine because she was an alien.

The first section, on Catharine's early life, is written without chronological order, but with related events together, because it is the way Catharine remembers it. It is merely an attempt to sketch out some of the various threads which led Catharine to her later conflict. The second section will be told in chronological order, an account of Catharine's life from the time she came to New Hampshire until the failure of her plans. This period, covering about three months' time, will be the central part of the book and the longest.

*Part 3*

# THE CRITICS

# Introduction

The relatively small number of secondary bibliographic entries in this volume reflects a general lack of attention to Shirley Jackson's work. Not surprisingly, "The Lottery" has elicited the largest response. Even these essays, however, are often note-length and fail to address Jackson's broader themes. Half of the selections herein are excerpts from some of the fullest treatments of "The Lottery." Also reprinted are three pieces that focus on several of Jackson's lesser-known stories, including the excellent "The Tooth." These essays range from biographical and myth criticism to Marxist and feminist approaches.

The many interviews Judy Oppenheimer conducted in the course of her research for *Private Demons: The Life of Shirley Jackson* (1988) provided biographical material available in no other commentaries on Jackson's fiction. Among the short stories to which Oppenheimer alludes are "Janice," "The Intoxicated," and "Got a Letter from Jimmy." She devotes several pages in her twelfth chapter to "The Lottery," frequently citing Jackson's "Biography of a Story." My excerpt from *Private Demons* mentions five of Jackson's other early stories from the 1940s; Oppenheimer's explanation of the "many levels" of "Like Mother Used to Make" is especially informative.

The next two selections introduce opposing concerns of Jackson's work, the attraction of home and the flight from home. James Egan in "Sanctuary: Shirley Jackson's Domestic and Fantastic Parables" (1989) argues that much of her writing is "either the expression of an idyllic domestic vision or the inversion of that vision into the fantastic and Gothic." Egan's essay merits a complete reading, but I omit many of his remarks on Jackson's semi-autobiographical family books, *Life among the Savages* and *Raising Demons*, along with his analysis of three of her novels, *The Sundial*, *The Haunting of Hill House*, and *We Have Always Lived in the Castle*. The balance of the essay discusses several short stories, among them "The Daemon Lover," "The Beautiful Stranger," and "Louisa, Please Come Home." Of special interest is Egan's application of Tzvetan Todorov's remarks on fantastic discourse to the bizarre effect of dislocation in some of Jackson's fiction.

Richard Pascal's "'Farther than Samarkand': The Escape Theme in Shirley Jackson's 'The Tooth'" (1982) is reprinted in full. Pascal's introductory paragraphs suggest that, for Jackson, "the fantasy of running away from it all was a constant fictional preoccupation." He points out that, not only in "The Lottery" but also in "The Summer People," "A Day in the Jungle," and "I Know Who I Love," Jackson's protagonists are oppressed by their families or larger communities. I disagree with the conclusion that Jim in "The Tooth" is Clara's escapist fantasy, yet, as Pascal says, the story is more disturbing than "a straightforward Freudian line of analysis would allow."

Helen E. Nebeker's "'The Lottery': Symbolic Tour de Force" (1974) is the earliest of this section's three excerpted commentaries on "The Lottery." I omit several paragraphs in which Nebeker summarizes much previous commentary about the story and explores the symbolism of the villagers' names. The passages reprinted below develop other "symbolic undercurrents" that draw us "toward the ultimate horror, where everything will fuse." Nebeker's emphasis on ritualistic aspects of the lottery (the solstice setting, the box, and the three-legged stool) is related to later discussions by Barbara Allen and James M. Gibson.

Nebeker was the first critic to call attention to the "patriarchal order" of the village, a central issue in Fritz Oehlschlaeger's and Peter Kosenko's discussions. Reprinted is a segment of "The Stoning of Mistress Hutchinson: Meaning and Context in 'The Lottery'" (1988), in which Oehlschlaeger views the story as "the depiction of a patriarchal society's way of controlling female sexuality." The reader may wish to consult the complete version of the essay for the parallels Oehlschlaeger draws between Tessie Hutchinson's situation and those of the woman accused of adultery in the Bible, Hardy's Tess of the D'Urbervilles, and Anne Hutchinson. I also omit his discussion of the similarities between "The Lottery" and Jackson's first novel, *The Road through the Wall*. The excerpt does include Oehlschlaeger's comments on the story's pitting of woman against woman, a conflict that can also be found in several stories I discuss in Part 1 (i.e., "Trial by Combat," "Flower Garden," and "Men with Their Big Shoes"). The final selection is an excerpt from Kosenko's "A Marxist/Feminist Reading of Shirley Jackson's 'The Lottery'" (1985), which emphasizes women's low standing in the capitalist structure of the village.

Although I question some of Oehlschlaeger's and Kosenko's conclusions, their essays provide a necessary focus on a common figure in Jackson's short and long fiction—the powerless female. The contributions of these last two critics must be weighed against Judy Oppenheimer's contention that Jackson "was no feminist. Her vision was personal, not political, and she would have strenuously resisted any effort to view her work in that way, even if she had survived into an era in which the personal had become the political" (*Private Demons*, 164). On the other hand, as Oppenheimer reminds us, Jackson's protagonists "are invariably women, and strangers in a land not theirs" (164).

# Judy Oppenheimer

[Shirley Jackson's] short-story writing proceeded apace, thanks in part to [Stanley Edgar Hyman's] insistence, and she was getting better and better. No longer was she simply transcribing from reality, as she often had in college; now she was becoming adept at taking the bare bones of reality and giving them a twist, infusing them with some of the fears and horrors and distortions swirling around in her own mind. It was not unlike witchcraft—you mixed a brew, threw in the people and incidents you decided on, and used your darker powers to charge the atmosphere with tension, control mood, set destiny. It was also a powerful medium for revenge, a way to control the final outcome. Her hand was growing surer all the time.

It did not, of course, hurt that Stanley was now at *The New Yorker*. In 1943 her stories began appearing there for the first time; for many years this would be her chief market. No fewer than four of her stories appeared there in 1943, another four in 1944, an almost unheard-of feat for a new writer. Her second *New Yorker* story, "Come Dance with Me in Ireland," published in May 1943, was even included in the collection *The Best American Short Stories, 1944*. Shirley was on a roll.

Most of her stories were set in a world of suburban conventionality—a familiar world, Geraldine's world, the world she had grown up in. But under Shirley's hand, that world became charged with something darker. In "After You, My Dear Alphonse," a young boy brings a black friend home for lunch; his genteel mother tries to handle it "charitably," offering the boy used clothes, carefully questioning him, revealing herself damningly with every word. In "Come Dance with Me in Ireland," three women bustle around, aglow with pride in their own virtue, fixing lunch for a tramp—who then insults them and leaves—"I never served bad liquor to my guests."[1]

It was Shirley's genius to be able to paint homey, familiar scenes like this, and then imbue them with evil—or, more correctly, allow a reader to see the evil that had been obvious to her all along, even in sunny Burlingame. One felt the presence of a grinning skull behind the cover of

From *Private Demons: The Life of Shirley Jackson* (New York: G. P. Putnam's Sons, 1988), 101–3. © 1988 by Judy Oppenheimer. Reprinted by permission of the Putnam Publishing Group.

surface gentility, homemade biscuits, shining floors, and this is what made the tales so disturbing. Shirley never had to search for exotic locales or strange characters. You see, her stories seemed to nudge lightly, insistently at the reader, it was right here, right in front of you all the time. Her earliest published stories did not yet play with the nature of reality itself—but that would come soon.

She liked to use odd pieces of real life in her stories, and her friends enjoyed bringing her anecdotes for possible inclusion. Once Frank Orenstein ran into a little girl in Brooklyn who had found a human leg lying on the street; he relayed this to Shirley right away and was pleased, later, to see "his leg" incorporated into a story, "Pillar of Salt."[2] Ben Zimmerman and Taissa Kellman, who lived in apartments next to each other, became the subjects of another tale, "Like Mother Used to Make." The story is of a rather fussy young man who plans a dinner complete with cherry pie for his female neighbor, in his neat, well-appointed apartment. After dinner, another man comes to visit the woman—and she allows him to think the apartment, as well as the pie, is hers. The man settles down, impressed with her homemaking skills; the actual owner, horrified and helpless, finally leaves.

"That was Ben—it was so Ben, specifically, that she actually asked permission before she published it," said Frank. Ben Zimmerman confirmed it. The story, he said, grew out of an incident in which Stanley and Taissa were sitting in his apartment and refused to leave even though he was expecting a guest. "I had to actually leave myself and meet my guest somewhere else." He did not mind, in fact enjoyed, appearing in Shirley's story.

Taissa, however, who was not informed beforehand, was less than pleased. "I thought: unfair. It made out that Ben knew all about cooking and I had taken advantage of him to impress the guy. It was the other way around: I was the cook. It was really kind of an act of anger to me. I thought she was more approving of me than that. I was fairly sexy-looking, had a lot of guys—maybe this was what Shirley felt resentment about." Certainly it had not escaped Shirley's quick eye that Stanley, too, appreciated Taissa's good looks. "She could never get over the fact that Stanley was so attracted to good-looking women. It was a constant irritant; all day long there was this barb in her flesh. But this was Stanley—you bought the package with Stanley."

Taissa did remember "sitting around listening to a lot of Shirley's stories being created, hacked out, fought out with Stanley, seeing a lot of things from around us being integrated into the stories. It was fun, but I think if

I'd known about the story about Benny and me, I would have confronted her: How dare you make me the villainess?"

The story then had many levels—it was a sly poke at Ben, a slap at Taissa, a disturbing little tale altogether. Yet somehow it was more disturbing than the mere facts seemed to warrant. The reader was left with a terrible unease—had the girl taken over the clean apartment forever? But things like that don't happen—do they? And suddenly, the comforting limits of the real world had dissolved, and the reader was left standing at a misty crossroads, gazing into an abyss—other worlds, other possibilities, unnamed terrors. This was Shirley's true territory. It was where she had always lived, and now, in her writing, she was able to convey it to others.

As time went on, she drew more and more on her own wide store of fears for her stories, from the specific—dentists, closed spaces, overhangs, traffic—to the general—chaos, loss of identity, disintegration. In "Pillar of Salt," a woman becomes agonizingly conscious of the decay, the rotting structure, of the city around her. At last she calls her husband; she has realized she is unable to cross the street. In "The Beautiful Stranger," a woman perceives her husband, suddenly, as someone completely new; the world itself seems new, fraught with fresh hope, until she is caught, standing on a suburban street, unable even to recognize her house: "Somewhere a house which was hers, with the beautiful stranger inside, and she lost out here," Shirley ended.[3]

They were personal fears, but through her skill they expanded to envelop the reader. Suddenly they were not the obscure terrors of one unknown woman but the reader's own, pressing in on him. Her stories broke down the barrier between reader and author so the reader himself felt the icy touch of panic, the sense of unreality. She wove her fears and visions into a web she flung out at the world; it clung there, delicate, invisible, but tenacious. Not every reader appreciated the experience of being drawn into Shirley's world, but no one escaped unaffected by it.

## Notes

1. "After You, My Dear Alphonse" and "Come Dance with Me in Ireland" were both originally published in *The New Yorker* in 1943 and later incorporated into her collection *The Lottery*.

2. Frank Orenstein interview.

3. "Pillar of Salt" was originally published in *Mademoiselle* in 1948 and later incorporated into *The Lottery*. "The Beautiful Stranger," written in 1946, was published in *Come Along with Me*.

# James Egan

Shirley Jackson is probably best known for her tales of latent evil and dark rituals, notably "The Lottery" (1948), and for such overtly Gothic pieces as *The Haunting of Hill House* (1959). Yet her range was considerable, including absurdist short stories, psychological thrillers, and two works of biographical domestic humor, *Life among the Savages* (1953) and *Raising Demons* (1957). Critical consensus about Jackson seems to hold that she had mastered both the familial and the macabre and could incorporate into each idiom a wit that was at times wry and self-deprecating, at times disquieting. One of her favorite but least discussed motifs is the domestic, the familial, and the rituals associated with it. I propose to argue that a substantial part of her work may be interpreted as either the expression of an idyllic domestic vision or the inversion of that vision into the fantastic and Gothic. Jackson controls the tenor of her domestic and fantastic parables primarily by her sophisticated use of wit, irony, and paradox and by juxtaposing the premises of her domestic tales to those of her fantastic ones. An awareness of Jackson's treatment of the familial and its opposite not only allows us to examine the ways in which she transforms domestic into horrific, but the evolution of her world view as well. . . .

Both before and after Jackson defines her domestic ideals in *Life among the Savages* and *Raising Demons*, much of her serious fiction revolved around the motif of the domestic—the creation, maintenance, and destruction of the familial idyll. Her characters often search for domestic sanctuary, and the places those searches lead to, the complications and illusions they set in motion, are a mainstay of her work. Versions of the sanctuary range widely, from the realistic to the fantastic and Gothic. In contrast to her later tales, "Men with Their Big Shoes," "Elizabeth," "I Know Who I Love," and "The Little House" could be classified as grim and sobering, but realistic just the same. "Men with Their Big Shoes" involves an aging and cynical maid, Mrs. Anderson, a disruptive invader from an unhappy marriage, who poisons the well of domestic bliss for her employer, young Mrs. Hart. A sort of domestic bully, Mrs. Anderson tries to force her employer to accept her version of domesticity, dropping hints about the

From "Sanctuary: Shirley Jackson's Domestic and Fantastic Parables," *Studies in Weird Fiction* 6 (Fall 1989): 15–24. Reprinted by permission of James Egan, Professor of English, the University of Akron, Akron, Ohio.

loose habits and moral undependability of husbands. She treats Mrs. Hart as a daughter, a daughter who should provide Mrs. Anderson with a place to live in case her husband throws her out of her own home. The innocent, trusting, romantically inclined younger woman is constantly prevailed upon to suspect the notion of marital happiness she had been living by. "Elizabeth" recounts the story of an unmarried New York professional woman who works as an editor in a marginal literary agency. Elizabeth cannot help but reflect on her drab, dreary apartment and office and dreams of making both more comfortable and homelike. She has a nominal romantic relationship with Robbie, her employer, but the relationship makes her feel as frustrated and depressed as her living quarters do, so much so that she reacts with hostility toward Daphne, the young secretary Robbie has recently hired. Though she seems to have given up on Robbie as a potential husband, Elizabeth cannot refrain from jealousy over Daphne as a potential rival. Faced with a shrunken daily life, devoid of domestic bliss or even comfort, she frantically makes a date with Jim Harris, a writer whose work she had previously handled. The story ends inconclusively, but images of escape and romance color Elizabeth's perception of Harris; she sees the possible realization of her dreams of the conventional and domestic.

"I Know Who I Love" details the domestic misery of a woman named Catharine, daughter of a prim minister of a father who regarded her as a "trap" and "an unnecessary expense."[1] She endures cruel treatment by her high school peers and eventually shoulders the burden of a hectoring, dying mother. Because of Catharine's wretched home life, her feelings of rejection and her parents' suspicious treatment of Aaron, the only man who showed her attention and affection, she faces a sad, empty life in New York City. Catharine has been so badly damaged by her upbringing that she simply accepts her present lot. Family failures have set the tone for her misery. Elizabeth, protagonist of "The Little House," has apparently found a domestic sanctuary, a tidy home left to her by a dead aunt. When she first arrives to take possession of the house, she feels the thrill of promise (*CAWM*, 173) and envisions rearranging the house to suit her. But Elizabeth's idyll quickly fades. Two neighbors, the elderly, maiden Dolson sisters, pay a "friendly" visit and suggest that her aunt was murdered, speculating about how the murderer might have gotten in. Elizabeth tries desperately to return to her first vision of the little house as a sanctuary but she becomes nervous and panics. Her dream has been shattered by rudimentary human evil—the gossip and meddling of the Dolson sisters.

Some searches for the domestic and familial lead Jackson's characters into the realm of the fantastic, resulting in tales which contain what Tzvetan Todorov and others consider the primary themes of fantastic discourse: metamorphosis; "Pan-determinism" (special causality); "fragmentation and multiplication of the personality; the collapse of the limits between subject and object . . . and the transformation of time and space."[2] Given the variety of fantastic variations of the familial theme, Lenemaja Friedman's claim that Jackson will occasionally introduce a fantastic twist to dislocate the normal amounts to a substantial understatement.[3] An early story, "Like Mother Used to Make," displays a bizarre domestic metamorphosis. Fussy David and sloppy Marcia, two neighbors in a city apartment building, arrange to have dinner at David's, a dinner he prepares with care in his tidy, comfortable, "private" flat, a place he considers a retreat from a "discourteous" outside world.[4] Marcia's apartment appears very much the opposite of his—disheveled, carelessly decorated, unharmonious. As the two sit down to dinner, they are disturbed by a knock on Marcia's door: Mr. Harris, one of Marcia's co-workers, has dropped by unexpectedly, and she invites him to dinner. Harris apparently thinks that David's apartment is Marcia's and that she has prepared the meal. Neither David nor Marcia disturbs the illusion. David proceeds to wait on the two and eventually serves dessert, but still Harris refuses to leave, settling in instead. Finally, David leaves his own apartment, walks over to Marcia's and begins to tidy it up. David's obsession with domesticity has led to a bizarre role reversal, a transformation. He becomes the "homey" Marcia the real Marcia refuses to become. Having had his own domesticity interrupted, he begins to create it again in a different location, a fantastic reversal of stereotypical male and female familial roles.

"The Beautiful Stranger" represents a more radical departure into the fantastic. As Margaret waits at the train for her husband to return from a business trip, she experiences an "intimation of strangeness" and an "odd sense of lost time" (*CAWM*, 58). At first, the man who steps from the train seems to be her husband, but she quickly comes to realize that he is not. A fantastic transformation of time and space has occurred, for the stranger knows things about Margaret and her daily life that he could not reasonably have known (Todorov, 120, 65). Yet she welcomes him and finds sanctuary in his mannerisms and plans for their life. The fantastic comforts her for awhile but another fantastic reversal occurs at the story's end. After going to town to buy a present for the stranger she returns to her home to face disorientation and confusion. She cannot identify her house and ends up alone and alienated, again caught up in a fantastic reversal of domesticity.[5] Fantastic motifs likewise surface in "The Daemon Lover," another early short piece, featuring an anonymous thirty-four-year-old woman who waits anxiously for her fiancé, James Harris, to arrive on their wedding day. She lives alone, without sanctuary, and Harris has offered her the prized domestic ritual of marriage. She waits but he does not arrive, so she sets out in search of him. Hostile strangers offer no help, constantly rebuffing the increasingly desperate woman. Eventually she gets a small clue and goes to an apartment where Harris was rumored to have lived. She knocks and hears voices but no one answers the door at his alleged last address. Her needs and illusions have sent her in pursuit of an illusion. Was there ever a James Harris? Have the limits between subject (her) and object (him) collapsed? The lines between real and imagined, self and Other, may have vanished. She reacts with confusion and anxiety to what she considers an impossibility, a predicament not uncommon in fantastic tales (R. Jackson, 30). The woman's yearning for the domestic may also have made her the victim of a metamorphosis in which her lover has become her torturer, leading her on an odyssey of humiliation.

Absurdity surfaces in the plight of Louisa in "Louisa, Please Come Home." Louisa feels stifled by the familial, by what she feels are the constraints of wealth, normality, and social status, so she runs away from home on her sister's wedding day. She likes her new freedom in a new city, Amityville, but ironically she quickly moves into another domestic sanctuary, a boarding house presided over by the motherly Mrs. Peacock. Paul, a friend when she lived with her family, finds Louisa and returns her to her parents, who have broadcast pleas on the radio for her to come back. Metamorphosis occurs when she confronts her parents: they don't recognize her. Louisa has been transformed into a stranger, even though she answers correctly several questions that, presumably, only she could have answered. Ironically, though she'd like to stay home now, her parents accuse her of a hoax, an experience they've suffered through several times in the past year. Jackson suspends the laws of probability here to suggest that Louisa's identity and personality have been dissolved; her parents are confounded by the illusion of a multiple personality, when, in fact, their missing daughter stands before them. In "Beautiful Stranger," "The Daemon Lover," and "Louisa, Please Come Home," Jackson's light domestic wit has become dark, relentless, ironic humor. She presents victims who are tricked and trapped. If comedy occurs here, the joke is on these unfortunate women. In Louisa's case a bizarre double reversal occurs—first she tricks her family by deserting them, and then they return the favor....

As we have seen, throughout her career Shirley Jackson examined the ways in which the ideals of the domestic and familial were created, nurtured, attacked from various quarters, escaped from, weakened, parodied, and destroyed. Particularly in *Life among the Savages* and *Raising Demons* she used the cathartic power of her humor to support her vision of a nurturing domestic world. Wit and the self-deprecating comic were a means of preserving order, of coping with life's daily disruptions, of avoiding entanglement in narcissistic illusions. Her comic domestic perspective concentrated on physical rather than psychological problems and troubling issues were largely excluded from that perspective. Even in her early short fiction, however, dissonance occurs. Characters can be found in bleak cosmetic settings, cut off from family love and support, or eager to escape from domestic lives which stifle them. Occasionally these characters simply accept the lack of the familial, and occasionally they reach out for domestic sanctuaries. As Jackson's fiction evolved over time, some of her protagonists reached desperately for the domestic tranquility absent from or distorted in their lives, and their yearning for sanctuary led them into the fantastic or Gothic, into situations which proved to be open-ended, unpredictable, paradoxical, and illusory. These searches lack the regenerative wit of the chronicles. If they contain humor at all, it tends to be dark and ironic, with the searchers the victims of cosmic jokes in many cases. That Jackson's world view darkened as she continued to write may be suggested by the way in which she evokes terror—by treating her domestic vision absurdly and ironically, fantastically, Gothically. Her readers have long been aware of her suspicions about the normative or "outside" world, and she certainly attacks the outside with full force in *Hill House* and *Castle*, apparently offering up the alternative of Gothic sanctuary.[6] Yet these "sanctuaries" are no more than intricate illusions built on parodies and reversals of her domestic perspective. We must not hurriedly conclude that Jackson necessarily advocates the alternatives to the normative world presented in these last two novels, for her Gothic sanctuaries are nihilistic, denials of escape from the Gothic maze, or endless processions of destructive illusions. Instead, she tempts us with the tantalizing paradox of the Gothic sanctuary, a paradox which sets up the reader for essentially the same metaphysical pratfalls several of her characters ultimately take.

## Notes

1. *Come Along with Me: Part of a Novel, Sixteen Stories, and Three Lectures*, ed. Stanley Edgar Hyman (New York: Viking, 1968), 46; hereafter cited in text.

2. Tzvetan Todorov, *The Fantastic: A Structural Approach to a Literary Genre,* trans. Richard Howard (Cleveland: Case Western Reserve University Press, 1973), 120, and Rosemary Jackson, *Fantasy: The Literature of Subversion* (New York: Methuen, 1981), 81; both hereafter cited in the text.

3. Lenemaja Friedman, *Shirley Jackson* (Boston: Twayne Publishers, 1975), 72.

4. *The Lottery and Other Stories* (New York: Farrar, Straus & Giroux, 1982), 29; hereafter cited in text.

5. See Eric S. Rabkin, *The Fantastic in Literature* (Princeton: Princeton University Press, 1976), 73 and 146 on fantastic reversals.

6. Stuart C. Woodruff, "The Real Horror Elsewhere: Shirley Jackson's Last Novel," *Southwest Review* 52 (1967): 153.

# Richard Pascal

To attentive readers of Shirley Jackson's work, it came as no surprise to discover that the novel she was working on at the time of her death was to be about a middle-class woman who has abandoned her lifelong home town and former identity. "I erased my old name and took my initials off everything, and I got on the train and left,"[1] says the heroine of "Come Along With Me," articulating the desire felt by many other Jackson protagonists to liberate themselves from communal and domestic obligations and referents. For the best-selling authoress of *Life Among the Savages* and *Raising Demons*, those sprightly autobiographical chronicles which reassuringly make light of the anxieties of bourgeois domestic life, the fantasy of running away from it all was a constant fictional preoccupation. In her stories and novels she explores with remarkable skill and insight the impulse to escape from the familial universe which her non-fiction implicitly celebrates. In this as in many other respects, the best of her fiction is deserving of wider critical interest than it has hitherto received. My objective in this discussion is to examine the escape theme in one of the most fascinating stories, "The Tooth," and to offer by way of introduction some suggestions about Jackson's treatment of it elsewhere and its relevance to other concerns apparent throughout her work.[2]

Prominent among the latter is the conception of the small communal group which is bound together less by love and respect than by fear, guilt, and dumb tradition. In story after story the small town or neighborhood is depicted as a nexus of sanctioned intrigue against whatever is individual, different, or alien, and in which the ties that bind may also strangle. In "The Lottery," even the individualism of valuing one's own life is ritualistically and horrifyingly exorcised by the community. In "The Summer People," two vacationers from the city who stay on in a small resort community past the traditional Labor Day leavetaking discover that that tradition is to the townsfolk a taboo, the breaking of which entails forfeiture of normal services and amenities and leads, ultimately, to dark hostility. Sometimes the communal group is simply the family, oppressively nuclear. Elsa Dayton in "A Day in the Jungle" leaves her home and husband

"'Farther than Samarkand': The Escape Theme in Shirley Jackson's 'The Tooth,'" *Studies in Short Fiction* 19 (1982): 133–39. © 1982 by Newberry College. Reprinted by permission.

because they represent a life of stifling quotidian regularity; marriage has been for her a succession of "hideous unprivate months" (*CAWM*, 130). Catharine Vincent in "I Know Who I Love," leaving home as a young woman, ceases immediately to think about her nagging parents, and does so only "dutifully" (*CAWM*, 48) after they have died. The sense of duty, inspired not by love or deep moral awareness, but by anxiety and insecurity, is to the family in Jackson's fiction what custom is to the small community: a bonding mechanism whose primary function is to ensure cohesiveness.

Opposed to the regulated world of the small group is the realm of freedom and self-centeredness represented, usually, by the city. To those in recoil from the confines of the small group, the city stands as a glistening dream of freedom in which communally inculcated patterns of self-abnegating behavior do not hold. Thus Elsa, during her day in the "jungle" of the downtown area to which she has fled from her suburban home, is "very much aware of the fact that for the first time she moved knowingly and of choice through a free world" (*CAWM*, 130). Such freedom, not merely to do what one likes, but to create a life and a self of one's own, is the promise which the city seems to hold. Yet the inverse of the freedom to create a new self is the destruction of the old, which the city also seems to portend. In "Pillar of Salt," the impression of things crumbling is continually with Margaret during her visit to New York, and she suspects that the disintegrating buildings, streets, and vehicles are symptomatic of the city's effect on people: it is the place where they "come apart."[3] At the end of the story she is utterly panicked by the swarming anonymity of the crowds on the streets outside, and at not being noticed familiarly. Similarly, Elsa Dayton's fears of accidental injury during her day downtown really amount to an insecurity about her ability to hold the jungle of an unfamiliar world at bay. Without the constant external verification of identity which the small community provides, the self may seem to lose its reality and the world may crumble crazily.

These, then, are the two realms between which many of Shirley Jackson's heroines gravitate. In the family or town or neighborhood the ties may chafe, but they do hold you together; in the city there are no ties, and *you* must hold you together—assuming there is a "you" which can exist independently, out of familiar context. Some of the most interesting moments in Jackson's fiction are those in which the flight from familiarity to the realm of strangeness and freedom causes a character's sense of identity to weaken or even vanish. Such experiences of fundamental tremors in the self's sense of who it is aren't easily explicable as schizoid disturbances or breakdowns, a line of analysis which assumes a preexistent central self to feel disturbed or break down. What seems to fascinate Shirley Jackson most is the possibility that behind the self which we ordinarily assume to be irrevocably ingrained, if not preordained, there is nothing immutably necessary which we can call our own: it is, for her, an idea which is both frightening *and* alluring.

In "The Tooth," Clara Spencer, a middle-class housewife, boards an evening bus for New York from the small town which is her home. The reason for the overnight journey is that she must see a dentist about a severe flareup of a toothache which she has suffered from intermittently for years. Just prior to her departure, she complains to her husband of feeling "so *funny*," and he expresses concern that there might be something seriously wrong with her. To this she responds uneasily, "It's just a *toothache* . . . nothing very serious about a *toothache*," and the reason for her unease is hinted at a moment later when, after shivering at the suggestion that the tooth might have to be pulled she says, "I just feel as if I were all tooth. Nothing else" (*MSJ*, 121). On the bus she feels "closed in alone with the toothache" (*MSJ*, 125), and later, in the dentist's office, her tooth seems to her to be "the only part of her to have any identity" (*MSJ*, 128). When told by the dentist that she must go to an extractionist, the questions she wants to ask him (though she refrains) are "What about me? or, How far down do the roots go?" He replies to her spoken question, "What will they do?" but also, in a sense, to the imagined ones by saying "They'll take that tooth out. . . . Should have been done years ago" (*MSJ*, 129).

In retrospect, then, her husband's earlier assertion that she has been having that same toothache off and on for as long as he has known her indicates clearly that the tooth represents the deeply rooted lifetime-old self inculcated by the domestically oriented small community, and further implies that she was never happy being that self. From their parting conversation at the bus station, we are given an impression of the life-style which the community instills. The talk is all of plans and duties, not of love or personal wishes, and the nearest her husband comes to a declaration of affection is this:

> "You know, Clara," he made his voice very weighty, as though if he spoke more seriously his words would carry more conviction and be therefore more comforting, "you know, I'm glad you're going down to New York to have Zimmerman take care of this. I'd never forgive myself if it turned out to be something serious and I let you go to this butcher up here." (*MSJ*, 121)

Their relationship is a somberly moral connection in which the important gratification is not erotic or emotional, just the satisfaction derived from knowing that one's weighty obligations have been discharged with impeccable conscientiousness. Once launched on her journey Clara never thinks of her husband or children, and what she and he are really concerned about in their farewell conversation is mutual reinforcement of faith in the mores of the family and the small community.

For Clara, the reinforcement is insufficient. Shortly after boarding the bus she is chatting with the bus driver without fully understanding why, "except that it was late at night and people isolated together in some strange bus had to be more friendly and communicative than at other times" (*MSJ*, 123). Faced with a universe of motion and darkness and armed only with the isolated self, Clara feels the Jackson "city experience" immediately upon departure from home. The world of structured familial and communal relationships seems very fragile to her as, sitting toward the back of the bus, she senses that "only the thin thread of lights along the ceiling of the bus held them together, brought the back of the bus where she sat along with the front of the bus where the driver sat" (*MSJ*, 125).

But sitting next to her then is "Jim," a stranger who, she is foggily aware, assists her in the roadside restaurants where the bus stops periodically, and who offers her his shoulder upon which to rest her head while she dozes. She is also dimly conscious of strange things he is telling her, about a beautiful island "farther than Samarkand" (*MSJ*, 124). Jim is clearly fantastic, a creation of Clara's overstrained mind. This is implied throughout the story: in a restaurant, for example, she asks him, "What do you want?" (*MSJ*, 126), and he points to a cup of coffee and a sandwich *she* then consumes; without having been told, he knows that she is going to see a dentist; when he leaves her in New York she does not see him go, even though she is watching very carefully; and at the end of the story, thinking she is running hand in hand with him "barefoot through hot sand," she doesn't notice the tellingly "curious glances" (*MSJ*, 136) of pedestrians passing by on the city sidewalk. A substitute for and alternative to not just her husband, but the entire domestic society which she has left behind, he provides guidance just when she feels most disorientedly apart from other people. As a creature of her imagination he is really an aspect of herself, of course, and for her to follow his directions and hearken to his seductive verbal travelog is to tell herself what to do and what to want.[4] But so used is she to thinking of the "Clara" identity as her very self that she cannot consciously assume proprietorship of her egocentric impulses, and so she must objectify them and render them somewhat distant in a dream figure.

In essence, it is the realm of passive, ego-centripetal wish-fulfillment, the world of pleasant dreams, that Clara seems to yearn for. The combined effects of codeine, whiskey, a sleeping pill, and lack of food have propelled her into a state of dreamlike altered consciousness, making her feel comfortable about "being carried along without effort of her own" (*MSJ*, 125). In the course of her drugged journey of enchantment, she doesn't quite have the *ultimate* dream, but, as it were, dreams of having it. The land "farther than Samarkand" described by "Jim" represents that ultimate dream, and its appeal is that it inverts the basic values and features of the tightly strictured communal group. This is apparent from the very nature of the place, which seems to be a tropic isle with an ambiance of lazy, unfocussed eroticism, in sharp contrast to the world of sterile matrimonial devotion which Clara has just left. More deeply, though, it is its asocial quality which is most alluring about the faraway land. There, there are voices and songs but, it would seem, no other people—or, at least, none who impress themselves upon one's attention. Similarly, life there is characterized by guiltless, recumbent passivity: "Nothing to do all day but lie under the trees" (*MSJ*, 125). When there is nothing to do, consequences are impossible, and so too are responsibility and decisiveness.

Ironically, however, when the enchantment is at its deepest and she is most passive, a new power of determination is liberated within her. Her state of dreamlike consciousness reaches its peak during the extraction as a result of the anaesthetic she has been given:

> First of all things get so far away, she thought, remember this. And remember the metallic sound and taste of all of it. And the outrage.
>
> And then the whirling music, the ringing confusedly loud music that went on and on, around and around, and she was running as fast as she could down a long horribly clear hallway with doors on both sides and at the end of the hallway was Jim, holding out his hands and laughing, and calling something she could never hear because of the loud music, and she was running and then she said, "I'm not afraid," and someone from the door next to her took her arm and pulled her through and the world widened alarmingly until it would never stop and then it stopped with the head of the dentist looking down at her and the window dropped into place in front of her and the nurse holding her arm.
>
> "Why did you pull me back,?" she asked, and her mouth was full of blood. "I wanted to go on." (*MSJ*, 131–32)

Clara's commands to herself to remember her sensations during the initial phase of the operation and her subsequent cry of "I'm not afraid" reveal that she is finally making an effort to embrace her mental and emotional life at its deepest level and to accept the consequences, hazards, and indignities of that commitment. In the midst of the disorienting whirl of unstructured mental and physical sensations, the figure of Jim reappears to provide guiding direction. It is still a dream at the end of that hallway, of course, as is made clear when she feels herself being pulled back into the world of waking reality which widens beyond the scope of control of her isolated ego. But the bravery and dignity of Clara's avowal that she wanted to go on cannot be attributed dismissively to an inability to face the alarming breadth of reality unaided by the wishful imagination. Jackson's careful rendering of the experience stresses that the difference between inability and unwillingness in this regard is not altogether meaningful or clear, and that Clara is admirably aware on some level of having chosen her own fate. Thus, moments after the operation, this exchange takes place: "'God has given me blood to drink,' she said to the nurse, and the nurse said, 'Don't rinse your mouth or it won't clot'" (*MSJ*, 132). She is willing to drink the blood in her mouth as an act of expiation, though more in payment than atonement, for the sin of choosing to live for herself. But the nurse misses the deeper implication of her words and seems, sanely proffering formulaic advice, shallow and automaton-like by comparison.

Subsequently, in the crowded Ladies' Room, Clara seems more self-sufficient and can cope almost calmly with the loss of her previous identity. With only a "slight stinging shock" she realizes that she has no idea which of the several faces reflected in the mirror is hers, and that "no one was familiar in the group, no one smiled at her or looked at her with recognition" (*MSJ*, 134). It is an extreme of the Jackson "city experience" of enswarming anonymity and loss of the identity-sustaining familiar context. Yet Clara's response is merely a "queer numbness in her throat" (*MSJ*, 134). On discovering which of the faces is hers, her reaction is only sullenness at not having a chance to "take" one of the pretty ones, and she immediately sets about letting her hair down, applying rouge to her pallid cheeks, and drawing "an emphatic rosy mouth" on her lips (*MSJ*, 136). The old Clara would never have done those things, not simply because they bespeak sexual self-awareness and narcissism, but even more so because they are done with such emphatic determination to seize control of self and circumstance. She proceeds to stride "purposefully" to the elevator (*MSJ*, 136), as the neurotically driven old Clara would never have done, to seek a lover the old Clara would never have admitted to herself that she desired, much less sought. When "Jim" appears out of the crowd to take her hand, she remembers that she has lost her bottle of painkilling codeine pills and left in the Ladies' Room a slip of paper containing the nurse's instructions for alleviating painful aftereffects of the extraction. But neither is needed, for the real pain she has suffered throughout her life was the result of being forced to maintain her old identity, and its absence seems an anodyne. Jim is a fantasy and she may be insane, but there is nonetheless a "happily ever after" ring to the story's ending: "her hand in Jim's and her hair down on her shoulders, she ran barefoot through hot sand" (*MSJ*, 136).

It should be noted, in conclusion, that Shirley Jackson intended the figure of "Jim" to be associated with James Harris, the "daemon lover" of Child Ballad 243, who entices a married woman to abandon her family and run away with him on a voyage which, she realizes too late, is destined for hell.[5] Thus some readers might be tempted to regard the story as a sort of Freudian version of the morality tale contained in the old ballad: the sin of feeling solipsistically happy and free, it might seem, is punished by the damnation of madness. Certainly the story's ending, while hardly moralistic, has the thrust of a cautionary warning about the consequences of succumbing to the seductive murmurings of that "daemon lover," one's wishful imagination. Yet even as the warning is imparted, the lure of the fantasy world is powerfully felt, and it is far from clear that the passing pedestrians who walk upon what they know to be the sidewalk are wiser or happier than Clara, running barefoot through imagined sand. Jackson's careful suspension of judgment at the end helps to explain why "The Tooth" is an oddly more unsettling story than a straightforward Freudian line of analysis would allow: she refuses to assume unblinkingly the value and desirability of the "reality principle," of remaining aware of things, people, and events as they objectively are (or are generally understood to be). It is, in her fictional universe, the small communal group which champions that principle, discouraging individual gratification in favor of duty and, necessarily therefore, instilling intense awareness of reality as sternly independent of the wishful self. But if self-gratification replaces communal responsibility as the supreme and guiding value for the individual, the world of private fantasy, or of reality as colored by personal desires, may come to seem a superior kind of reality. Rarely concerned with the moral implications of the quest for self-gratification and pure personal freedom, for Shirley Jackson the intriguing considerations tend to be strategic: whether and how the self can make good its escape, and what the rewards and consequences might be. She knows very well that running away with the daemon lover may mean going to hell. But she knows equally well why so many individuals thrill to his talk of a land "farther than Samarkand."

# Notes

1. *CAWM*, 4. References to this volume will henceforth be incorporated into the text.

2. Book reviews aside, critical works on Shirley Jackson amount to a comparative handful. To date there has been one book about her, Lenemaja Friedman's *Shirley Jackson*, Twayne's United States Authors Series No. 253 (Boston: Twayne, 1975). Friedman offers a bibliography of secondary sources, but, as she says, many of these contain "only a sentence or two, and none very helpful" (Friedman, 170–71). Readers interested in criticism of Jackson should supplement Friedman's list with the following: Stuart C. Woodruff, "The Real Horror Elsewhere: Shirley Jackson's Last Novel," *Southwest Review* 52 (Spring 1967): 152–62; Robert L. Kelly, "Jackson's 'The Witch': A Satanic Gem," *English Journal* 60 (December 1971): 1204–1208; Helen E. Nebeker, "'The Lottery': Symbolic Tour de Force," *American Literature* 46 (March 1974): 100–107; Steven K. Hoffman, "Individuation and Character Development in the Fiction of Shirley Jackson," *Hartford Studies in Literature* 8 (1976): 190–208; John G. Parks, "The Possibility of Evil: A Key to Shirley Jackson's Fiction," *Studies in Short Fiction* 15 (1978): 320–23, and "Waiting for the End: Shirley Jackson's *The Sundial*," *Critique* 19.3 (1978): 74–88. Even much of the best of her work, however, remains unexplored. Friedman and Hoffman are the only commentators who discuss "The Tooth," for example, and they do so only briefly and superficially.

3. *MSJ*, 35. References to this volume will henceforth be incorporated into the text.

4. In this qualified sense I agree with Hoffman, who sees Jim as a "contra-sexual projection of Clara's mind." He also regards Jim as a Jungian "animus" figure, however, an interpretation which I find rather forced. Whatever else Jim may represent, it is not "the will to power and an opinionated personality," which are, Hoffman says, the characteristics manifested by the animus. See Hoffman, 200–201.

5. A portion of that ballad was included in the collection of stories in which "The Tooth" first appeared, and the Jim Harris character recurs through several of the other stories contained therein. See *The Lottery*, 305–306.

# Helen E. Nebeker

The symbolic overtones [of "The Lottery"] become evident as early as the fourth word of the story when the date of June 27th alerts us to the season of the summer solstice with all its overtones of ancient ritual. Carefully the scene is set—the date, the air of festivity, release, even license. The children newly freed from school play boisterously, rolling in the dust. But, ominously, Bobby Martin has already stuffed his pockets with stones and Harry Jones and Dickie Delacroix follow his example, eventually making a great pile of stones in the corner which they guard from the raids of other boys. By the end of just two paragraphs Jackson has carefully indicated the season, time of ancient excess and sacrifice, and the stones, most ancient of sacrificial weapons. She has also hinted at larger meanings through name symbology. "Martin," Bobby's surname, derives from a Middle English word signifying ape or monkey. This, juxtaposed with "Harry Jones" (in all its commonness) and "Dickie Delacroix" (of-the-Cross), urges us to an awareness of the Hairy Ape within us all, veneered by a Christianity as perverted as "Delacroix," vulgarized to "Dellacroy" by the villagers. Horribly, at the end of the story, it will be Mrs. Delacroix, warm and friendly in her natural state, who will select a stone "so large she had to pick it up with both hands" and will encourage her friends to follow suit. Should this name symbology seem strained, superimposed, a little later we shall return to it and discover that every major name in the story has its special significance.

Returning to the chronology of the story, the reader sees the men gather, talking of the planting and rain (the central issues of the ancient propitiatory rites), tractors and taxes (those modern additions to the concerns of man). The men are quieter, more aware, and the patriarchal order (the oldest social group of man) is quickly evidenced as the women join their husbands and call their children to them. When Bobby Martin tries to leave the group and runs laughing to the stones, he is sharply rebuked by his serious father, who knows that this is no game. Clearly this is more than the surface "idyllic" small-town life noted by Heilman;[1] the symbolic under-

From "'The Lottery': Symbolic Tour de Force," *American Literature* 46 (1974): 100–7.
© 1974 by Duke University Press. Reprinted by permission.

currents prepare us to be drawn step by step toward the ultimate horror, where everything will fuse.

In the fourth paragraph, Mr. Summers, who ironically runs the "coal" business, arrives with the postmaster, Mr. Graves, who carries the three-legged stool and the black box. Although critics have tended to see the box as the major symbol, careful reading discloses that, while the box is referred to three times in this paragraph, the stool is emphasized four times and in such strained repetition as to be particularly obvious. Further, in the next two paragraphs it will be stressed that the box rests upon, is supported by, the *three-legged stool*. It would thus seem that the stool is at least as important as the box: in my opinion, it is the symbol which holds the key to Jackson's conclusive theme. In the interest of structure and coherence, this point must be developed later in the article.

Returning to the symbol of the box, its prehistoric origin is revealed in the mention of the "original wood color" showing along one side as well as in the belief that it has been constructed by the first people who settled down to make villages here (man in his original social group). The chips of wood, now discarded for slips of paper, suggest a preliterate origin. The present box has been made from pieces of the original (as though it were salvaged somehow) and is now blackened, faded, and stained (with blood perhaps). In this box[2] symbol, Jackson certainly suggests the body of tradition—once oral but now written—which the dead hand of the past codified in religion, mores, government, and the rest of culture, and passed from generation to generation, letting it grow ever more cumbersome, meaningless, and indefensible.

Jackson does not, however, attack ritual in and of itself. She implies that, as any anthropologist knows, ritual in its origin is integral to man's concept of his universe, that it is rooted in his need to explain, even to control the forces around him. Thus, at one time the ritual, the chant, the dance were executed precisely, with deep symbolic meaning. Those chosen for sacrifice were not victims but saviors who would propitiate the gods, enticing them to bring rebirth, renewal, and thanking them with their blood. This idea explains the significance of Mrs. Delacroix's comment to Mrs. Graves that "there's no time at all between lotteries any more" and her reply that "Time sure goes fast." To the ancients, the ritual was a highly significant time marker: summer solstice and winter solstice, light versus dark, life versus death. These modern women only verify the meaninglessness of the present rite. Later, in a similar vein, when one of the girls whispers, "I hope it's not Nancy," Mr. Warner replies, "People ain't the way they used to be," implying that, anciently, honor and envy were accorded those chosen to die for the common welfare. Another neat symbolic touch tied to the meaningful ritualistic slaughter of the past is suggested by the character Clyde Dunbar. He lies at home, unable to participate in this year's lottery because of his broken leg. This reminds us that in every tradition of propitiation the purity and wholeness of the sacrifice was imperative. This "unblemished lamb" concept is epitomized in the sacrifice of Christ. In view of the interweaving of these ideas, it is difficult to see only "incidental symbolism" or to overlook the immediate and consistent "symbolic intention" of the narrative....

Now we understand the significance of the three-legged stool—as old as the tripod of the Delphic oracle, as new as the Christian trinity. For that which supports the present day box of meaningless and perverted superstition is the body of unexamined tradition of at least six thousand years of man's history. Some of these traditions (one leg of the stool if you like), are as old as the memory of man and are symbolized by the season, the ritual, the original box, the wood chips, the names of Summers, Graves, Martin, Warner (all cultures have their priesthoods!). These original, even justifiable, traditions gave way to or were absorbed by later Hebraic perversions; and the narrative pursues its "scapegoat" theme in terms of the stones, the wooden box,[3] blackened and stained, Warner the Prophet, even the Judaic name of Tessie's son, David. Thus Hebraic tradition becomes a second leg or brace for the box.

Superimposed upon this remote body of tradition is one two thousand years old in its own right. But it may be supposed the most perverted and therefore least defensible of all as a tradition of supposedly enlightened man who has freed himself from the barbarities and superstitions of the past. This Christian tradition becomes the third support for the blood-stained box and all it represents. Most of the symbols of the other periods pertain here with the addition of Delacroix, Hutchinson, Baxter and Steve.

With this last symbolic intention clearly revealed, one may understand the deeper significance of Jackson's second, below-the-surface story. More than developing a theme which "deals with 'scapegoating,' the human tendency to punish 'innocent' and often accidentally chosen victims for our sins,"[4] or one which points out "the awful doubleness of the human spirit—a doubleness that expresses itself in blended good neighborliness and cruelty,"[5] Shirley Jackson has raised these lesser themes to one encompassing a comprehensive, compassionate, and fearful understanding of man trapped in the web spun from his own need to explain and control the incomprehensible universe around him, a need no longer answered by the web of old traditions.

Man, she says, is a victim of his unexamined and hence unchanged traditions which engender in him flames otherwise banked, subdued. Until enough men are touched strongly enough by the horror of their ritualistic, irrational actions to reject the long-perverted ritual, to destroy the box completely—or to make, if necessary, a new one reflective of their own conditions and needs of life—man will never free himself from his primitive nature and is ultimately doomed. Miss Jackson does not offer us much hope—they only talk of giving up the lottery in the north village, the Dunbars and Watsons do not actually resist, and even little Davy Hutchinson holds a few pebbles in his hands.[6]

## Notes

1. Robert B. Heilman, *Modern Short Stories; A Critical Anthology* (New York, 1959), 384.

2. Etymologically, the closeness of our words "box" and "book" is indicated in the [Old English] derivation from words meaning "evergreen tree or shrub" and "beech tree," probably from the habit of carving runic characters on the beech. The Latin words *codex* and *liber* have the same similarities.

3. The Ark of the Covenant itself is one of the earliest representations of the literal box.

4. Virgil Scott, *Studies in the Short Story*, Instructor's Manual (New York, 1968), 20.

5. Cleanth Brooks and Robert Penn Warren, *Understanding Fiction*, 2d edition (New York: Appleton-Century-Crofts, 1959), 76.

6. This paper was written under a grant from Arizona State University.

# Fritz Oehlschlaeger

In a 1979 article John H. Williams notes what he takes to be a "flaw" in the two-stage process by which the victim is selected in Shirley Jackson's "The Lottery." Readers of the story will recall that the first round of the drawing determines a household from which the victim is to be drawn; the second round, the single victim from within that household. Williams points out that under such a system "individuals who are members of smaller families are more likely to be chosen as the sacrificial victim," and he then proposes a new plan that would keep the two-stage process but have the same effect as simply "selecting one individual at random from the village."[1] But perhaps instead of correcting the "flaws," we should look at the lottery as Jackson designs it for a key to its meaning. The nature of the process by which the victim is selected gives each woman a very clear incentive to produce the largest possible family. Each child she has gives her a better chance of surviving if the marked paper falls to her household in the first round. What I am suggesting, then, is that one way the story can be seen is as the depiction of a patriarchal society's way of controlling female sexuality. Helen Nebeker has argued that the story presents a ritual that has outlived the fertility function it once had in an earlier myth-oriented time.[2] Such an argument overlooks the real and continuing function of the lottery as it is organized. That function remains the encouraging of fertility within marriage, along with the patriarchal domination that accompanies it.

A conflict between male authority and female resistance is subtly evident throughout "The Lottery." Early in the story, the boys make a "great pile of stones in one corner of the square," while the girls stand aside "talking among themselves, looking over their shoulders at the boys."[3] Later, as the Hutchinsons file up to draw their papers from the box, it is a girl who whispers, "I hope it's not Nancy" (300). This girl's expression of a purely personal feeling is perceived by Old Man Warner as a threat to the social order, as is indicated by his bitterly exclaiming, "It's not the way it used to be" (300), when presumably everyone subordinated personal feelings to the social demands of the ritual. It is also a woman, Mrs. Adams,

From "The Stoning of Mistress Hutchinson: Meaning and Context in 'The Lottery,'" *Essays in Literature* 15 (1988): 259–65. Reprinted by permission of Western Illinois University.

who presents the story's most significant challenge to the lottery. When at one point her husband Mr. Adams remarks that "over in the North village they're talking of giving up the lottery" (297), Old Man Warner gives vent to a tirade on the folly of departing from what has always served its purpose. Mr. Adams makes no response, but his wife does, pointing out to the Old Man that "some places have already quit lotteries" (297), an oblique but nevertheless real gesture of resistance. That Jackson wants us to read Mrs. Adams's statement as a gesture of resistance is reinforced by what she does with the Adamses at the end of the story. Mr. Adams is at the front of the crowd of villagers as they set upon Tessie Hutchinson. No mention, however, is made of Mrs. Adams's being involved in the stoning.

There is a strong pattern of detail in the story, then, suggesting that those who are most discomfited by, or resistant to, the lottery are women. On the other hand, men control the lottery. Mr. Summers and Mr. Graves are its official priestly administrators, and when they need help, they inquire whether any of the "fellows" (292) might want to give a hand. The lottery is arranged by families and households, women being assigned to the households of their husbands, who draw for them in the initial round. That the society is a heavily patriarchal one is suggested in many other ways as well. As the people gather at the outset of the story, the women stand "by their husbands," and Jackson sharply distinguishes female from male authority: when Mrs. Martin calls her son Bobby, he "ducked under his mother's grasping hand and ran, laughing, back to the pile of stones," but when "his father spoke up sharply," Bobby "came quickly and took his place between his father and his oldest brother" (292). Later when Mrs. Hutchinson complains that the draw has been unfair, her husband tersely and authoritatively commands her, "Shut up, Tessie" (299). And when it becomes clear that Tessie has drawn the marked paper, Bill "forced the slip of paper out of her hand" and "held it up" for the crowd to see (301). The details Jackson chooses to describe the administrator of the lottery, Mr. Summers, and his wife further clarify the nature of male power and female submission in the lottery's community. Mr. Summers is given his position because people feel "sorry for him" as one who "had no children" and whose "wife was a scold" (292). The woman who is without children is dismissed as a "scold," a challenge to male authority. The childless man, on the other hand, is elevated to a place of special responsibility and even sanctity. . . .

. . . Tessie fails to be a heroine, and the way that she does so testifies to the success with which the male-dominated order has imposed itself upon her. It is crucial to note that her most grievous failure lies in betraying another woman, her married daughter, by suggesting that she be considered a member of the Hutchinson household for the second stage of the lottery. Jackson emphasizes women's turning against one another, too, through her pointed depiction of the brutality of Mrs. Delacroix and Mrs. Graves in setting upon Tessie. At the beginning of the story, the girls stand together watching the boys gather the stones, but as those girls become women, the involvement in marriage and childbearing that the lottery encourages pits them against one another, blinding them to the fact that all power in their community is male.

## Notes

1. John H. Williams, "A Critique of the Sampling Plan Used in Shirley Jackson's 'The Lottery,'" *Journal of Modern Literature* 7 (1979): 543–44.

2. Helen Nebeker, "'The Lottery': Symbolic Tour de Force," *American Literature* 46 (1974): 104.

3. *L*, 291. Future citations will be given parenthetically.

# Peter Kosenko

No mere "irrational" tradition, the lottery is an *ideological mechanism*. It serves to reinforce the village's hierarchical social order by instilling the villagers with an unconscious fear that if they resist this order they might be selected in the next lottery. In the process of creating this fear, it also reproduces the ideology necessary for the smooth function of that social order, despite its inherent inequities. What is surprising in the work of an author who has never been identified as a Marxist is that this social order and ideology are essentially capitalist.

I think we need to take seriously Shirley Jackson's suggestion that the world of the lottery is her reader's world, however reduced in scale for the sake of economy. The village in which the lottery takes place has a bank, a post office, a grocery store, a coal business, a school system; its women are housewives rather than field workers or writers; and its men talk of "tractors and taxes."[1] More importantly, however, the village exhibits the same socio-economic stratification that most people take for granted in a modern, capitalist society.

Let me begin by describing the top of the social ladder and save the lower rungs for later. The village's most powerful man, Mr. Summers, owns the village's largest business (a coal concern) and is also its mayor, since he has, Jackson writes, more "time and energy [read money and leisure] to devote to civic activities" than others (292). (Summers's very name suggests that he has become a man of leisure through his wealth.) Next in line in the social hierarchy is Mr. Graves, the village's second most powerful government official—its postmaster. (His name may suggest the gravity of officialism.) And beneath Mr. Graves is Mr. Martin, who has the economically advantageous position of being the grocer in a village of three hundred.

These three most powerful men who control the town, economically as well as politically, also happen to administer the lottery. Mr. Summers is its official, sworn in yearly by Mr. Graves (294). Mr. Graves helps Mr. Summers make up the lottery slips (293). And Mr. Martin steadies the lottery box as the slips are stirred (292). In the off season, the lottery box is stored

From "A Marxist/Feminist Reading of Shirley Jackson's 'The Lottery,'" *New Orleans Review* 12 (Spring 1985): 27–32. Reprinted by permission of the *New Orleans Review*.

either at their places of business or their residences: "It had spent one year in Mr. Graves' barn and another year underfoot in the post-office, and sometimes it was set on a shelf in the Martin grocery and left there" (293). Who controls the town, then, also controls the lottery. It is no coincidence that the lottery takes place in the village square "between the post-office and the bank"—two buildings which represent government and finance, the institutions from which Summers, Graves, and Martin derive their power.

However important Mr. Graves and Mr. Martin may be, Mr. Summers is still the most powerful man in town. Here we have to ask a Marxist question: what relationship is there between his interests as the town's wealthiest businessman and his officiating the lottery? That such a relationship does exist is suggested by one of the most revealing lines of the text. When Bill Hutchinson forces his wife, Tessie, to open her lottery slip to the crowd, Jackson writes, "It had a black spot on it, the black spot Mr. Summers had made the night before with [a] heavy pencil in [his] coal-company office" (301). At the very moment when the lottery's victim is revealed, Jackson appends a subordinate clause in which we see the blackness (evil) of Mr. Summers's (coal) business being transferred to the black dot on the lottery slip. At one level at least, evil in Jackson's text is linked to a disorder, promoted by capitalism, in the material organization of modern society. But it still remains to be explained *how* the evil of the lottery is tied to this disorder of capitalist social organization.

Let me sketch the five major points of my answer to this question. First, the lottery's rules of participation reflect and *codify* a rigid social hierarchy based upon an inequitable social division of labor. Second, the fact that everyone participates in the lottery and understands *consciously* that its outcome is pure chance gives it a certain "democratic" aura that obscures its first codifying function. Third, the villagers believe *unconsciously* that their commitment to a work ethic will grant them some magical immunity from selection. Fourth, this work ethic prevents them from understanding that the lottery's actual function is not to encourage work *per se* but to reinforce an inequitable social *division* of labor. Finally, after working through these points, it will be easier to explain how Jackson's choice of Tessie Hutchinson as the lottery's victim/scapegoat reveals the lottery to be an ideological mechanism which serves to defuse the average villager's deep, inarticulate dissatisfaction with the social order in which he lives by channeling it into anger directed at the *victims* of that social order. It is reenacted year after year, then, not because it is a mere "tradition," as Helen Nebeker argues, but because it serves the repressive ideological function of purging the social body of all resistance so that business (capitalism) can go on as usual and the Summers, the Graves and the Martins can remain in power.[2]

Implicit in the first and second points above is a distinction between universal participation in the lottery and what I have called its *rules* of participation. The first of these rules I have already explained, of course: those who control the village economically and politically also administer the lottery. The remaining rules also tell us much about who has and who doesn't have power in the village's social hierarchy. These remaining rules determine who gets to choose slips in the lottery's first, second and third rounds. Before the lottery, lists are "[made] up of heads of families [who choose in the first round], heads of households [who choose in the second round], [and] members of each household in each family [who choose in the last round]" (294). The second round is missing from the story because the family patriarch who selects the dot in the first round—Bill Hutchinson—has no married male offspring. When her family is chosen in the first round, Tessie Hutchinson objects that her daughter and son-in-law didn't "take their chance." Mr. Summers has to remind her, "Daughters draw with their husbands' families" (299). Power in the village, then, is exclusively consolidated into the hands of male heads of families and households. Women are disenfranchised....

The final major point of my reading has to do with Jackson's selection of Tessie Hutchinson as the lottery's victim/scapegoat. She could have chosen Mr. Dunbar, of course, in order to show us the unconscious connection that the villagers draw between the lottery and their work ethic. But to do so would not have revealed that the lottery actually reinforces a *division* of labor. Tessie, after all, is a woman whose role as a housewife deprives her radically of her freedom by forcing her to submit to a husband who gains his power over her by virtue of his place in the work force. Tessie, however, rebels against her role, and such rebellion is just what the orderly functioning of her society cannot stand. Unfortunately, her rebellion is entirely unconscious.

Tessie's rebellion begins with her late arrival at the lottery, a *faux pas* that reveals her unconscious resistance to everything the lottery stands for. She explains to Mr. Summers that she was doing her dishes and forgot what day it was. The way in which she says this, however, involves her in another *faux pas*: the suggestion that she might have violated the village's work ethic and neglected her specific job within the village's social division of labor: "Wouldn't have me leave m'dishes in the sink, now, would you Joe?" (295). The "soft laughter [that runs] through the crowd" after this

181

remark is a nervous laughter that indicates, even more than the village women's singling out of the Dunbars and the Watsons, the extent of the village's unconscious commitment to its work ethic and power structure (295). When Mr. Summers calls her family's name, Tessie goads her husband, "Get up there, Bill" (297). In doing so, she inverts the power relation that holds in the village between husbands and wives. Again, her remark evokes nervous laughter from the crowd, which senses the taboo that she has violated. Her final *faux pas* is to question the rules of the lottery which relegate women to inferior status as the property of their husbands. When Mr. Summers asks Bill Hutchinson whether his family has any other households, Tessie yells, "There's Don and Eva. . . . Make them take their chance" (299). Tessie's daughter Eva, however, *belongs* to Don and is consequently barred from participating with her parents' family.

All of these *faux pas* set Tessie up as the lottery's likeliest victim, even if they do not explicitly challenge the lottery. That Tessie's rebellion is entirely unconscious is revealed by her cry while being stoned, "It isn't fair" (302). Tessie does not object to the lottery *per se*, only to her own selection as its scapegoat. It would have been fine with her if someone else had been selected.

In stoning Tessie, the villagers treat her as a scapegoat onto which they can project and through which they can "purge"—actually, the term *repress* is better, since the impulse is conserved rather than eliminated—their own temptations to rebel. The only places we can see these rebellious impulses are in Tessie, in Mr. and Mrs. Adams's suggestion, squelched by Warner, that the lottery might be given up, and in the laughter of the crowd. (The crowd's nervous laughter is ambivalent: it expresses uncertainty about the validity of the taboos that Tessie breaks.) But ultimately these rebellious impulses are channeled by the lottery and its attendant ideology away from their proper objects—capitalism and capitalist patriarchs—into anger at the rebellious victims of capitalist social organization. Like Tessie, the villagers cannot articulate their rebellion because the massive force of ideology stands in the way.

The lottery functions, then, to terrorize the village into accepting, in the *name* of work and democracy, the inequitable social division of labor and power on which its social order depends. When Tessie is selected, and before she is stoned, Mr. Summers asks her husband to "show [people] her paper" (301). By holding up the slip, Bill Hutchinson reasserts his dominance over his wayward wife and simultaneously transforms her into a symbol to others of the perils of disobedience.

# Notes

1. *The Lottery*, 291. Further page references will occur in the body of the paper.

2. Helen E. Nebeker, "'The Lottery': Symbolic Tour de Force," *American Literature* 46 (1974): 103.

# Chronology

| | |
|---|---|
| 1916 | Shirley Hardie Jackson is born 14 December in San Francisco, first of two children of Leslie Hardie Jackson, a lithograph company executive, and Geraldine Bugbee Jackson, descendent of San Francisco architects. |
| 1930–1933 | At Burlingame (California) High School keeps a diary, writes poetry and stories, plays in the school orchestra, and attends movies regularly. |
| 1933 | Family moves to Rochester, New York, traveling via ship to New York City by way of Cuba. Shirley decides to become a lawyer. Spends senior year at Brighton High School, graduating in 1934. |
| 1934–1936 | Studies at the University of Rochester, where she reads Lewis Carroll, François Villon, and commedia dell'arte and writes stories. |
| 1936 | Ends several years of keeping a diary in May; withdraws from the University of Rochester with low grades in June. Period of mental depression. |
| 1936–1937 | Stays at home, writing about a thousand words daily. |
| 1937 | Enrolls at Syracuse University, intending to become a writer; changes major from journalism to English, with a speech minor. |
| 1938 | Publishes her first story, "Janice," in a creative-writing-class collection at Syracuse, attracting the attention of Stanley Edgar Hyman, her fellow student. Is fiction editor of the *Syracusan*, a campus literary magazine that prints several of her stories, including "Y and I and the Ouija Board." |

| | |
|---|---|
| 1939 | With Hyman, founds and edits the *Spectre*, a magazine that publishes her poetry and stories through its fourth and final issue in summer of 1940. Their editorials explore the race issue on campus and defend the *Spectre* against threats of censorship. |
| 1940 | Graduates from Syracuse University in June and on 13 August marries Hyman in New York City after he wins a *New Republic* contest and becomes an editorial assistant. (After marriage Jackson gives 1919 as her birth year.) Writes for a radio station, then sells books at Macy's, but quits after Christmas. |
| 1941 | Works for an advertising agency. Near year's end moves with Hyman to a New Hampshire cabin, where both write for several months. The *New Republic* buys "My Life with R. H. Macy" for $25, her first national publication. |
| 1942 | Laurence Jackson, her first of four children, born. Hyman becomes a staff writer at the *New Yorker*. |
| 1943 | The *New Yorker* publishes "After You, My Dear Alphonse" in January, first of 12 stories she sells to the magazine, most of them in the mid-1940s. |
| 1944 | "Behold the Child among His Newborn Blisses" is published in *Cross-Section: A Collection of New American Writing*, with stories by Jane Bowles, Ralph Ellison, Norman Mailer, and others. Publishes "Little Old Lady," the first of several stories in *Mademoiselle*. "Come Dance with Me in Ireland" is reprinted from the *New Yorker* in *Best American Short Stories, 1944*. |
| 1945 | Family moves to North Bennington, Vermont, where Hyman teaches at Bennington College. Daughter Joanne Leslie born. |
| 1948 | First novel, *The Road through the Wall*, set in California, is published by Farrar, Straus & Co. "The Lottery," published by the *New Yorker* on 26 June, provokes hundreds of letters to the editor. "Charles," the first of many semi-autobiographical family stories, appears in *Mademoiselle*. Daughter Sarah Geraldine born. |

1949  *The Lottery; or, The Adventures of James Harris* is widely reviewed and sells extremely well for a short-story collection; listed among "Best Fiction of 1949" by editors of the *New York Times Book Review.* "The Lottery" is reprinted in *Prize Stories of 1949: The O. Henry Awards*; one judge cites its superb narrative quality. *Woman's Home Companion* and *Good Housekeeping* both publish the first of many stories. Jackson teaches briefly at Bennington College.

1950  Meets Dylan Thomas, to whom she dedicates "A Visit." "The Lottery" is adapted for television by Ellen Violett and broadcast on NBC's "Cameo Theater" 14 June.

1951  *Hangsaman*, second novel, dedicated to her children, is set in a college environment similar to Bennington. *Best American Short Stories, 1951* selects "The Summer People." Son Barry Edgar born.

1952  Publishes 12 stories, including the popular "The Night We All Had Grippe."

1953  First of two family chronicles, *Life among the Savages*, incorporates several autobiographical stories, including "Charles" and "The Third Baby's the Easiest," into a continuous narrative. Brainerd Duffield adapts "The Lottery" for stage in a one-act play.

1954  *The Bird's Nest*, novel about a split personality, receives enthusiastic reviews.

1956  Makes first of several appearances at the Suffield Writers' Conference in Connecticut. *The Witchcraft of Salem Village*, nonfiction in the Landmark series, is published for a teenage audience. *Best American Short Stories, 1956* reprints "One Ordinary Day, with Peanuts."

1957  Publishes second family chronicle, *Raising Demons*, integrating several family stories written since *Life among the Savages*. Lectures at Syracuse University in July. The film *Lizzie*, based on *The Bird's Nest*, released.

1958  *The Sundial*, a novel dedicated to her agent, Bernice Baumgarten, is the last book Jackson publishes with Farrar, Straus & Cudahy. Writes *The Bad Children*, a one-act comedy, for her children.

1959 Viking publishes *The Haunting of Hill House*, novel dedicated to Leonard Brown, Jackson's English teacher at Syracuse University. The book is a popular success and named to the *New York Times Book Review's* "Best Fiction of 1959."

1960 Contributes several essays to a book from which she later dissociates herself, *Special Delivery: A Useful Book for Brand-New Mothers*, published by Little, Brown. *Haunting of Hill House* is nominated for National Book Award.

1961 "Louisa, Please . . ." wins the Edgar Allan Poe Award.

1962 *We Have Always Lived in the Castle* is one of *Time* magazine's "Ten Best Novels" of the year and on the *New York Times Book Review's* list of "Best Fiction of 1962." Three years of intensive work on the book are followed by mental depression that leads Jackson to seek psychotherapy.

1963 Popular film adaptation of *The Haunting of Hill House*—*The Haunting*, starring Julie Harris and Claire Bloom—is released. *9 Magic Wishes* appears in Modern Masters Books for Children series; among other authors in the series are Robert Graves, Arthur Miller, and Richard Wilbur.

1964 *Best American Short Stories, 1964* reprints "Birthday Party" from *Vogue*. Jackson lectures at Breadloaf writers' colony; her journal writing helps relieve depression.

1965 Reads from works-in-progress, the novel "Come Along with Me" and a children's book, at Syracuse University in April. Lecture tour in May includes University of Chicago. Selected to receive Arents Pioneer Medal for Outstanding Achievement, highest honor at Syracuse University, but does not attend the ceremony. In June briefly visits Flannery O'Connor's mother in Georgia. Dies of cardiac arrest while taking her afternoon nap at home on 8 August. "The Possibility of Evil" appears in the *Saturday Evening Post* in December, with an appreciation by Hyman; the story wins a posthumous Edgar from the Mystery Writers of America the next spring.

1966      Second children's book, *Famous Sally*, is published. Hyman collects 11 stories from *The Lottery*, together with *The Bird's Nest, Life among the Savages*, and *Raising Demons*, in *The Magic of Shirley Jackson*, named to the *New York Times Book Review*'s "Best Fiction of 1966."

1967      Hyman donates the Shirley Jackson Papers, including many unpublished short stories, to the Library of Congress.

1968      Hyman edits *Come Along with Me: Part of a Novel, Sixteen Stories, and Three Lectures*, listed among the "Best Fiction of 1968" by the *New York Times Book Review*.

# Selected Bibliography

## Primary Works

### Short Story Collections

*Come Along with Me: Part of a Novel, Sixteen Stories, and Three Lectures.* Edited with a preface by Stanley Edgar Hyman. New York: Viking, 1968. "Janice," "Tootie in Peonage," "A Cauliflower in Her Hair," "I Know Who I Love," "The Beautiful Stranger," "The Summer People," "Island," "A Visit" (originally published as "The Lovely House"), "The Rock," "A Day in the Jungle," "Pajama Party" (originally published as "Birthday Party"), "Louisa, Please Come Home" (originally published as "Louisa, Please . . ."), "The Little House," "The Bus." "The Night We All Had Grippe" is printed after the lecture "Experience and Fiction," and "The Lottery" follows the lecture "Biography of a Story."

*The Lottery; or, The Adventures of James Harris.* New York: Farrar, Straus, 1949. Reprinted as *The Lottery and Other Stories.* Farrar, Straus & Giroux, 1982. "The Intoxicated," "The Daemon Lover" (originally published as "The Phantom Lover"), "Like Mother Used to Make," "Trial by Combat," "The Villager," "My Life with R. H. Macy," "The Witch," "The Renegade," "After You, My Dear Alphonse," "Charles," "Afternoon in Linen," "Flower Garden," "Dorothy and My Grandmother and the Sailors," "Colloquy," "Elizabeth," "A Fine Old Firm," "The Dummy" (originally published as "Dummy"), "Seven Types of Ambiguity," "Come Dance with Me in Ireland," "Of Course," "Pillar of Salt," "Men with Their Big Shoes," "The Tooth," "Got a Letter from Jimmy," "The Lottery."

*The Magic of Shirley Jackson.* Edited with a preface by Stanley Edgar Hyman. New York: Farrar, Straus & Giroux, 1966. Part 1 reprints 11 stories from *The Lottery*: "The Daemon Lover," "My Life with R. H. Macy," "Colloquy," "Pillar of Salt," "The Renegade," "Flower Garden," "Elizabeth," "Come Dance with Me in Ireland," "Of Course," "The Tooth," "The Lottery."

### Uncollected Short Stories

"About Two Nice People." *Ladies Home Journal*, July 1951, 48–49, 124–25, 127.

"Account Closed." *Good Housekeeping*, April 1950, 52–53, 104, 106, 109–10, 113.

## Selected Bibliography

"All She Said Was 'Yes.'" *Vogue*, 1 November 1962, 142–43, 169, 171, 174–75.

"All the Girls Were Dancing." *Collier's*, 11 November 1950, 36.

"Alone in a Den of Cubs." *Woman's Day*, December 1953, 42–43, 107–8.

"Aunt Gertrude." *Harper's*, April 1954, 50–53.

"The Bakery." *Peacock Alley*, November 1944, 98, 100–101.

"Behold the Child among His Newborn Blisses." In *Cross-Section: A Collection of New American Writing*, edited by Edwin Seaver, 292–98. New York: L. B. Fischer, 1944.

"The Box." *Woman's Home Companion*, November 1952, 25, 82–83.

"Bulletin." *Magazine of Fantasy and Science Fiction*, March 1954, 46–48.

"Call Me Ishmael." *Spectre* 1, no. 1 (Fall 1939): 30–31.

"The Clothespin Dolls." *Woman's Day*, March 1953, 36, 163–65.

"Concerning . . . Tomorrow." *Syracusan* 4, no. 6 (March 1939): 8.

"Daughter, Come Home." *Charm*, May 1944, 75, 94–95.

"Day of Glory." *Woman's Day*, February 1953, 32, 87, 89.

"Don't Tell Daddy." *Woman's Home Companion*, February 1954, 42–43, 57, 64, 66–67.

"Every Boy Should Learn to Play the Trumpet." *Woman's Home Companion*, October 1956, 36–37, 77–79.

"Family Magician." *Woman's Home Companion*, September 1949, 22–23, 92–93, 98, 100.

"The First Car Is the Hardest." *Harper's*, February 1952, 79–83.

"The Friends." *Charm*, November 1953, 118–19, 140–45.

"The Gift." *Charm*, December 1944, 66, 130, 135–36.

"A Great Voice Stilled." *Playboy*, March 1960, 57–58, 91.

"Had We but World Enough." *Spectre* 1, no. 3 (Spring 1940): 28–31.

"Happy Birthday to Baby." *Charm*, November 1952, 94–95, 132–36.

"Home." *Ladies Home Journal*, August 1965, 64–65, 116, 118.

"The Homecoming." *Charm*, April 1945, 66, 114–17.

"The House." *Woman's Day*, May 1952, 62–63, 115–16, 118–19.

"An International Incident." *New Yorker*, 12 September 1953, 92, 95–96, 98–101.*

"It Isn't the Money I Mind." *New Yorker*, 25 August 1945, 46, 48–49.

"It's Only a Game." *Harper's*, May 1956, 36–39.

"Journey with a Lady." *Harper's*, July 1952, 75–81.

"Liaison à la Cockroach." *Syracusan* 4, no. 7 (April 1939): 10, 24.

"The Life Romantic." *Good Housekeeping*, December 1949, 165–67.

---

* *New Yorker* page numbers are of the metropolitan New York edition; the page numbers for the edition of the same issue published outside New York vary slightly.

"Little Dog Lost." *Charm*, October 1943, 29, 92.

"A Little Magic." *Woman's Home Companion*, January 1956, 28–29, 93–94.

"Little Old Lady." *Mademoiselle*, September 1944, 243–45.

"The Lovely Night." *Collier's*, 8 April 1950, 14–15, 66–68.

"Lucky to Get Away." *Woman's Day*, August 1953, 26, 117–19.

"The Missing Girl." *Magazine of Fantasy and Science Fiction*, December 1957, 42–52.

"Monday Morning." *Woman's Home Companion*, November 1951, 21, 57, 60.

"The Most Wonderful Thing." *Good Housekeeping*, June 1952, 49, 252–56.

"Mother Is a Fortune Hunter." *Woman's Home Companion*, May 1954, 48, 69, 74, 77.

"Mrs. Melville Makes a Purchase." *Charm*, October 1951, 92–93, 114–19.

"My Friend." *Syracusan* 4, no. 4 (December 1938): 19.

"My Life in Cats." *Spectre* 1, no. 4 (Summer 1940): 36–37.

"My Son and the Bully." *Good Housekeeping*, October 1949, 38, 218–20.

"Nice Day for a Baby." *Woman's Home Companion*, July 1952, 34–35, 47–48, 50.

"Nothing to Worry About." *Charm*, July 1953, 80–84.

"The Omen." *Magazine of Fantasy and Science Fiction*, March 1958, 118–30.

"On Being a Faculty Wife." *Mademoiselle*, December 1956, 116–17, 135–36.

"On the House." *New Yorker*, 30 October 1943, 77–79.

"One Last Chance." *McCall's*, April 1956, 52–53, 112, 114, 116.

"One Ordinary Day, with Peanuts." *Magazine of Fantasy and Science Fiction*, January 1955, 53–61.

"The Order of Charlotte's Going." *Charm*, July 1954, 74–79.

"The Phantom Lover." *Woman's Home Companion*, February 1949, 24–25, 95–98, 100. Another version of "The Daemon Lover."

"The Possibility of Evil." *Saturday Evening Post*, 18 December 1965, 61–64, 68–69.

"Queen of the May." *McCall's*, April 1955, 47, 73, 75, 78.

"Root of Evil." *Fantastic*, March–April 1953, 124–29, 162.

"Shopping Trip." *Woman's Home Companion*, June 1953, 40–41, 85–87.

"The Sneaker Crisis." *Woman's Day*, October 1956, 29, 101–102.

"*So* Late on Sunday Morning." *Woman's Home Companion*, September 1953, 40–41, 47–48.

"The Strangers." *Collier's*, 10 May 1952, 24–25, 68–71.

"Strangers in Town." *Saturday Evening Post*, 30 May 1959, 18–19, 76–77, 79.

"The Third Baby's the Easiest." *Harper's*, May 1949, 58–63.

"Visions of Sugarplums." *Woman's Home Companion*, December 1952, 42–43, 53.

"When Things Get Dark." *New Yorker*, 30 December 1944, 40–43.

"Whistler's Grandmother." *New Yorker*, 5 May 1945, 59–61.

"The Wishing Dime." *Good Housekeeping*, September 1949, 34–35, 223–28.

"Worldly Goods." *Woman's Day*, May 1953, 10–11, 178–79.

"Y and I." *Syracusan* 4, no. 2 (October 1938): 21, 30.

"Y and I and the Ouija Board." *Syracusan* 4, no. 3 (November 1938): 6.

## Novels

*The Bird's Nest*. New York: Farrar, Straus & Young, 1954.

*Hangsaman*. New York: Farrar, Straus & Young, 1951.

*The Haunting of Hill House*. New York: Viking, 1959.

*The Road through the Wall*. New York: Farrar, Straus, 1948.

*The Sundial*. New York: Farrar, Straus & Cudahy, 1958.

*We Have Always Lived in the Castle*. New York: Viking, 1962.

## Nonfiction

"The Case for Dinner-Table Silence." *Good Housekeeping*, March 1960, 42, 44, 47–48.

"Fame." *Writer*, August 1948, 265–66.

"Go Down, Faulkner (in the Throes of William Faulkner's *Go Down, Moses*)." In *The Best of Bad Faulkner*, edited by Dean Faulkner Wells, 129–32. San Diego: Harcourt Brace Jovanovich, 1991.

"Karen's Complaint." *Good Housekeeping*, November 1959, 38, 40, 42, 46.

"List Found in a Coat Pocket." *Vogue*, 15 April 1953, 59, 108.

"A Little Test for Mothers." *Good Housekeeping*, October 1960, 54, 56, 58.

"Look Ma, We're Moving." *Good Housekeeping*, February 1952, 49, 173–75.

"The Lost Kingdom of Oz." *Reporter*, 10 December 1959, 42–43.

"Love and Terror under a Fairy Spell." Review of *The Unicorn*, by Iris Murdoch. *Cosmopolitan*, May 1963, 24.

"Mother, *Honestly!*" *Good Housekeeping*, September 1959, 24, 26–27.

"The Muse Hits Syracuse" (with Stanley Edgar Hyman). *Spectre* 1, no. 4 (Summer 1940): 13–16.

"No, I *Don't* Want to Go to Europe." *Saturday Evening Post*, 6 June 1964, 8, 10.

"Out of the Mouths of Babes." *Good Housekeeping*, July 1960, 36, 38, 40.

"Questions I Wish I'd Never Asked." *Good Housekeeping*, March 1961, 50, 52.

Review of *The Children Grew*, by Eleanor Choate Darnton. *New York Times Book Review*, 28 November 1954, 38.

Review of *In Darkest Childhood*, by Richard G. Hubler. *New York Times Book Review*, 28 November 1954, 38.

Review of *Just Be Yourself*, by Mary Bard. *New York Times Book Review*, 7 October 1956, 29.

Review of *Out of the Red*, by Red Smith. *New York Times Book Review*, 7 May 1950, 18.

Review of *Parson Austen's Daughter*, by Helen Ashton. *New York Times Book Review*, 11 September 1949, 9.

Review of *Pemberley Shades*, by D. A. Bonavia-Hunt. *New York Times Book Review*, 11 September 1949, 9.

Review of *Story: Fiction of the Forties*, edited by Whit Burnett and Hallie Burnett. *New York Times Book Review*, 20 November 1949, 48.

Review of *The Stumbling Stone*, by Aubrey Menen. *New York Times Book Review*, 10 July 1949, 4.

Review of *Women and Children First*, by Bernard DeVoto (Cady Hewes, pseudonym). *New York Times Book Review*, 25 November 1956, 32.

"Santa Claus, I Love You." *Good Housekeeping*, December 1959, 38, 40, 42.

*Special Delivery: A Useful Book for Brand-New Mothers*, by Shirley Jackson et al. Introduction by Edmund N. Joiner III, M.D. Boston: Little, Brown, 1960. Republished as *And Baby Makes Three*. New York: Grosset & Dunlap, 1960.

"Three Sonnets." *Spectre* 1, no. 2 (Winter 1940): 16.

"We the Editor" (with Stanley Edgar Hyman). *Spectre* 1, no. 1 (Fall 1939): 2–5; 1, no. 2 (Winter 1940): 2–3; 1, no. 3 (Spring 1940): 2–3; 1, no. 4 (Summer 1940): 2–4.

"What I Want to Know Is, What Do Other People Cook With?" *Good Housekeeping*, July 1961, 14, 17.

## Memoirs

*Life among the Savages*. New York: Farrar, Straus & Young, 1953.

*Raising Demons*. New York: Farrar, Straus & Cudahy, 1957.

## Works for Children

*The Bad Children: A Musical in One Act for Bad Children*. Music by Allan Jay Friedman. Chicago: Dramatic Publishing, 1959.

*Famous Sally*. Illustrated by Charles B. Slackman. New York: Harlin Quist, 1966.

*9 Magic Wishes*. Illustrated by Lorraine Fox. A Modern Masters Book for Children. New York: Crowell-Collier, 1963.

*The Witchcraft of Salem Village*. Landmark Books. New York: Random House, 1956.

# Secondary Works

## Interviews

Breit, Harvey. "Talk with Miss Jackson." *New York Times Book Review*, 26 June 1949, 15.

Ciccolella, Cathy. "Jackson Credits SU with Writing Start." [Syracuse University] *Daily Orange*, 28 April 1965, 1, 5.

Hutchens, John K. "On the Books." *New York Herald Tribune Book Review*, 8 May 1949, 17.

Kunitz, Stanley J., ed. "Shirley Jackson." *Twentieth Century Authors*, 483–84. First Supplement. New York: Wilson, 1955.

Nichols, Lewis. "Demonologist." *New York Times Book Review*, 7 October 1962, 8.

"On an Author." *New York Herald Tribune Book Review*, 5 July 1953, 2.

## Book-Length Studies

Friedman, Lenemaja. *Shirley Jackson*. Boston: Twayne Publishers, 1975.

Metcalf, Linda Trichter. "Shirley Jackson in Her Fiction: A Rhetorical Search for the Implied Author." Ph.D. diss. New York University, 1987.

Miller, Raymond R. Jr. "Shirley Jackson's Fiction: An Introduction." Ph.D. diss. University of Delaware, 1974.

Nardacci, Michael L. "Theme, Character, and Technique in the Novels of Shirley Jackson." Ph.D. diss. New York University, 1980.

Oppenheimer, Judy. *Private Demons: The Life of Shirley Jackson*. New York: G. P. Putnam's Sons, 1988.

Parks, John Gordon. "The Possibility of Evil: The Fiction of Shirley Jackson." Ph.D. diss. University of New Mexico, 1973.

## Articles and Parts of Books

Allen, Barbara. "A Folkloristic Look at Shirley Jackson's 'The Lottery.'" *Tennessee Folklore Society Bulletin* 46 (December 1980): 119–24.

Bagchee, Shyamal. "Design of Darkness in Shirley Jackson's 'The Lottery.'" *Notes on Contemporary Literature* 9, no. 4 (1979): 8–9.

Brinkmann, Horst. "Shirley Jackson, 'The Lottery' (1948)." In *Die amerikanische Short Story der Gegenwart*, edited by Peter Freese, 101–9. Berlin: Erich Schmidt, 1976.

Brooks, Cleanth, and Robert Penn Warren. "'The Lottery': Interpretation." In *Understanding Fiction*, 72–76. 2d ed. New York: Appleton-Century-Crofts, 1959.

Carpenter, Lynette. "Domestic Comedy, Black Comedy, and Real Life: Shirley Jackson, a Woman Writer." In *Faith of a (Woman) Writer*, edited by Alice Kessler-Harris and William McBrien, 143–48. Westport, Conn.: Greenwood Press, 1988.

_____. "The Establishment and Preservation of Female Power in Shirley Jackson's *We Have Always Lived in the Castle.*" *Frontiers* 8, no. 1 (1984): 32–38.

Church, Joseph. "Getting Taken in 'The Lottery.'" *Notes on Contemporary Literature* 18, no. 4 (1988): 10–11.

Cleveland, Carol S. "Shirley Jackson." In *And Then There Were Nine . . . More Women of Mystery*, edited by Jane S. Bakerman, 199–219. Bowling Green, Ohio: Bowling Green State University Popular Press, 1985.

Coulthard, A. R. "Jackson's 'The Lottery.'" *Explicator* 48, no. 3 (Spring 1990): 226–28.

Downing, Janay. "Much Ado about Nothing: Narrative Strategies in Shirley Jackson and Teresa Bloomingdale." *WHIMSY* 1 (1983): 206–8.

Egan, James. "Sanctuary: Shirley Jackson's Domestic and Fantastic Parables." *Studies in Weird Fiction* 6 (1989): 15–24.

Gibson, James M. "An Old Testament Analogue for 'The Lottery.'" *Journal of Modern Literature* 11 (March 1984): 193–95.

Hoffman, Steven K. "Individuation and Character Development in the Fiction of Shirley Jackson." *Hartford Studies in Literature* 8, no. 3 (1976): 190–208.

Kelly, Robert L. "Jackson's 'The Witch': A Satanic Gem." *English Journal* 60 (December 1971): 1204–8.

Kittredge, Mary. "The Other Side of Magic: A Few Remarks about Shirley Jackson." In *Discovering Modern Horror Fiction*, edited by Darrell Schweitzer. *Starmont Studies in Literary Criticism*, no. 4, 3–12. Mercer Island, Wash.: Starmont House, 1985.

Kosenko, Peter. "A Marxist/Feminist Reading of Shirley Jackson's 'The Lottery.'" *New Orleans Review* 12 (Spring 1985): 27–32.

Lainoff, Seymour. "Jackson's 'The Lottery.'" *Explicator* 12 (March 1954): item 34.

LeCroy, Anne. "The Different Humor of Shirley Jackson: *Life among the Savages* and *Raising Demons.*" *Studies in American Humor*, n.s. 4 (Spring–Summer 1985): 62–73.

Lootens, Tricia. "'Whose Hand Was I Holding?': Familial and Sexual Politics in Shirley Jackson's *The Haunting of Hill House.*" In *Haunting the House of Fiction: Feminist Perspectives on Ghost Stories by American Woman*, edited by Lynette Carpenter and Wendy K. Kolmar, 166–92. Knoxville: University of Tennessee Press, 1991.

Nebeker, Helen E. "'The Lottery': Symbolic Tour de Force." *American Literature* 46 (March 1974): 100–107.

Newman, Judie. "Shirley Jackson and the Reproduction of Mothering: *The Haunting of Hill House*." In *American Horror Fiction: From Brockden Brown to Stephen King*, edited by Brian Docherty, 120–34. New York: St. Martin's Press, 1990.

Oehlschlaeger, Fritz. "The Stoning of Mistress Hutchinson: Meaning and Context in 'The Lottery.'" *Essays in Literature* 15 (Fall 1988): 259–65.

Parks, John G. "Chambers of Yearning: Shirley Jackson's Use of the Gothic." *Twentieth Century Literature* 30 (Spring 1984): 15–29.

———. "The Possibility of Evil: A Key to Shirley Jackson's Fiction." *Studies in Short Fiction* 15 (Summer 1978): 320–23.

———. "Waiting for the End: Shirley Jackson's *The Sundial*." *Critique* 19, no. 3 (1978): 74–88.

Pascal, Richard. "'Farther than Samarkand': The Escape Theme in Shirley Jackson's 'The Tooth'" *Studies in Short Fiction* 19 (Spring 1982): 133–39.

Schaub, Danielle. "Shirley Jackson's Use of Symbols in 'The Lottery.'" *Journal of the Short Story in English* 14 (Spring 1990): 79–86.

Sullivan, Jack. "Shirley Jackson." In *Supernatural Fiction Writers: Fantasy and Horror*, edited by E. F. Bleiler, 1031–36. Vol. 2. New York: Charles Scribner's Sons, 1985.

Terry, James S., and Peter C. Williams. "Literature and Bioethics: The Tension in Goals and Style." *Literature and Medicine* 7 (1988): 1–21.

Welch, Dennis. "Manipulation in Shirley Jackson's 'Seven Types of Ambiguity.'" *Studies in Short Fiction* 18 (Winter 1981): 27–31.

Whittier, Gayle. "'The Lottery' as Misogynist Parable." *Women's Studies* 18, no. 4 (1991): 353–66.

Williams, Richard H. "A Critique of the Sampling Plan Used in Shirley Jackson's 'The Lottery.'" *Journal of Modern Literature* 7 (September 1979): 543–44.

Woodruff, Stuart C. "The Real Horror Elsewhere: Shirley Jackson's Last Novel." *Southwest Review* 52 (Spring 1967): 152–62.

## Bibliographies

Hall, Joan Wylie. "Shirley Jackson." *Facts on File Bibliography of American Fiction: 1919–1988*. Edited by Matthew Bruccoli et al., 266–67. Vol. 1. New York: Facts on File, 1991.

Herrick, Casey. "Shirley Jackson's 'The Lottery.'" *Bulletin of Bibliography* 46, no. 2 (June 1989): 120–21.

Phillips, Robert S. "Shirley Jackson: A Checklist." *Papers of the Bibliographical Society of America* 56, no. 1 (January–March 1962): 110–13.

———. "Shirley Jackson: A Chronology and a Supplementary Checklist." *Papers of the Bibliographical Society of America* 60, no. 2 (April–June 1966): 203–13.

# Index

# The Author

Joan Wylie Hall received her Ph.D. from the University of Notre Dame and is an instructor of English at the University of Mississippi. She has written on Ruth McEnery Stuart, Willa Cather, Marilyn French, and Shirley Jackson for reference works and for such journals as the *Colby Library Quarterly*, the *Cather Yearbook*, and *Studies in Short Fiction*. She has served as a tutor at Harvard University and as an instructor at Notre Dame and Saint Mary-of-the-Woods (Indiana) College.

# The Editor

General editor Gordon Weaver earned his B.A. in English at the University of Wisconsin-Milwaukee in 1961; his M.A. in English at the University of Illinois, where he studied as a Woodrow Wilson Fellow, in 1962; and his Ph.D. in English and creative writing at the University of Denver in 1970. His novels include *Count a Lonely Cadence, Give Him a Stone, Circling Byzantium,* and *The Eight Corners of the World.* Many of his short stories are collected in *The Entombed Man of Thule, Such Waltzing Was Not Easy, Getting Serious, Morality Play, A World Quite Round,* and *Men Who Would Be Good.* He edited *The American Short Story, 1945-1980: A Critical History,* and is currently editor of *Cimarron Review.* He is professor of English at Oklahoma State University and serves as an adjunct member of the faculty of the Vermont College Master of Fine Arts in Writing Program.